BIOGRAPHIES
of
ALASKA-YUKON PIONEERS

1850-1950

—Volume 5—

Compiled and Edited
by
Ed Ferrell

HERITAGE BOOKS
2008

HERITAGE BOOKS
AN IMPRINT OF HERITAGE BOOKS, INC.

Books, CDs, and more—Worldwide

For our listing of thousands of titles see our website at
www.HeritageBooks.com

Published 2008 by
HERITAGE BOOKS, INC.
Publishing Division
100 Railroad Ave. #104
Westminster, Maryland 21157

Copyright © 2004 Ed Ferrell

Other books by the author:

Biographics and Genealogical Abstracts from Hardin County, Illinois Newspapers, 1872-1938

Biographies of Alaska-Yukon Pioneers, 1850-1950 Volumes 1-5

Frontier Justice: Alaska 1898—The Last American Frontier

The Dangerous North

All rights reserved. No part of this book may be reproduced or transmitted in any form or by any means, electronic or mechanical, including photocopying, recording or by any information storage and retrieval system without written permission from the author, except for the inclusion of brief quotations in a review.

International Standard Book Numbers
Paperbound: 978-0-7884-2503-5
Clothbound: 978-0-7884-7217-6

ACKNOWLEDGEMENTS

I am grateful to my wife Nancy Warren Ferrell, an author and researcher in her own right, for the countless hours she spent in typing biographies, often from hard-to-read photo copies of early day newspapers.

COMPILER'S NOTES

I did not modernize the spelling, punctuation, or capitalization of the biographies; the entries were typed "as is," reflecting the style of the original writer. However, I did edit out Victorian phrases along with "fluff" common to biographies. My selections are based on what I find on the microfilms. I have used brackets in the entries to clarify dates and information. Brackets with [?] indicate I was unable to read the paper because of poor copy and there is some question on the date, number, etc.

Ed Ferrell
Juneau, Alaska

DEDICATION

To the memory of the women who pioneered the Last frontier and have long since gone over The Long Trail. For the most part, their stories go untold.

GEORGE R. ADAMS

George R. Adams was born in 1845[?]. In 1865 he joined the Robert Kennicott expedition to Alaska.

The first American who ever set foot in the Yukon basin is in Dyea.. His name is George R. Adams. He will engage in the general merchandise business in this city. He is a pioneer of pioneers. Many years have passed since first he set foot in the frozen north, yet he is still one of the handsomest and best preserved men who walked the streets of Dyea. His hair and mustache are white, but Mr. Adams is strong and active and as full of hope as ever. As he has cast his lot in Dyea, a few facts of his history will be interesting.

Nearly thirty-three years ago Maj. Robert Kennicott of Cleveland, Ohio sailed from San Francisco for St Michael at the mouth of the mighty Yukon in command of an expedition for the purpose of exploring the coast of Alaska for the Russian-American telegraph line. With him was a youth of twenty summers, strong, hardy and energetic George R. Adams. The party of thirteen sailed for the north on the bark Golden Gate and late in September established winter quarters at Unalaklik, at the mouth of the river of that name. Lieut. Adams for that was his title in the service to which he had enlisted, was placed in charge of the first expedition to penetrate the Yukon valley. He was the first American to set foot in the Yukon basin. With a half breed Russian and an Indian guide, he penetrated the interior during the winter of 1865 as far as Nulato, making a portage from the headwaters of the Unalaklik.

Mr. Adams lived in Alaska for twelve years following this in the employ of the Alaska Commercial company. His experiences in Alaska have been extensive and his knowledge of the Yukon country is large. Back of the plain story of hardship and danger which Mr. Adams can tell when he feels like indulging in reminiscences, is a story of romance which is a part of the history of Alaska. To tell this story one would have to describe the death by his own hand of Maj. Kennicott, who was in charge of the party, and whose failure to reach Fort Yukon, where he expected to meet another party from the Frazer river so preyed on his mind that he took a dose of strychnine. Another incident in that memorable campaign was a long, mind-killing wait at St. Michael, for the steamers which were to bring supplied to the little party, and the ragings of two men who, when the steamers arrived after all hope had vanished, succumbed to the territory mental strain and were put in irons and sent back to the states, both total wrecks.

Mr. Adams said that shortage of food is an old story in Alaska. When he organized his expedition he explored the Yukon basin from Unalaklik, food was exceedingly scarce at St. Michael. Sugar was worth $5 per pound, and they were most willing to pay that unusual price. Ice was beginning to form in the Unalaklik river when with the Russian and Indian he started in a skin canoe for its headwaters. He found an easy portage from its source to Nuluto. After establishing a base of operations at this point, he returned to Unalaklik for provisions. After securing these he started again for Nulato, this time over the frozen surface of the river with dog teams, which he had obtained at Cape Romanoff. Several times the journey was made between the two points for provisions, which were very scarce and hard to get. During that winter Lieut Adams and his two companions were forced to subsist on supplies obtained largely from the Indians. As they proceeded they found that the natives were short of food and some even on the verge of starvation. A diet of bean soup, plentifully salted, was the rule.

"Even under such circumstances," said Mr. Adams, "I grew stout and hearty. It was when we returned to Unalaklik in the summer of 1866 and waited until the surface of Norton Sound was a glittering sheet of ice, and still the supply boats did not come, that the awful terrors of a winter in that latitude without food dawned upon us. We had all arranged to scatter over the country hoping to live with the natives during the winter. I had prepared to set out on a trip down the coast alone when a storm came up and the ice was broken. A few days later the steamer Wright which was the flagship of the expedition, and the ship Nightingale appeared in the harbor, laden with supplies and bringing the first intelligence from civilization we had enjoyed in fourteen months. Of course we were overjoyed. The strain, however, was too much for two unfortunate fellows, Green and Cotter. Both became raving maniacs and were put in irons. Both died some years later without having fully recovered from that awful experience."

THE DYEA TRAIL, Jan. 19, 1898

LYNN B. ADSIT

Lynn B. Adsit, aged 46 years, pioneer of Juneau and widely known throughout Alaska, died of cancer of the stomach in Los Angeles, Calif., one day last week. He is survived by his widow who lives in Juneau and by his mother and sister, who were with him when the end came.

Mr. Adsit went to Juneau with his parents in 1891. His father engaged in business there, after a time representing a number of outside wholesale houses in the capital city, as well as Alaska generally.

After the death of his father in 1910, Mr. Adsit took over the various lines held by him and continued the business. Three years later he became associated with B. C. Delzelle and enlarged the business materially. This partnership lasted more than a decade. In recent years, Mr. Adsit has maintained his business alone, and until some months ago covered a large part of the Territory.

Mr. Adsit was a native of Chicago, Ill., being born there on October 11, 1884.

ALASKA WEEKLY, March 28, 1930

ALEXANDRA ALBERTSTONE

Alexandra Albertstone, the late beloved wife of Reuben Albertstone died Sunday the 15th inst.

Mrs. Albertstone was for along time president of the St. Nicholas Benevolent Society and in that capacity was the means of much good work–being accomplished by the members.

She was a dutiful and loving wife, and fond mother. The coffin was carried from church by the ladies, received by the bearers and borne to the Russian cemetery where it was consigned to its final resting place by the side of the deceased sister, Mrs. P. Cochran.

THE ALASKAN, Jan. 21, 1899 (?)

F. A. T. ALDRICH (See Vol.2)

Mr. Aldrich was born in Fort Waine, Indiana, Sept. 22nd, 1857. His parents emigrated to Dubuque, Iowa, 1859. At the age of 15 he ran away from home and took a position as cabin boy on a steamer on the Mississippi River. In 1876, at the age of 19 years, Mr. Aldrich joined General Terry's Indian expedition in the Sioux war, serving as a teamster and general emergency man. In 1877 he was a teamster with General Miles in the Nez Perce war when Chief Joseph was captured. Continuously since 1879 Mr. Aldrich has followed the fortunes of a prospector and miner over the territories of Montana, Alberta, Alaska, the Yukon and in Siberia. He served as a member of the house for the first Territorial legislature of Alaska; was re-elected to the Senate of the second and third Territorial assemblies.

ALASKA MAGAZINE May 1917

GEORGE ALLEN

George Allen, who with his brother Gene Allen, founded the famous Klondike Nugget [newspaper] in the days of the gold rush, died this week in Eastern Washington as the result of a heart attack.

In recent years he has been in Topennish, where he was editor of the weekly paper.

He is survived by his widow and two daughters, Mrs. Ruth Allen McGreedy and Mrs. Eileen James, and by a son,

Merrit.

With his brother Gene, George Allen went into the Klondike during the rush, freighting plant and equipment over the White Pass and down the river to Dawson, where they started the Nugget. In the face of tremendous odds they succeeded in getting out the paper, which has since become a noted example at frontier journalism. His brother Gene is now residing in Seattle.

ALASKA WEEKLY, Sept. 13, 1935

JOHN W. ALLEN

John Allen died on Monday morning[?], succumbing to the fever from which he was suffering.

John W. Allen was born February 15th, 1840, in Oliver township, Jefferson county, Penn. When only 24 years old he left home for Montana, but returned in a year or two to his native place where he married. In 1867 he came west again with the Custer expedition and was the first discoverer of gold in the Black Hills. Settling there he became quite wealthy and was for several years chairman of the board of county commissioners of that place. He remained in the Black Hills until the year 1887, exercising considerable influence and was highly respected.

One of those freaks of fortune, however, peculiar with a miners' life left him in rather reduced circumstances, so in the spring of '87 he started north. Arriving in Alaska he proceeded at once into the Yukon gold fields and remained there for one season. He then returned to Juneau, where his family has been stopping meanwhile, and turned his attention to mining in this vicinity. He soon acquired an interest in the "Last Chance" placer mine between here and the Basin, with Nelson Bros and some parties in Spokane Falls. About three months ago he went below on business, and immediately after his return was stricken with the malady which has at length proved fatal.

A bereaved wife and two little girls are now left to mourn the loss of a loving husband, an affectionate father, and a devoted

friend.
JUNEAU CITY MINING RECORD, Nov. 27, 1890

LEONARD ALLEN

Mr. Allen has been with the office of Indian Affairs at Ketchikan since November 1933 as principal and community worker. He received his A. B. Degree from the Central State Teachers' College at Mt. Pleasant, Michigan in 1930 and in 1934 received his M. A. Degree from the University of Michigan.

Mr. Allen taught a rural school for two years at Meecham, Gratiot County, Michigan. For three years Mr. Allen was superintendent at the high school at Crystal, Michigan, and prior to coming to Alaska, was for five years Superintendent of Schools at Otter Lake, Michigan.

Making their home in Juneau, Mr. and Mrs. Allen and son, Robert, will for the present occupy the resident of George Simpkins at 604 Fifth Street.
DAILY ALASKA EMPIRE, June 2, 1943

LOLA ALLEN

Mrs. Lola Allen, 69, magazine writer and former publisher of a weekly newspaper at Skagway, died in a hospital here Friday, following a prolonged illness.

Mrs. Allen published the mimeographed *Moose Pass Miner, Alaska* after leaving Skagway and then taught at Ninilchik until she retired because of failing health.
ARROWHEAD PRESS & SITKA SENTINEL, Aug. 2, 1948

JOHN AMES

John Ames, pioneer Alaskan, and a resident of Anchorage for many years was found dead in his home in that city as a result of a self-inflected rifle wound, apparently taking that means of ending a long illness.

He was born in Colorado and went to Alaska many years ago, living at Kodiak for a time before going to Anchorage. He

is survived by his widow, a daughter, four sons, and a sister, all residing in Anchorage except the daughter and two older sons. The daughter and one son live in fairbanks and the other son lives in Juneau.
THE ALASKA WEEKLY, Mar. 29, 1935

ERWIN ANDERS

Erwin Anders died Wednesday evening July 9th at his apartment at the Baranoff Hotel which he has occupied for a number of years. By birth a German, he came to this country in 1859 and in 1862 he enlisted in the Marine Corps and served through the civil war and continued in the service until 1886, when he was given his discharge from the service at Sitka. He then entered the service of Mr. DeGroff as clerk, and in 1895 he was appointed Deputy Collector of Customs at St. Michaels, by Collector Ben Moore, he returned to Sitka in 1898 where he has lived since that time. Mr. Anders was stationed on the "Vandalla" US Naval vessel which took Gen. Grant around the world.

Beside relatives in Germany Mr. Anders leaves a sister at Madison, Wisconsin, a nephew at St. Louis, and a niece in Illinois.
THE ALASKAN, July 12, 1902

ALYCE E. ANDERSON

Alyce E. Anderson was born at Bishop Hill, Illinois, on August 17, 1868, and received all her schooling, including the preparation for teaching, in that state.

She taught three years in the Bishop Hill schools, and five years at Kirkland, Washington, before coming to Alaska in 1911.

In Alaska, she taught one year in Juneau, three years at Unga, eight years at Ninilchik, three years at Chignik, seven years at Naknek, three years at False Pass, two years at Sanak, and one at Portlock, and was scheduled to teach at Portlock again this year. Her teaching service in Alaska was continuous after her arrival, except for the five-year period of 1929-1934, when she was in business at Ninilchik. This made a total of 36 years teaching service, eight in the states, and twenty-eight in Alaska.

She died in Anchorage in August 1940, as the result of an operation.

ALASKA SCHOOL BULLETIN, Sept. 1940

BISHOP ANTHONY

Bishop Anthony has lived in Alaska from 1897 to 1907. He was in charge of the Sitka Cathedral and was also superintendent of the Alaska churches. After leaving America as an Archimandrite he was lost sight of. Very little is known of his work in Russia. At one time there was a rumor that he had perished in the Baltic Sea. during the war.

Bishop Anthony is well known to many Alaskans. He is a man of culture and education and his appointment will be hailed by adherents of the Russian church as well as the American public.

THE STROLLER'S WEEKLY, Oct. 1921

SAMUEL ARCHER

Samuel Archer, a member of the firm of Archer, Ewing & Co., was born in West Virginia in 1868, but calls himself a Missourian, since he was raised in that state. When a boy he learned the printer's trade, and was connected with the publishing business in every capacity from printer's devil to editor and proprietor, locating at one time or another in nearly every state and territory west of the Mississippi river. He came to Alaska as a prospector in 1897, going to the Klondike over the Skagway trail. With his present business associate, W.W. Ewing, he organized the well known mercantile firm of Archer, Ewing & Co. in 1899, which operated stations in Seattle, Wash., and Nome, Solomon and Dickson, Alaska. Mr. Archer has resided on Seward Peninsula since the early days of Nome; is at present in charge of the company's extensive business interests at Solomon and Dickson, and is identified with other enterprises throughout the district. Being a man of affairs and experience, and public spirited in disposition, he takes great interest in political affairs affecting Alaska; was elected a member of the second city council of Nome, and is at present United States Commissioner for the Solomon district. Mr. Archer is eminently qualified to represent this district at the coming convention with honor and credit both to himself and the Seward Peninsula.

NOME SEMI-WEEKLY NEWS MINING EDITION, Oct. 13, 1905

O.W. ASHBY

If any man can claim to be a real Alaskan it is O.W Ashby. He came to this country in 1884 from Missouri, where he was born in 1862. He mined for many years on the tributaries of the Yukon river, before the existence of Dawson, and was one of the first to enter the camp after its discovery. The discovery of Nome diggings brought him here with one million board feet of lumber. He has conducted large mining enterprises. He is associated with the Topkok ditch, which bought water for the Daniel creek operation. When he first came to Alaska he was accompanied by his brother Tom who still remains and is also engaged in mining.

NOME SEMI-WEEKLY NEWS MINING EDITION, Oct. 13. 1905

THOMAS H. ASHBY

Thomas H. Ashby, pioneer mining man of Alaska and now a resident of Juneau, on May 11, celebrated the fiftieth anniversary of his arrival in Juneau. He has resided in the North ever since that time and was in the Yukon more than a decade before the Klondike was discovered.

Mr. Ashby, his brother, Oscar, and three nephews of Richard T. Harris who with Joe Juneau discovered gold here, landed in Juneau on May 11, 1884, all of them going to Alaska from Missouri upon receipt of the word of the discovery.

After remaining at Juneau for two years, Mr. Ashby went farther north in search of new gold field. He was on the Stewart River, a tributary of the Upper Yukon River, in 1886, and the next year found him in the thriving camp at Forty-Mile.

Five years there and he pulled his stakes and went to Hootalinqua and prospected in that district until 1895 when he shifted down river to Circle. He was in that camp when word of the strike at Klondike River came through. With Billy Leake and two other oldtimers he mushed upriver over the ice and landed in that camp in the spring of 1897.

There he remained mining and prospecting until the Fall of 1900 when he came in the States to spend the winter. The next spring he joined the rush to Nome where for 13 years he continued in the placer mining game.

In 1913 he returned to Juneau and has made his home there ever since. "For 40 years out of the half-century I have lived in the North, I was engaged in placer mining and prospecting for quartz. It's a real game and I am still going strong," Mr. Ashby declared.

ALASKA WEEKLY, May 25, 1934

ELLEN GRACIA CALHOUN BACH

Ellen Bach died at Douglas City, Alaska, Saturday July 4th, 1903. Ellen Gracia beloved wife of Frank Bach, mother of Lenora, Alice, Frankie and Cecil Bach, daughter of Mrs. And Mrs. J. J. Calhoun, sister of Mrs. Ed. Webster, Frank and Carl Calhoun, a native of Oakfield, Wisconsin, aged 34 years, 11 months and 4 days.

Ellen Gracia Calhoun was born at Oakfield, Wisconsin, August 1, 1868. On Sept. 17, 1888, she arrived in Juneau, with her parents and brother and sister. On August 1st 1889 she became the wife of Frank Bach of Douglas. With the exception of but a few months, her entire married life was spent in this city. Six children, three boys and three girls, came to bless their home.

One boy and one girl were taken from the little flock, and the other four are left to comfort the sorrow stricken father. They are Lenora aged 12; Alice aged 11; Frankie 2 /1/2; and Cecil, a little over a year old.
DOUGLAS ISLAND NEWS, July 8, 1903

GARY BACH

Gary Bach, pioneer transportation man in Alaska, was claimed by death at his home on Pine street in Ketchikan last Friday morning [August 20, 1943] from a heart attack.

He was born in Carlton, Wisconsin in 1873. He was a purser on the Admiral line vessels for years before settling in Anchorage where he was married 22 years ago.

Survivors include his widow, and son, Gary in the Coast Guard, who is now in Ketchikan, and a niece in Durham, No. Carolina. He will be buried in Seattle.
. WRANGELL SENTINEL, Aug. 27, 1943

GEORGE W. BAILEY

On the 20th of October the U. S. Revenue cutter *Richard Rush* arrived in this port after a six months cruise in Alaska waters, her flag at half mast, and reported that the commander, Captain Geo. W. Bailey, had been lost overboard in the dark, during a strong gale and boisterous sea. The Captain had been ill and retired to his cabin after exchanging a few words with the officers of the deck, and then was seen no more. His loss was not discovered until some hours later, when nothing could be done beyond a futile search of the vessel, which had been running before the wind at the rate of 9 miles an hour. The accident occurred on the morning of October 16th, about 300 miles west of the mouth of the Columbia river.

Captain George W. Bailey was a native of New London, Conn., 43 years of age, and had been in the Revenue service fourteen years, having been made a Captain in 1874. His numerous friends and the public at large will sympathize with his

grief-stricken widow and his aged mother, whose sole support he had been for many years.
ALASKA APPEAL, Oct. 30, 1879

OPHELIA BARANOVITCH
On Tuesday morning Ophelia Baranovitch and F.F. Frobese were united in holy wedlock at the Catholic chapel in this town.[Sitka]
THE ALASKAN, Sat. April 11, 1888

CHARLES VINCENT BARANOVICH
Charles Vincent Baranovich, who came to Alaska in the early sixties and married the daughter of Francois, cook for the garrison of Russian Soldiers stationed at Fort Wrangell. His wife was born in the stockade, remnants which are still visible. Baranovich engaged in trading with the natives, and in 1865 was granted a concession at Karta Bay; his being one of the twenty-one concessions granted by the Russian government
Baranovich established a trading post at Karta Bay, to which natives from Tolstoy, Wrangell, and even as far away as Sitka brought furs and skins.
THE PATHFINDER, August 1920

JOHN BARONOVITCH
Captain Hamilton of the Truth came into port last Sunday he reported that John Baronovitch had been lost overboard and was probably drowned.
The launch had left Karta Bay Saturday evening bound for Loring. Baronovitch had put out the side lights and afterwards went below and put on his overcoat. He went on deck again and was not missed until the boat pulled into Loring. Here the captain went to waken him and found his bunk empty. A search of the boat was made but the missing man could not be found. Sometime during the night he had evidently slipped overboard and sunk.

Baranovichi was thirty-eight years old and was born in Kasaan. He was married but had no children. His brother in the hope of finding some trace of him is offering a hundred dollars reward for his discovery.

The deceased was the brother of Mrs. T. J. Case of this place.

WRANGELL SENTINEL, August 4, 1910

E. B. BARBEE

Staff Sergeant E. B. Barbee, retired of the U.S. Signal Corps, died recently in San Francisco, Calif. He was known from Nome to Ketchikan, and was a veteran in the Alaska service.

Mr. Barbee was in the Seattle office in the early days under Col. William A. Glassford. He came to Alaska and helped run the line from Valdez to Fairbanks and served time on the trail. He was stationed at Valdez for several years, was located at the key in Juneau for a number of years, and was known by hundreds in this city, served at Sitka, then in Seattle and came north again and ended his "hitch" at Sitka, retiring after 30 years service.

During the forepart of the World War, Barbee was stationed in Seattle, then went to Juneau and remained there for two years.

Mr. Barbee was a Spanish American war veteran serving in the Philippines.

ALASKA WEEKLY, May 14, 1926

ELLA ROBINSON BARNES   (See Vol. I, George Barnes)

Wrangell friends received a brief wire last week from Elton J. Barnes of Modesto, California, stating that his mother, Mrs. George Barnes had passed away on April 2.

Mrs. Barnes was one of the early missionaries of the Presbyterian Church in Alaska, having been sent to Wrangell about 1878 as a teacher in the mission school.

She married within a year or two after her arrival and for about 40 years was a resident. She is survived by her son, Elton

and his son, Elton, Jr.
WRANGELL SENTINEL, April 13, 1934

MARY BARONOVICH

Mary Baronovich of Kasaan, passed away recently. She was born in the old Russian fort of Wrangell many years before Alaska was purchased by the United States. She was the daughter of the steward of the post, and her age is about 90 years old. In early life she married Charles Vincent Baronovich the first white man to go to Kasaan, in which village he established a store more than sixty years ago He died in 1879.

Mrs. Baronovich was the mother of ten children, five of whom survive her. They are: Mrs. T. J. Case of Wrangell; Joe Baronovich of Ketchikan; Mrs. Frobese of Seattle; Nick Baronovich of Kasaan; Mrs Carrie Young of Seattle.
HYDER WEEKLY HERALD, Sept. 30, 1925
WRANGELL SENTINEL, August 13, 1925

W. H. BARRACLOUGH

References were made from several church pulpits of Vancouver early this month in the loss suffered by the United Church, particularly in the West, by the sudden death at Kitchener of Rev. W. H. Barraclough. His work in British Columbia, pastorates and especially in Dawson, Yukon Territory, during the difficult days of the gold rush were feelingly spoken of and general regret was expressed in his passing. The late Mr. Barraclough was born at Ingersoll, Ont., August 30, 1865. His parents were greatly devoted to church work his mother being a sister to the late Rev. Thomas Crosby, one of the most noted missionaries who ever did work in British Columbia. At the age of 16 he was licensed as an exhorter by the Rev. W. W. Ross and soon became a lay preacher. After his early education in the public schools at Ingersoll and the collegiate institute of that place, he entered Victoria College from which he obtained his B. A. For some time he taught school and during his period did much devoted service as a lay preacher. At the age of 18 he began work as an evangelist and was in 1885 at the age of 20 called to the active work of the ministry. During the years of probation he traveled the Wellandport and Cainsville circuits, where he enjoyed great success. During his term at college a man was required for Niagara Street church, St. Catherines, and it was here he met his future wife, Miss Edith Rowe, a daughter of Rev. R. B. Rowe, one of the active and energetic ministers of the Hamilton conference.

Mr. Barraclough was ordained in 1891 in the Hamilton conference. After ordination he traveled the Springford and Teeterville circuits with great success, at the end of which time he volunteered for mission work was accepted and appointed to the Indian Mission at Chillwick, B. C. This was about 1896.

After a few years he was invited to Centennial church, Victoria, where he conducted a successful ministry. He was then asked to go to Central Methodist church, Sarnia, and was thus transferred to the London conference. Since that date he filled important pastorates in London, Ont., Moncton and St. John, N. B., and since then at Kitchener, Ont., where his death occurred.

DAWSON NEWS, June 1, 1926

GEORGE T. BARRETT, SR   (See Vol. 1)

Eighty-five years of life, filled to the brim with stirring adventure from early youth until recent years, closed early Monday morning for George T. Barrett, Sr. as the result of a heart attack suffered at the home of his son, George T. Barrett, principal of Wrangell Institute, who after the first of the year went to Minneapolis to bring his father back to Alaska.

Barrett was born in News Brunswick, Canada on January 14, 1854.

THE WRANGELL SENTINEL, March 24, 1939

SAM G. BARTHOLOMEW

Captain Sam G. Bartholomew, pioneer Alaskan and

resident in Ketchikan for the past 24 years, died at the Ketchikan General Hospital on April 6, a few hours after suffering a stroke on the Zapora, less than two hours after the vessel left Ketchikan for Wrangell.

Captain Bartholomew was one of the best known mariners in the Ketchikan district where he had been a boat operator for 20 years. He was president of the Alaska Transportation Company which operates the Evelyn Berg and the Zapora.

He is survived by his wife, a daughter 19 and a son 14, a brother, Ralph Bartholomew, and a sister, Mrs. George Svenson of San Francisco. In keeping with the tradition of the sea and in accordance with his last wishes, his body was taken to Seattle for cremation, the ashes to be scattered over the sea.

WRANGELL SENTINEL, April 24, 1936

EDWARD "BOB" L. BARTLETT

Bob Bartlett's mother read about the Klondike gold rush in 1898 and traveled to Skagway and over the bleak Chilkoot. In Fairbanks she met a big, broad-shouldered man named Ed Bartlett, who was packing supplies into the wilderness for the frenzied gold seekers. His firm of Bartlett Brothers was the most noted packing enterprise in the North. The couple were married and on April 20, 1904, a son Edward, Jr., was born.

As soon as he was old enough to read, Edward L. Bartlett became known as "Bob." He grew up in Fairbanks, pioneer trading center in Alaska's "Golden Heart." At the age of 15 he went with his father on a pioneering trip into the Circle region. There were no roads and the elder Bartlett drove a team and wagon over the jolting ground to Chatanika. It took them 11 days to travel the 109 miles from Chatanika to Eagle Creek, a trip now made in three hours by car and 20 minutes by plane. Bob saw many famous Alaskan pioneers on that trek, but only three were now living-Bob himself, Jack Burrington, a picturesque prospector, and Wilber Jewell, who still lives in Circle.

Bob left high school one semester to go with his father to the Kantishna mining district, where Ed Bartlett was freighting ore for Tom Aitken. They used snowshoes most of the way. It was a tough, hard trip and Bob remembers falling all over the big. Webbed feet until he got used to them. Snowshoes require strong leg muscles and he was exhausted by the time camp was reached.

Bob graduated from high school at Fairbanks and then attended the University of Alaska. He is the first graduate of Alaska' s college-the farthest north university in the world-to sit in the halls of Congress. In 1927 he went to work as a reporter for the Fairbanks News Miner, after having gotten some preliminary experience there under a famous old Alaskan editor, W. F. Wrong Font Thompson.

Bob was the main writer for the News Miner until 1932, learning much journalistic lore from Hjalmar Nordale, who will rank in Bob's book of friends very near the top. In 1932 Alaska elected a new delegate in Congress-a tall, lean lawyer from Valdez, named Anthony J. (Tony) Dimond. He was destined to be one of the Territory's best known public servant and to serve long in Congress than any other man in Alaskan history. When he went to Washington, Tony took Bob Bartlett with him as his principal secretary.

For four years Bob continued in this capacity. He had a chance to study government and to become acquainted with the federal departments handling Alaskan business. Then in 1936 he felt the call of the North Country, luring him across a continent of space and time. He returned to Alaska with his family and moved from Fairbanks to Circle, operating a gold mine on Independence Creek.

In the shadow of the Arctic Circle Bob's two children grew up. Doris Ann is now 11 and Susan is four. His wife, Vide is also a native Alaskan, and, like her husband, a graduate of the University of Alaska.

In 1939 President Roosevelt appointed this Far Northern gold miner to be Secretary of Alaska, a position second only to that of governor. As chairman of the Alaskan Unemployment Compensation Commission, Bob's work had come favorably to the President's attention. In the position of Secretary of Alaska, Bob became a close friend and follower of Governor Ernest Gruening, who for more than two decades had been a prominent figure in American journalism and in the American progressive movement.

ALASKA LIFE, April 1945

HARRY W. BAUER

Dr. Harry W. Bauer was educated after leaving high school in the North Pacific Dental college of Portland, taking a three year's course, and following this he worked with Dr. C. H. Waston of Seattle, one of the leading dentists of the country and who was for many years the dean of the Des Moines, Iowa, Dental college. After a most thorough course of study under a man of great practical experience Dr. Bauer made a trip to Alaska in search of a permanent location and finally decided to come to Ketchikan. The doctor has within a comparatively short time build up a good business. He was born in New York City in 1882 and some years later his family moved to Portland, Oregon, where he grew to manhood.

ALASKA MINING JOURNAL, Jan. 1907

R. M. BECKER

R.M. Becker was one of the earliest pioneers of Alaska and a resident of Skagway for ten years, passed his 78th mile stone last Friday.

Mr. Becker was born in Middleburg, N.Y., Oct. 22, 1831. He came to Alaska in 1863 going to Wrangell and mining on the Stikine river. Later Mr. Becker went below and located on a farm on an island near Anacortes, Wash. He sold the farm and was proprietor of the Commercial hotel in Seattle at the time of the big fire. He then went to Honolulu and was there during the troublesome time following the dethroning of Queen Lil. Mr.

Becker came to Skagway ten years ago and has resided here since except for an occasional trip to the outside.
DAILY ALASKAN, Oct. 26, 1907

CHARLES O. BENJAMIN

Charles O. Benjamin, 66, widely known pioneer merchant, died Sunday following a heart attack.

Mr. Benjamin came to Alaska in 1903 and mined in the Anchorage section until 1907 when he came to Wrangell and entered the mercantile business.

He was a member of the Territorial House of Representatives in 1925 and 1927, and member of the Senate in 1929. He served on the Wrangell City Council for many years.

Benjamin is survived by his widow, a son Lloyd, both of Wrangell, and a daughter Marjorie, now in Seattle.
PETERSBURG PRESS, Nov. 17, 1939

B. E. BENSON

B. E. Benson, Alaska pioneer passed away at an early hour yesterday morning at St. Ann's Hospital at the age of 75 [?].

Born in Ellicottville, New York, Mr. Benson came to Alaska in January 1899, and lived at Haines and Skagway and later in Juneau. For a number of years he has had a farm on the Loop Road near Mendenhall Glacier.

He is survived by his widow Mary C. Benson, a daughter, Mrs. Caroline Tresing of Brooklyn, New York, and a daughter, Mrs. Beatrice Murphy of Seattle.
DAILY ALASKA EMPIRE, Sept. 8, 1936

CHARLES BERESFORD

Charles Bresford, an inmate of the Pioneers' Home at Sitka, died at the institution January 20th. Beresford was born in Sheffield, England, 59 years ago and came from Montana to the North about fifteen years ago to accept a position as mining engineer with Col. J. H. Conrad, at Carcross, Yukon, who was operating the Conrad Consolidated Mines in the vicinity of Windy Arm. He was with Conrad for a number of years and then went to the Porcupine country back of Haines, where he secured a number of claims which he was unable to dispose of to advantage. He was at one time one of the most prominent mining engineers of the northwest.

PETERSBURG WEEKLY, March 16, 1923

LUDWIG BERG

Ludwig Berg, Wrangell pioneer, passed away Wednesday morning at 7:30 at his home. He had been in failing health for some time. Mr. Berg was born in Trondheim, Norway, 88 years ago. He and Mrs. Berg, who survives him, were married March 27, 1882 in Ramsdalen, Norway and came to America in 1891, settling in Michigan. A short time later they returned to Norway where two of their children were born, and came back to Michigan in the latter 1890s and finally settled in Wrangell in 1900. During his long residence here Mr. Berg was variously engaged in dairying, fish buying and mining. He was one of the early-day leaders in business and community life and contributed much to the development of the community until age forced his retirement but, true Alaskan that he was, he never lost interest in his mining properties which are located at Berg's Bay and which he worked, with the aid of his sons, until very recently.

In March, 1942, Mr. and Mrs. Berg celebrated their 60th wedding anniversary in Wrangell with a dinner given by their daughter and son-in-law, Mr. and Mrs. Cope G. Munday.

Surviving Mr. Berg, besides his wife are J. E. Berg, long a resident of Ketchikan, now of California; John Berg of Pasadena, Calif.; and Mrs. S. A. Shepard of Seattle who arrived here before their father passed away; Mrs. Ed Christensen of Anchorage; Mrs. Munday; and L. C. Berg of Sitka.

The Bergs also had three other children. Two are buried in Norway and one, Alfred, died in Petersburg some years ago and is buried there.

Twelve grandchildren and eleven great-grandchildren and a sister, Mrs. Bertina Tingstad of Seattle also survive.

WRANGELL SENTINEL, June 2, 1944

EMIL BERGMAN

Fort Yukon Postmaster Emil Bergman was appointed to office June 22, 1926. He succeeded Mrs. Grace Brooks.

The post office in Fort Yukon was established in 1899 and housed first in the old N.A.T. Co. building.

Emil came to Alaska in 1909, walking to Fairbanks from Valdez with his two brother, Oscar, who later worked with the Alaska Railroad for many years and Eric, now located at Manley Hot Springs. He has raised a family of 8 children, 5 of whom are now married with families of their own. Daughter Adeline finished high school in Fairbanks this spring, winning a scholarship award to the University of Alaska.

JESSEN'S WEEKLY, July 18, 1947

CLARENCE J. BERRY

Clarence J. Berry, multi-millionaire oil man and former Alaskan, died following an appendicitis operation in Los Angeles last night.

The Fairbanks News-Miner said, "Of all the men who took fortunes in gold out of Yukon Territory and Alaska, Clarence J. Berry probably became the richest. A stake that was founded in the Klondike increased swiftly until Berry was reported to be worth over $30,000,000.

"He is remembered by old-timers as one who was willing to stretch out a helping hand to pioneers in need. His benefactions to old friends and acquaintances amounted to thousands of dollars yearly. It is said that in addition to those he gave temporary aid Berry always provided funds which provided sole support for over a hundred persons.

"With his brothers Fred and Frank, Clarence Berry secured and mined some of the richest ground in the Klondike.

About 1905 he came to Fairbanks and obtained ground on lower Ester, from which he took out another fortune.

"After remaining here three or four years Berry went to the States and made his home there from then until the time of his death. Still seeking wealth from the ground, Berry got into the oil game and the 'black gold' paid him fabulous returns, making him one of the richest men in the West.

"Berry spent his boyhood in Fresno, Calif., and except for the years he lived in the Yukon Territory and Alaska made California his home practically all his life.

"For many years past he made his headquarters in San Francisco. He maintained an elaborate suite of rooms at the St. Francis Hotel as well as owning a palatial home.

"Berry was 63 or 64 years old. Surviving him are his widow and two brothers, Frank and Fred, and his aged mother, who is living in Long Beach, Calif. Another brother, Henry was killed last year in an automobile accident."

THE KUSKO TIMES, Nov. 8, 1930

DONALD BERRY

Died, in this city, on Friday July 24, 1903, Donald Berry a native of St. Andrews, New Brunswick, Canada, aged 69 years.

Donald Berry was a carpenter and millwright by trade, and in his younger days worked for some time in Boston. He afterwards came west to Virginia City, Nevada, and from there to California, where he was employed in the different mining camps. He came to Alaska in 1886 on the steamer, Idaho, landing in Juneau on Jan. 16th He was employed at Treadwell in the construction of the 240 mill and afterwards in other work, and Douglas was his home until his death.

Berry is survived by a daughter at San Francisco.

DOUGLAS ISLAND NEWS, July 29, 1903

JAMES J. BETTLES

Captain James Bettles died at his home in Oak Harbor,

Washington on September 4th, 1939, at the advanced age of 83 years, having been born January 22, 1856.

At seventeen, he left home and operated a pack train in the Okanogan district in Washington.. In 1883 (?), he went to Sitka and later to Chenega where he married Alena Sistososs in 1891 and operated a trading post there. Here he engaged in ship building and owned the first steam boat on Prince William Sound, the June. James Bettles was one of the first to chart that region and carried the mail for many years between Valdez and Cordova.

During his experience on the Sound he rescued 40 of the 80 people from the wrecked S.S. Olympia, one a t a time by using a net, having to go "bow on" for each one. Because of the terrific storm that caused a pack of ice, he froze his lungs. He was forced to retire from active shipping.

After coming to Washington in 1918, he has lived on his farm near Whidby Island.

Captain James J., Bettles is survived by two daughters, Anna, now Mrs. Jas. Alexander, and Alice, Mrs. George Kirk; one son, Joe A. Bettles, of Pendleton, Org.; a sister, Mrs. Charlotte Sheld, of San Diego; a brother, Albert, of Los Angeles, and another brother, Gordon Bettles, of Seattle.

THE ALASKA WEEKLY, Sept. 8, 1939

BEULEH CHAFREL BIGGS

Beuleh Chafrel Biggs, a well known pioneer of Alaska and wife of Harry E. Biggs, died Sunday night [Feb. 19] at the family home on East and Fifth street.

Deceased was born in Georgia, Oct. 16, 1876 and was married Nov. 1892. She came to Juneau in 1901. She is survived by her husband and adopted son, William; a married daughter and two grandchildren in Pittsburgh, Kan.; and a half brother in Texas.

JUNEAU SUNDAY CAPITAL, Feb. 26, 1922

FRED R. BIRCH

Fred R. Birch was a pioneer of the Northland. He went to Atlin, B. C. in 1899; remained there until 1900, and then returned to Seattle, where he engaged in the practice of law. In 1915, he again went north, going to the Nelchina district, a new camp, to the north of the Matanuska coal field. Birch remained in that camp, which was more or less a fizzle, for a season, and again returned to Seattle, where he since resided. In the Nelchina district, Birch was dreaming of a snow motor, or something of the sort, and after he came outside, put his ideas into concrete form, perfecting a machine that seems to do the work–on the outside, at least. How the snow motor will work in Alaska is a matter that will be determined on this long journey. The snow motor is now produced by the Snow-Motors, Incorporated, of Detroit, Michigan, and Gordon Scott will have charge of the three machines to be employed on the expedition.

ALASKA WEEKLY, Jan. 15, 1926

JOSEPHINE MEYERS BISHOP

The daughter of the publisher of Juneau's first newspaper, who was born in this city in 1891, is revisiting her birth place this week.

Mrs. Josephine Meyers Bishop of Seattle stopped over to look up friends while on her return to her home. She has been visiting with a daughter in Fairbanks. Yesterday she flew by Alaska Coastal Airlines for a day of visiting in Sitka where her father published a newspaper for a year, in 1887, before he moved to the mining camp of Juneau, which had been located seven years earlier.

Mrs. Bishop brought with her several issues of the early day newspaper, The Juneau City Mining Record. The paper was published here for seven years by her father, Frank F. Meyers. She has a file of the newspapers for the first year it was published, in 1888, which she left with her daughter.

Mrs. Bishop was just three years old when her father sold

his newspaper and moved his family to Port Townsend, Wash., where he managed the newspaper, The Leader, for many years.

Mrs. Bishop's three sisters also were born in Alaska. The eldest, Clara, was born in 1887 in Sitka; Vivian was born in 1889; and Ruhamah in 1893 in Juneau.

The Juneau born visitor is making her second trip to Alaska since she left. She spent some time with her daughter in Fairbanks four years ago. Mrs. Bishop, now a widow, says she will "settle down" for a while now in her home of the Seattle-Ballard district and, "recall the pleasure of this visit and make plans for another, soon again, I hope."

THE DAILY ALASKA EMPIRE, Sept. 27, 1957

ALBERT F. BIXBY

Albert F. Bixby, U. S. Army veteran and longtime Alaska and Juneau resident, died July 21, at Port Angeles, Wash.

Mr. Bixby was born Nov. 25, 1878 in Idaho. He joined the U.S. Army as a youth to serve in the Boxer Rebellion and made the army his career for most of his life, serving also in the Spanish American war, the Mexican Campaign, and World War I with the First Division. When the United States entered into World War II, he was given the choice of working as a civilian employee of the army or being recalled to service. He chose the later.

More than 40 years of Mr. Bixby's life was spent in Alaska, chiefly with the Army. He served at Nome, Anchorage and Port Chilkoot out of Haines.

His total services extended over 30 years and he received his honorable discharge October 12, 1925 in Plattsburg, N.Y. A noted trumpeter, Mr. Bixby was assigned to sound taps at the burial of President McKinley in Canton, Ohio.

Mr. Bixby came to Juneau in 1933 and has made his home in Juneau and this area since that time except for the past year.

Surviving him are his widow, Violet, two daughters: Mrs. Howard Summona of Juneau; and Mrs. Georgia Wood of

Compton, Calif.; a son, Gil Bixby of Juneau and Elfin Cove; six grandchildren; and one great-grandchild.

JUNEAU EMPIRE, July 26, 1955

EDITH BLAKE

Edith Blake, who went to Nome in 1899, where she spent three winters looking after her claims on Dexter and Anvil creeks came out on the last trip of the Ohio laden with gold dust.

In addition in looking after her property in the Far North, Miss Blake, who is an accomplished musician as well as a writer of note, has found time during the long winter months to teach the young mind how to shoot, contribute to the social gaiety of the town, and furnish interesting matter to the Midnight Sun.

After a brief visit among friends and relatives in California and the East, Miss Blake will return on the last boat to Nome preferring as she does the winter life in there to even the sunny clime in Southern California where she was born.

THE MIDNIGHT SUN, Sept., 1903

WALTER C. BLANTON

Walter Blanton came to Alaska from Seattle in January, 1901, and has been at Valdez, at Fairbanks in the spring of 1904; Anchorage, 1915, and Hyder from 1920. He is in the second year of his office as treasurer of Hyder Igloo and is proprietor of the Silver Grill in Hyder. He enlisted in the United States army in 1917 from Anchorage and has seen ten months overseas service with the 216th Aero squadron.

ALASKA DISPATCH, May 5, 1922

MARY WORTH BONE

Mrs. Scott T. Bone, 82, widow of Alaska's former governor and former Seattle newspaper editor, died Thursday in Los Angeles, relatives here reported. Mary Worth was born in Anderson, Indiana, and she had seven children.

Mrs. Bone and her husband who died in January 1936,

lived in Alaska for four years from 1921 to 1925 while he served as governor of the Territory.

Bone was the first city editor of the Washington Post and then founded the Washington Herald.

THE NOME NUGGET, June 28, 1948 [?]

SCOTT CARDELLE BONE   (See Vol. 4)

Scott Cardelle Bone, Republican, served as the tenth governor of Alaska from 1921 to 1925. He was born in Shelby County, Indiana, on Feb. 15, 1860. He was married to Mary Worth of Anderson, Indiana on June 15, 1887 and had seven children by her, Paul Myers, Roger Morse, Mildred (Mrs. John Ford Starr), Scott Worth, Carroll Alfred, Robert Douglas, and Marguerite.

Bone was a journalist by profession. He served in various capacities on Indiana newspapers from 1881-1888. Following this for a 17-year period he was news editor and then managing editor of the Washington D.C. Post. He was editor and principal owner of the Washington Herald from 1906-1911.

He then moved to Seattle, and served as editor-in-chief of the Seattle Post-Intelligencer from 1911- 1918. During his Seattle residence he was chairman of the Alaska Bureau of the Seattle Chamber of Commerce, 1914-1915, and made a trip to Alaska, thus becoming familiar with its problems. He served as director of publicity for the Republican National Convention in 1919 and in 1921 was appointed Governor of Alaska by President Harding, assuming his duties of office in May of that year. He did not seek the governorship, but was chosen as a result of a factional struggle for the position between two prominent Alaskans.

The governorship of Alaska was the first and only office Bone ever held. His wide acquaintance in the newspaper world gave the Territory much valuable publicity and he kept an optimistic eye busy in an effort to make Alaska better known to the world.

Scott C. Bone died in Santa Barbara, Calif. January 27, 1936.

ALASKA DAILY PRESS, Jan. 28, 1936

JOSEPH BOSKOWITZ

Joseph Boskowitz, organizer of the Boskowitz Steamship Company and the Alaska Commercial company, died today, aged 88. He came here in 1862 and formed the Victoria Sealing company but retired from that enterprise after the signing of the treaty affecting sealing. He then entered the fur business with the Alaska Commercial company, which secured the sealing rights of the Pribiloff Islands. Later, seven of his ships were seized on the contention that sealing was prohibited, but the government made restitution however.

As a young man he was associated with a group of commercial men who were instrumental in inducing Secretary Seward in purchasing Alaska from Russia; His firm was then heavily interested in the Alaska fur trade.

KETCHIKAN CHRONICLE, March 21, 1923

BERTHA J. BOYD

Mrs. Bertha J. Boyd, pioneer woman of the Kuskokwim country, passed away in Anchorage one day last week, according to recent reports.

She is survived by a daughter, Mrs. Bernarit [?] of McGrath.

Mrs. Boyd came to the Kuskokwim country to teach in the native school at Bethel more than 20 years ago. While at Bethel, she also served in the capacity of nurse, administering to the needs of the natives who regarded her as a mother. Many natives who are alive today, give her credit, for their staying alive.

While down river, she spent some time in isolated spots on the Bering Sea, in charge of checking out school supplies to small, out-of-the-way schools. She came from Bethel to teach school in Takotna. While teaching here, she became interested in

The Kusko Times, then owned and operated by A. X. Grant. Some time later, she gave up teaching and devoted her whole time to assisting Mr. Grant in publishing the paper.

Mrs. Boyd was associated with Kusko Times over a period of 15 years, during which time she became well known throughout the entire country.

THE KUSKO TIMES, Feb. 26, 1937

HERBERT J. BRADLEY

Herbert J. Bradley, born 27 years ago in Wrangell, has a record of achievement in which he may well take pride. He became a wage earner at fourteen years of age when he began working during the fishing season for his grandfather, the late John Bradley, one of the most highly respected of the older Indians in Wrangell. By the time he was 19 years old he had earned his own boat and since that age has been an independent fisherman. He has had much experience, besides on the fishing grounds as a representative of local fish buyers.

When but 23 years old he was elected president of the local camp of the Alaska Native Brotherhood, a position which he held for three successive years. Under his presidency, plans were initiated and carried through for the building of the A. N. B. hall, under the circumstances a striking achievement in itself, both for young Bradley and the organization which he headed. During these years he served as a grand camp officer and is now on the local A. N. B. council and treasurer of the organization.

In the spring of 1934 with his father, James Bradley, and two others, he organized the Stikine Gillnetters Association to which he was elected president, re-elected by the 70 white and Indian members last year and again re-elected recently for the coming year.

We believe Herbert Bradley is entitled to the support of the voters. We are endorsing Herbert Bradley and asking that voters give his candidacy for the city council consideration.

WRANGELL SENTINEL, April 3, 1936

JOHN GREEN BRADY (See Vol. 3)

The Verstovian, published in the interest of the Sheldon Jackson School at Sitka, in honor of Founders Day, April 17, pays a fitting tribute to the late John Green Brady, the founder as follows:

"John Green Brady arrived in Sitka in March of 1878 and immediately called the natives together in the old Baranof Castle building and announced his mission. His auditors were rude and uncivilized, with bare feet, long hair and painted faces.

Nothing had been done toward their education. On April 17th, 1878, Mr. Brady and Miss Fannie Kellogg opened the first Protestant native school in Sitka in an upstairs room of the soldiers' barracks. The present Sheldon Jackson School is the lineal descendant.

Governor Brady was a firm believer in industrial education. So strongly was he of the opinion that this type of work was of first important that he determined to withdraw from service of the Mission Board and devote himself to the industrial training of the natives. He started a sawmill, took a homestead and in many other ways stimulated the movement toward individual homes and attainment of self-support.

In 1897 he was appointed Governor of Alaska by President McKinley and held this office for nine years with fidelity to duty and great benefit to the territory. The closing years of his life were spent in active efforts to build up the civil and commercial interests of the territory which he had done so much to establish. His death occurred on the evening of December 17, 1918, at the old homestead at Sitka. His body was laid to rest in a little knoll in the military cemetery at Sitka, which thus has the distinction of giving a resting place to the early remains of the only governor buried within the boundaries of the territory of Alaska."

ALASKA WEEKLY, June 11, 1926

ROBERT S. BRAGAW   (See Vol. 1)

Robert S. Bragaw, better known to Anchorage folks as "Dad" Bragaw, died at his home in that city recently from a stroke of paralysis.

He was a direct descendent of the family Bourgon Brouchard and his wife, Catherine Le Febre, French Huguenots, from Manheim on the Rhine, who landed on Manhattan Island in 1675. They bought an estate in old Nassau and there established the family whose members are now variously known as Bragau, Bragaw and Brokaw. During the Revolutionary war the old home, then owned by Richard Bragaw, was a rendezvous for patriots and all of the members of the family bore arms in the struggle for independence.

Robert Bragaw was born at New London, Conn. October 1, 1851. He was educated in the public schools of his native state and his first occupation was in a wholesale grocery house in New York City. At the age of 23 he moved west to Denver and engaged in the mining and real estate business. In 1883 he cast his destiny with the Couer d'Alenes and two years later married.

The official career of Mr. Bragaw began when he was appointed recorder of Kootenal county and he served in that capacity until 1890, when he was elected clerk of the district court and ex-officio county auditor and clerk of the county commissioners. He held that office until 1899. In that year he was appointed forest supervisor of the Priest River forest reserve and resigned that office in 1904 to become state auditor to which office he was elected by a majority of 20,000 votes.

In 1906 Mr. Bragaw moved to Spokane and engaged in the real estate business with his son. He moved to Los Angeles later and went to Anchorage in 1917, having resided there since that time.

ALASKA WEEKLY, March 9, 1928

JOHN BRANNEN (See Vol. 1)

John Brannen, who succeeds J. J. Jolley as chief of police,

was born in Clarion county Pennsylvania, 47 years ago. While quite young his parents moved to the Pacific coast, where his father engaged in trading in British Columbia. Young Brannen attended So. Louis college in Victoria, Hermann Piper of the city being the classmate of Mr. Brannen's. Subsequently, Mr. Brannen became a coal miner and worked for several years in the coal mines of British Columbia.

In 1889 he removed to Seattle and still followed his occupation of coal miner at Newcastle, Carbonado and other places. Having run many narrow escapes from death in the coal mines, he quit the business and took up a farm in Kitsap country, Wash., later removing to Seattle where he was given a position as patrolman on the police force. He was promoted to lieutenant and made drill instructor of the police corps, subsequently being promoted to captain of police, serving in these capacities for six years.

He resigned when Boltch Rogers became chief of police. For years Mr. Brannen was a member of the national guard of Washington

Mr. Brannen came to Nome in the spring of 1900, his intention being to engage in the freighting business, but he lost his horses on route and after he arrived here. He had brought 25,000 feet of lumber from Seattle as a speculation, the price had dropped before he got it landed, and with J. D. Gardner erected a building and opened a liquor house now known as the Candle City saloon. Mr. Brannen, though conducting a saloon, has not tasted liquor of any kind for 30 years. He has a wife and seven children, who reside in Seattle.

NOME NUGGET, Jan. 17, 1903

THOMAS E. BRIGGS

At 9:40 o'clock last night Thomas E. Briggs breathed his last at the White Pass and Yukon hospital in Skagway at the age of 47.

Deceased has been railroading continuously since 1881 when he was engaged in the mechanical department of the New York & New England railroad. He worked two years on the Baltimore & Ohio and then on the Carribean & Manganese in South America. From South America he came to the White Pass and has been in its service for five years and up to the time of his demise.

Deceased leaves a wife and two daughters in Nunda, N.Y., and a mother at Stormville in the same state.

THE DAILY ALASKAN, Jan. 26, 1904

SOPHIA LIND BRITT (See Vol. 2)

Mrs. William Britt died in Baltimore, Maryland at the home of her daughter-in-law, Mrs. Jacob Britt. Daughter of the prominent Lind family of Norway, Mrs. Britt came to Skagway early in the century as the bride of William Britt who had been a tutor in her home. Their son was born in Skagway where Mr. Britt was the proprietor of a pharmacy, and they lived there until Britt started a in business here [Juneau]. He was a member of the Territorial legislature for several sessions. Jacob Britt was appointed to Annapolis. He was the Captain of the Asheville which was lost in the South Pacific in 1942. William Britt died in an automobile accident in 1932.

ALASKA STATE HISTORICAL LIBRARY, Biography File (Daily Alaska Empire (?), dated Mar. 22, 1951)

DAVID BROWN

The oldest employee of the Treadwell and Alaska-Juneau mines, David Brown, was presented yesterday with a beautiful gold Elgin watch by more than 100 of his mine associates for his 40 years of service here.

Brown, accompanied by Mrs. Brown, will sail for the states Monday on the Yukon for his first trip outside since 1913.

He handed in his resignation to the AJ staff yesterday morning and at that time was given the watch by Walter Scott, mill superintendent.

"It's been 40 years last April, since I first started to work at Treadwell," Brown told an Alaska Press reporter today.

"That was back in 1895. In the fall of 1898 I took a trip to the old country, Scotland, and was gone for six months. In 1902 and 1910 I went out for a month each time, and in 1913 I spent three days in the states, but that's the last time."

The past spring Brown took his first air ride, and like it fine. "It was just like sitting in an easy chair in our parlor," he said. The flight was made to Goddard Hot Springs.

The 67 year old miner doesn't know if he'll ever return to Alaska again. "I'm going to California," he explained, "and if I can stand the heat I may stay there. You know, it's quite a change from the 24 years I've spent in Douglas Island and the 16 in Juneau."

Mr. and Mrs. Brown will visit their son, Sinclair Brown, in California, and Mr. Brown's brother, James S. Brown in Manteca, Calif. Mrs. Arthur Bringdale, their daughter, will occupy their home on Sixth and Park streets while they're gone.

On Mr. Brown's gold chain which he bought in Alaska in the gold rush days of 1898 will hang his new gold watch on which is inscribed, the "compliments of the men of the Alaska Juneau Mill to David Brown. . . .Sept. 30, 1935."(sic)

ALASKA DAILY PRESS, Sept. 28, 1935

LESTER BUCEY

Lester Bucey, Alaskan for 29 years, died in Anchorage after a brief hospitalization. He was one of the Territory's veteran newspaper men since the time he started his own paper in Seldovia in 1918 shortly after going to Alaska. For many years he owned and published the Seward Gateway until the plant burned in 1942.

Later in Anchorage, he joined in organizing the Anchorage

News and became advertising manager. Last June he resigned to enter into the real estate business to get away from the routine of office hours. In his sixties, his keen mind and sense of humor, and his active, kindly interest in the world and its people, kept him a much younger man in spirit than in body. He had friends of all ages.

He is survived by his wife, Mary; a son, James; and an adopted daughter Bettie, who, with her husband Capt. B. F. Adams, Jr, is in Frankfort, Germany.

ALASKA WEEKLY, May 2, 1947

PETER BUCKLEY

Among the pioneers of Alaska, Peter Buckley is a familiar name. Mr. Buckley is now a resident of Decoto, a suburb of Berkeley, California. Peter Buckley was born in New York state, and his early wandering experiences were gained in California, Hawaii, the Fiji Islands, Australia and Mexico.

In 1893 he went to Alaska, where he remained three years. He then returned to the states, remained a month and again hit the northern trail. That was 1896. He took his 14-year-old son with him and went over the Chilcoot Pass and on down to Circle City on the Yukon. The son, J. J. Buckley, is now a deputy U. S. marshal at Fairbanks.

The father returned to the states in 1900 and left for South America, where he engaged in extensive mining in Columbia for a few years, later going on a prospecting venture in the Philippine Islands and in South Africa. Mr. Buckley lived in Seattle during the year of the great fire, and later had property in Auburn, Seattle, and Belleview.

He has had much experience in prospecting and mining ores and placer deposits, much of which could not be worked profitably because of ineffectual treatment processes and inadequate transportation. He is still intensely interested in mineral development and metallurgical work. His daughter, Mrs. Katherine Buckley Griffiths, of Seattle, recently presented to him the plans of the new metallurgical process sponsored by General Research Foundation Society of Seattle, with which she is identified, at which Mr. Buckley expressed the desire to immediately embark upon an expedition to install the new process on his unworked property.

ALASKA WEEKLY, Sept. 3, 1926

ARCHIE BURNS

Archie Burns, then who there was no more familiar figure among the hardy pioneers of the great Northland, recently passed away in Fairbanks.

Archie Burns is a name known in every part of the North from the Fraser river to Nome. In the score or more years he spent on the frontier he blazed more thousands of miles of trail than any other man in the country. Several times the possessor of comfortable wealth, he was not contented, and pushing on the new camps would lose all. But a short time would pass before his indomitable energy and industry would yield another fortune. It was on the eve of another big success that death came, as the deceased had located a rich homestead, and was doing a big business in freighting, a calling he has followed intermittently the whole of his life.

First coming to Alaska in the early eighties, Burns joined the rush to the old Fortymile diggings. He located on a bar at the mouth of O'Brien creek, and soon had rocked out gold enough to support him in ease the remainder of his life. He was outside for a time but returned in 1896.

He was bringing a scow load of beef cattle down the Yukon late in the fall, when he got caught in the ice off the mouth of a stream then known as the Trondak. But a few short months and the Anglaized name, the Klondike, was in the headlines of every newspaper on the continent. The rush followed, and of course Burns' beef jumped to incredulous value. He abandoned the trip to Circle and returned outside with the returns of his venture in meat dealing. He could not stand the quiet and lack of adventure, and the winter of !898 found him on the Dyea trail, operating the famous "Burns' tram" from the summit of Chilkoot to the base of the great incline. In the two seasons he conducted the trams he cleaned at least $100,000 clear.

Just about the time the Nome excitement offered temptations many, and strong to those trying to accumulate a measure of Alaska's gold. As he had been a figure in every stampede for years he was in the lead of the movement to Nome. He put in two years at profitable freighting, and again took a look at the outside world. His stay was brief, his next destination being Dawson. The old days gone from that camp, he joined a party starting for the remote Koyukuk diggings. There he mined with McNamer. Then he mushed to Nome before the end of the season. The winter of 1901-02 he spent freighting on the Yukon between Dawson and Whitehorse. In the spring of 1902 he again went into the Koyukuk district. Next, he stampeded into the Tanana country. He was first to rattle over roads carved form a virgin wilderness in a wagon built by himself. The vehicle is of primitive make, his wheels having been cut from planking nailed together. With this he moved to Fairbanks creek and first boiler over taken out there. To accomplish this he had to open a trail.

In the deceased estate is the 320-acre homestead across the river. This is one of the most valuable pieces of property about the camp, though by reason of certain privilege of the statutes, its holder could not realize from the property for several years. It was the first homestead staked under new United States homestead act. The deceased was about 50 years of age.

NOME SEMI-WEEKLY NEWS, Jan. 14, 1905
DAILY ALASKA DISPATCH, Dec. 13, 1904

CHARLES W. BUSH

Charles W. Bush, for twenty years a resident of Alaska, first going to Valdez and later taking up a residence in Anchorage, accompanied by Mrs. Bush and son, came south on the steamer Alameda, and plans to quit the Northland. He will probably live in Portland, Oregon, his home before he departed for Alaska nearly a quarter of a century ago.

Mr. Bush, who is an asset in any city he lives in, and his brother-in-law, "Dad" Ingram, opened a tobacco store in Valdez when that town was the only terminus of the Richardson Highway, before the Copper River & Northwestern railroad was build. Bush, Always a lover of clean sports, was active in baseball, basketball and the like, while Ingram, who was something of a politician, was sent to the first Alaska legislative assembly from the Third division.

When the Alaskan Engineering Commission established the city of Anchorage, Mr. Bush moved to that point, while Ingram came outside. Bush took a position with the big mercantile firm in that city and Seward. He soon was installed as manager of the Anchorage branch for two successive terms and was mayor of the city when he resigned to come outside.

ALASKA WEEKLY, Jan. 15, 1926

HARRY BUZBY

Harry Buzby was born in [unable to read place] Oct. 12, 1863. Mr. Buzby removed to Illinois with his parents when he was a lad nine years of age, and later the family went to Nebraska. When he started life on his own he traveled west to Montana and for several years followed surveying. Later, he went into the cattle ranching business there.

Soon after the Dawson stampede he moved his family to Willamette, Ore. and went to Nome in 1901. In that year he moved his family to Skagway where he became interested in a molybdenum mine. He went to fairbanks in the early days of that camp.

He was one of the very early ranchers in Interior. He took up a homestead soon after his arrival at Fairbanks, locating on the banks of the Chena river. He cleared land and started to market which at the time was thought impossible to grow in the Interior. He contributed much to the knowledge to farming and stock

raising in Alaska.
Harry Buzby died in Fairbanks in February 1931.
KUSKO TIMES, Feb. 21, 1931

SAM CALLAHAN

Sam Callahan has left us. He was a noble, independent old pioneer soul, who, in his 76th year of life, mushed 7,000 miles to Seattle to again try his luck on Lonesome River, a tributary of the Innoko, where he found a prospect twenty years ago . We bade him goodbye as he sailed away on the first trip of the Victoria last June when his parting words were "I'm not coming out of Alaska any more. I love the country and want to be buried there. However, I am going to find pay on Lonesome River first"

We wave at him as the boat pulled away from the dock and had one cheery letter from him since, which stated that he was going to pole his outfit up the Yukon and the Innoko rivers and get established in a cabin before the freeze up came. He would be "out of communication for the winter," he said, "but would sure strike pay."

Callahan was found frozen to death inside his cabin but three days after arrival at his destination–striving and struggling over 11,000 miles to get back to that prospect he uncovered on Lonesome River twenty years ago.

We quote the lead paragraph of a story published in The Alaska Weekly, April 29, 1932, anent this grand old pioneer who had just arrived in Seattle: "His courage unfaltering, his frame a little bit warped but headed back for the Yukon where he spent twenty-three of his seventy-six years of life. Sam J. Callahan sauntered into the office of The Alaska Weekly yesterday having hitchhiked and mushed 7,000 miles to reach Seattle from which point he hopes to take passage again to the Northland."

And again we quote the concluding paragraph of the story which states: "Well, all we have to say in that despite the fact that Sam Callahan lost portions of his hands and feet in the 'Nigger' Jim stampede into Coal Creek in the early days of Dawson, he is still battling alone in his own independent way, and is on the trail back to the Yukon where he found a prospect years ago.

Sam Callahan arrived in Dawson in 1898 where he prospected and mined. Several years later he wandered into Rampart where, with the assistance of Sam E. Heeter, he edited and published a little weekly sheet known as the Yukon Valley News. A few years after the Iditarod was struck he went to that town and edited the Iditarod Pioneer for the late George Arbuckle. He was a member of the Texas Rangers under the famous Capt. Pat Dolan and shot his last buffalo in that state over fifty years ago.

We are indebted in the Kusko Times [Nov.15, 1932] for news of Sam Callahan's tragic end. This little newspaper published by A. X. Grant, dean of newspaper men in interior Alaska. In substance states that Joe Stickmann, Felix Andrews and another prospector met Sam Callahan as he was poling his outfit up the Innoko river. They were traveling in a gas boat and gave him a tow up Lonesome River where he decided to make headquarters in an abandoned cabin. The boys helped him unload his outfit, then pulled out back to the Innoko. Several days later they decided to cross overland and assist him in making his cabin comfortable for the winter. It was cold weather and on arrival they found the frozen body of the old prospector just inside the canvas door of his cabin. Apparently he had passed away a few hours after arrival at the journeys end.

Returning to the Innoko, the boys struck out for Ophir where they informed U. S. Commissioner Chris Bolgen of the facts. It was a long overland journey and occupied seven days. The commissioner instructed them to bury the body and on return to the cabin they found no lumber available to make a casket. He took their old friend's boat to pieces and made a coffin. Today his mortal remains rest in a rude coffin made from the timbers of the boat he poled up the Yukon to again try his luck on the Lonesome River. He rests in the Land he Loved so Well.

ALASKA WEEKLY, Jan. 6, 1933

J. FRANK CALLBREATH

J. Frank Callbreath is dead! The best known citizen of the Cassiar has passed on, leaving a vacancy that can never be filled.

Mr. Callbreath was born on the Springfield ranch in the Caribou country in British Columbia about 65 years ago. He was a son of Capt. John G. Callbreath who came west from the state of New York. A portion of Frank's early life was spent in the east. As a young man he entered the employ of the Southern Pacific Railway and at one time was president of the Order of Railway Conductors in southern California.

Frank Callbreath's father established a trading post at Telegraph Creek in 1874. Frank made several trips into the Cassiar when he was a young man, and finally in 1895 he gave up railroading to take over the business established by his father 21 years previously. He at once began catering to big game hunters, and for the past 35 years has made a speciality of outfitting big game hunters each fall.

The class of people who go on big game hunts are usually people of wealth, and are often people of such prominence as to be of national or international note. His clientele in the past quarter of a century has included numerous European Princes, Lords and Counts. There are few men living in any part of the world who have enjoyed a wider acquaintance among prominent people from many countries than was the privilege of this genial packing contractor, living in an isolated Indian village in the wilds of the Far North.

There was no toadyism in Mr. Callbreath's nature. While he knew the meaning of the world service, and always endeavored to please his patrons, his attitude toward the multimillionaire was no different from when he was dealing with a stranded prospector. No one who knew him could imagine him ever trucking to the rich and powerful for the sake of gaining their favor. It is therefore not surprising that a man of his type should have made many fast friends among rich and poor alike.

His big game hunting business was never advertised like the big game hunts in Africa or in the Himalayas, yet each fall big game hunters came to him from different parts of the world as a result of the kind words spoken in his behalf by other big game hunters who had been outfitted by him for a hunt in the Cassiar at some previous time.

Mr. Callbreath is survived by three grown children: Roy, Charles, and Jeanette.

THE WRANGELL SENTINEL, Feb. 27, 1930

ARCHIBALD JOHN CAMPBELL

A.J. Campbell died February 22, 1899 in Skaguay from heart failure. Dr. Campbell was a native of Scotland, but spent the greater part of his life in Canada and the United States. In early life he studied medicine and later turned his attention to teaching and the ministry. Formerly a Presbyterian minister, he was ordained in the clergy of the Episcopal church at Olympia, Wash. a little more than three years ago. He afterwards came to Ketchikan, Alaska and shortly afterwards to this place where he presided as minister of the Episcopal flock until relieved by the present minister.

He leaves three daughters and a son. His wife preceded him to the grave over twenty years ago.

THE SKAGUAY NEWS, Feb. 24, 1899

H. D. CAMPBELL

H. D. Campbell, 79, pioneer of the gold rush days, died here Saturday night of pneumonia after a week's illness.

He came north from Portland, Oregon, in the spring of 1898, was a carpenter on the sternwheeler Elwood bound for the Klondike via the Stikine River, Dease Lake and MacKenzie River. The route was not feasible. Campbell continued to freight on the Stikine. Wrangell was then a tent city.

Campbell went into building in town and built most of the early day buildings and many of the modern ones. He served under Harding, Coolidge, Hoover and Roosevelt as Deputy U. S. Marshal in the Wrangell district. He retired from active business seven years ago.

He was born in New Perth, Prince Edward Island, Canada in 1861. He was a member of the first Wrangell school board and early councils, was active in fraternal and civic groups through the years. He died in Wrangell Alaska on December 7, 1940.

He is survived by his widow in Wrangell, two sons, Ernest and Leonard, Wrangell merchants, three brothers, Ernest and Richard in Victoria and Josiah in New Perth.

PETERSBURG PRESS, Dec. 13, 1940

JOHN L. CAMPBELL

John Campbell, one of the camp's best known pioneers, and owner of Campbell boarding house died in Tacoma, Washington. He was one of early pioneers of the North, having come to Alaska and the Yukon during the great Klondike gold rush. At later periods he resided with Mrs. Campbell in various parts of Alaska, including the Nome district, where he spent several years.

Coming to Hyder with Mrs. Campbell in 1918, he remained a resident of the district throughout the remainder of his life, save for a few short visits to the States. He is said by friends to have been born in the southern states and he was about 70 years of age.

HYDER WEEKLY HERALD, Feb. 1, 1938.

CHARLES CAMSELL

Dr. Charles Camsell, Canada's deputy minister of mines, arrived in Wrangell Wednesday afternoon on his first visit since the spring of 1899 when he made his last trip in the fulfillment of a contract into which he had entered to carry his Majesty's mail from Wrangell to Telegraph Creek. Dr. Camsell was born in 1876 at Fort Liard. His father was chief factor for the Hudson's Bay company and two years later moved to Fort Simpson, located still farther in the northern wilderness at the confluence of the Liard and Mackenzie rivers.

When he was eight years old Mr. Camsell and his brother Fred were sent to school at Winnipeg. They were three months in arriving at their destination and remained there until they were graduated from the University of Manitoba in 1897. Shortly after their return home reports of the Klondike gold discovery reached them at Fort Norman and they came up the Mackenzie, the Liard and Dease rivers by canoe to Francis lake. From there they attempted to get to the Pelly river and into Dawson. Their ambition was frustrated and for a month and a half they wandered in that waste of land on the verge of starvation. Getting back to the Dease river they eventually made their way to Telegraph Creek where they secured the mail contract for the winter of 1898-1899. The next spring, the young adventurers, hearing of a mine excitement in Great Slave lake district, started by canoe from Dease lake and went to the headwaters of the Mackenzie only to find after all their toil and hardship that the reports of gold were without foundation. They were without resources except the canoe which they sold to the Bishop of Mackenzie for $25, and with the stake of $12.50 each they went trapping that winter. When they came out in the following spring of 1900 with their fur catch, Dr. Camsell joined a Dominion survey party which went to explore the shores of Great Bear lake. This was his first connection with the Dominion government. The party reached Edmonton in 1901 and Dr. Camsell was definitely established in his career as a geologist. Two years later he enrolled at Harvard and then at Boston Tech, receiving a doctor's in geology.
WRANGELL SENTINEL, Aug. 2 1935

J. H.   CANN

Captain J. H. Cann, a Alaskan figure for the last thirty years, died in Juneau Monday [June 17, 1935].

Accompanied by his wife, he first went to Alaska in 1906 and cruised the coast of the territory for the succeeding thirteen years, engaging in general trading and doing some casual prospecting. Gradually he became more and more interested in prospecting, and in 1919 he discovered and located this Apex-El Nido gold lode group situated on Chichagof Island, in the Lislanski Inlet section. The property was developed through his efforts and mill installation and profitably operated. At the time of his death Captain Cann was engaged with the representatives of English capital in arranging for further development and the operation of the property on a large tonnage basis. Cann had a wide acquaintanceship and numbered among his friends many notables in the theatrical world. Lionel Barrymoire was one of his close friends, and Dolores Costello was a house guest of he and Mrs. Cann for a week recently. His only known surviving relatives are his widow, Mrs. June Cann, and a nephew, Jack Cann, both at present in Juneau.

ALASKA WEEKLY, June 21, 1935

ALBERT CARLSON

When Charles Carlson returned to his cabin near St. Ann hospital yesterday morning a terrible sight met his gaze. Lying on the bed with a terrible wound on the side of his head and a bullet hole in his abdomen, was his brother, Albert Carlson, dead.

The bed, walls, and floor were saturated with blood, and a rifle, the evident instrument of death, lay within reach of the deceased.

A Coroner's jury found that neighbors heard five shots fired in the cabin Sunday evening at about 10:30 o'clock. The shots were about five minutes apart. There was no evidence that the man had an enemy in the world, nor was there any known reason why the man should take his own life.

Albert Carlson was a native of Gottland, Sweden, aged 43 years, 8 months and 10 days. He had lived in Douglas a number of years and bore a good reputation.

DOUGLAS ISLAND NEWS, June 1, 1910

W. H. "Bill" CARNEY

Carney's ice cream parlor dishes out homemade ice cream. The machine is an arrangement exactly like the ones this generation used to turn as kids on a hot Sunday afternoon. The difference being that Bill's freezer has a 5 gallon capacity, and is powered by a gasoline motor.

The ice cream parlor is located in what Fort Yukon calls Carney's hall, which houses the only movie in the town and a pool table. After the evening show is over the theater is converted to a dance floor by shoving the seats to the walls.

Bill, an oldtimer, opened the first motion picture house in Fort Yukon in 1926. A small cabin served as the theater. Prior to establishing himself in Fort Yukon, Bill spent his earlier Alaskan days in and around Tanana where he operated a pool hall, mined near Ruby and ran a roadhouse at Gold Mountain. He came to Alaska in 1902. Now Bill, Mrs. Carney and children think of Fort Yukon as home.

JESSEN'S WEEKLY, July 18, 1947

HERBERT WILLIS CARR

Herbert Willie Carr, one of the men of 1897, died at his home 3627 Ashworth Avenue, Seattle on November 13, 1937. In company with Judge W. D. Wood, former mayor of Seattle, he stampeded to the Klondike. Going via St. Michael he transferred to the steamer May West, which was caught by the winter ice near Rampart. Judge Wood of the Seattle-Yukon Transportation Co. was establishing a line of steamers on the river to help carry the crowds hurrying up the Yukon. Not to be stopped by the ice, Wood and Carr went on to Dawson by dog team and completed the business arrangement of the company at that end of the line.

Later in the winter Mr. Carr went out over the Dyea Trail to Seattle, was married and with his bride returned via the Pass and down the river to Dawson. After the transfer to the S.Y.T. Co. to the N.C.Co., Mr. Carr worked with Thomas W. Lippy in his development of the rich claims on Bonanza Creek. He later connected with the Dawson Electric Light and Power Company, with whom he came back to Seattle to make his future home. During the World War he served as auditor of the Western division of the supply department of the Red Cross.

ALASKA WEEKLY, Jan. 7, 1938

EDNA BAHOVEC CASE

Mrs. Edna Case, widow of Lawrence Case, who died in Ketchikan on May 2nd succumbed May 9th at Bishop Howe General Hospital where she had been admitted the previous Thursday.

Mrs. Case was born 40 years ago at Kake. She was a student at Sheldon Jackson School before her marriage to Fred Bahovec. She had been a resident of Wrangell for about 15 years.

She is survived by Her eleven-year-old daughter, Nora Case; son Lawrence Bahovec; and two daughters in Chicago, Gertrude and Louise Bahovec; her mother Mrs. S. N. Harvie; and sister, Mrs. Henry Willard.

WRANGELL SENTINEL, May 14, 1937

EMMA BARANOVICH CASE (Ssee Vol. 4)

Emma Case died March 22 following burns she received when her night gown caught fire from a bathroom heater. Her son, George, hearing her cries, ripped the clothes from her, and smothered the flames with a blanket, but Mrs. Case was very frail and failed to rally.

Emma Case was born at Kasaan on Oct 23, 1870. She came to Wrangell with her husband, Tom, 1898, landing with a barge on the beach. Mr. Case established a store on the present Case property and the family has lived there since. He was in partnership with Tom Wilson, another pioneer.

The case had five children: Tom Jr., Dolly, Oscar, Lawrence and George of whom only Tom and George are still living. She has a great granddaughter in Wrangell, Mrs. Ray Wheeler, and a great granddaughter, Shemya Wheeler, also a brother, Joe Baranovich, who was a legislator from Ketchikan in 1935, and a nephew, Erwin Baranovich.

THE ALASKA WEEKLY, April 10, 1953.

WILLIAM W. CASEY

William Casey, one of Juneau's best known and most prominent citizens, was stricken with apoplexy and immediate death at Ketchikan last Sunday. He came to Juneau in 1896 and except for a time during the Klondike rush, when he was engaged in packing on the Chilkoot trail, he has resided in Juneau ever since. He was the first chief of the fire department, a member of the third and fourth legislatures, 1917 and 1919. Mr. Casey was owner of the Juneau Transfer, a partner in the Juneau Hardware Company, stockholder in the First National Bank and an extensive property owner.

THE ALASKA PRESS, Nov. 2, 1934 (Ten Years Ago–From the Files of the Stroller's Weekly)

NELLIE CASHMAN   (See Vol. 2)

The news that Nellie Cashman died in a Victoria hospital a few days ago will be received with sadness by every oldtimer in Alaska and by many more who were in the North during the earlier days.

The mining lure possessed Nellie Cashman half a century or more ago, her first experience being in the silver camps of Arizona in the late 1870s when she was a young woman. Ten years later found her in the Cassiar and Old Caribou districts and a second ten years found her in the Klondike, and during the past 27 or 28 years there has not been a discovery in the North, Alaska or Yukon, but has numbered her among its earlier stampeders. As Service says, 'twas not the gold but the excitement of finding it that lured Nellie Cashman, and in every camp, she ever visited she was a veritable angel of mercy, nursing the sick, steeping spruce boughs for those afflicted with scurvy and diffusing sunshine wherever she happened to be.

In the early Dawson days when beans constituted the principal diet, it was Nellie Cashman who when she heard of a sick miner whom the very mention of beans would nauseate, would go to the mangers of the big stores and browbeat them into giving her something that the sick man could eat. These store managers invariably surrendered when they saw Nellie coming-or if they held out for awhile their surrender was all the more unconditional after she had told them a few things.

Nellie Cashman was an experienced dog driver and in the absence of dogs, she could shoulder a pack and keep step with the most hardy Nova Scotia Scotch, Quebec French or Montana Yankee that ever went on a stampede and when they camped to eat on the trail, it was Nellie who prepared the meal.

WRANGELL SENTINEL, Jan 15, 1925

ANNIE CASIDY

Last Friday in Juneau, one of the earliest pioneers of Skagway passed over the last trail. Mrs. Annie Casidy, who came to Skagway early in the summer of 1897 died at St. Ann's Hospital in Juneau of heart failure.

Mrs. Casidy was the proprietor of the first restaurant in Skagway. The restaurant was in a tent and stood on the lot now occupied by the iron warehouse opposite the Catholic church on lower Fifth avenue. Mrs. Casidy was very well known in Skagway and her kindly deeds will long be remembered.

She is survived by a daughter, Mrs. Gehri, who at present lives at Tacoma, a son, Kenneth, and a grandson, Cassie Kossuth, who resides in Skagway.

DAILY ALASKAN, April 17, 1911

WILLIAM W. CASEY

William Casey, one of Juneau's best known and most prominent citizens, was stricken with apoplexy and immediate death at Ketchikan last Sunday. He came to Juneau in 1896 and except for a time during the Klondike rush, when he was engaged in packing on the Chilkoot trail, he has resided in Juneau ever since.

He was the first chief of the fire department, a member of the third and fourth legislatures, 1917 and 1919. Mr. Casey was owner of the Juneau Transfer, a partner in the Juneau Hardware Company, stockholder in the First National Bank and an extensive property owner.

THE ALASKA PRESS, Nov. 2, 1934 (Ten Years Ago–From the Files of the Stroller's Weekly)

J. HARMON CASKEY

J. Harmon Caskey, one of the best known newspaper men of the North, died in Los Angeles on May 19, with internment at Forest Lawn Cemetery.

In life J. Harmon Caskey was ever a building, a newsman who always wanted to see what lay beyond the horizon. Of a cheery, optimistic disposition, he made friends wherever he went, and what is more, kept them.

He came to Seattle from his birthplace in Wooster, Ohio in1893, and in this city established two newspapers. However, the urge of travel was on him and being offered the management in Guatemala, he tracked south and held that position for a number of years.

Central America at that time was quiet and Caskey longed for more action. He returned to Seattle and about that time tales of placer gold were coming out of Alaska, so together with his wife he started for Dawson, intent on starting a newspaper there. He arrived in Dawson during the hectic days of "98" and started the Dawson News. He was for years in the Yukon Metropolis but moved to Fairbanks when the strike was made in the Tanana. There he founded and published the Alaska Citizen, at that time the only democratic newspaper in the Territory. In 1920 the plant was completely destroyed by fire, and the Caskeys moved to

California where he started another paper, the Belvedere Citizen, at a suburb of Los Angeles. He edited and published this paper up to the time of his death.

THE ALASKA WEEKLY, May 28, 1937

EDWARD CHAMBERLAIN

Edward Chamberlain passed away at Sitka on November 25 after an illness of more than a year. At one time Mr. Chamberlain was in the custom service and for several years he was connected with the publication of the Sitka Alaskan. He was a member of the Camp Sitka No. 6 of the arctic Brotherhood. Mr. Chamberlain was born in Edinburgh, Scotland, where he was educated. He was a man of kind disposition, genial and generous at all times, scholarly and intellectual, an accomplished public speaker, and was often called upon to deliver lectures at all public occasions in Sitka and Southeastern Alaskan towns. The funeral services were conducted by the Arctic Brotherhood, according to their beautiful and impressive ritual.

THE DOUGLAS ISLAND NEWS, Dec. 21, 1910

ELMER CHAMBERLAIN

Elmer Chamberlain, one of Skagway's early pioneers, died at 9:45 o'clock last night at his home on Sixth between Main and State streets of tuberculosis and other complications. He had been in ill health for about two years partly as the result of injuries which he received in Haines at that time. Mr. Chamberlain came to Skagway in May, 1899, and has resided here continuously ever since. He has a mother living in Noank, Conn., and a brother in New York. Mr. Chamberlain was about 50 years old.

THE DAILY ALASKAN, June 1, 1909

HENRY H. CHAPMAN

Rev. Henry H. Chapman, formerly rector at St. Matthews's Episcopal Church in Fairbanks, but for the past year stationed at Anvik, in the lower Yukon river country, and Mrs. Chapman came south this week on the steamer Yukon, and will enjoy a years vacation.

Rev. Chapman having been granted a leave of absence for this period of time, has been assisting his father, Rev. John Chapman, in mission work at Anvik.

The Chapmans expect to remain on the coast only a few days before department for North Carolina, the home state of Mrs. Chapman, after which they will go to New York City to meet Rev. Chapman's sister, who left Fairbanks for the metropolis in 1926.

Mr. and Mrs. Chapman were married in Anvik in the early spring, where Mrs. Chapman had served as a teacher in the mission school for six years.

ALASKA WEEKLY, Sept. 7, 1928

WILLIAM CHAPUT

Born in Maine, Father Chaput's parents emigrated to South Dakota where he spent his boyhood. He was ordained at the University of Ottawa in 1909, and at that time came West, becoming the pastor of Moxee City, Utah

When the war broke out, he enlisted with the 309th Motor Transport Company, and was later transferred to the 2nd Pioneer Infantry as chaplain. Due to his World War record and activities, he is now the chaplain of the American Legion of Alaska.

When the World War ended, Father Chaput came to Seattle and became pastor in the Monroe Parish and chaplain of the Monroe Reformatory.

In 1936 he came to Seward. The war, the reformatory, and travel have given Father Chaput a deep and tender understanding of human problems, and have fitted him as few men are fitted for the position he now enjoys.

ALASKA LIFE, March 1940

P. G. CHARLES

P. G. Charles has been in all the important towns of

Alaska, coming here from Seattle in January, 1900. He has been president of Iditarod Igloo No. 10 and is secretary of Ketchikan Igloo No. 16. He is an accountant for the Tongas Trading Company.

ALASKA DISPATCH, May 5, 1922

JAMES M. CHASE

Mr. and Mrs. James M. Chase are celebrating the anniversary of their fiftieth wedding anniversary today at the home of their daughter and son-in-law, Mr. and Mrs. Albert F. Parker at Gustavus.

James was born March 1, 1880 to Mr. and Mrs. Marsh Chase at their country home in Saline County, Nebraska. Nora Blauvelt Chase was born to Mr. and Mrs. Sylvester Blauvelt in the same county, Dec. 6, 1879. The couple first met the day of young "Jimmy's" birth when he was placed in the crib beside tiny Nora by Mrs. Blauvelt, who had gone in the Chase home to assist in the arrival of the new son.

James and Nora grew up together as children and were married in the home of the bride's parents near Belvidere, Nebr., September 12, 1900. After the ceremony they went immediately to their new home at Tobias, Nebraska where they remained until 1904, when they and their small son Archie, moved to Edison, Nebr. where daughter Jennie and a son, Marvan, were born.

In 1912 the family moved to Kansas City, Mo. But left shortly thereafter when a severe epidemic of polio swept the city.

In 1914 the family again tried city life when they moved to Omaha, where they remained until they came to Alaska.

These long time residents of Alaska first came to the Territory in March 1925 and lived on a Fox Island in Tibenkoff Bay until September of that year when they came to Juneau and established a home.

Mr. Chase was with the Juneau Motors Co., for five years, when it was owned by the late Harry Lucas. In 1930 he, with his sons opened the Service Motors in the A.B. Hall and operated until 1939 when he retired from active business.

THE DAILY ALASKA EMPIRE, Sept. 12, 1950

NORA BLAUVELT CHASE

Injuries from a fall Sunday proved fatal to Mrs. Nora B. who died early this morning in Gustavus. Only a month ago, she and her husband, James M. Chase, were honored at a gala celebration of their fiftieth wedding anniversary, happy to be surrounded by their descendants, all of whom live in the Territory. The Chases were married in Belvidere, Neb. September 12, 1900.

The family lived in Juneau for 14 years, taking a prominent place in business and civic affairs. Mrs. Chase was active in the Juneau Woman's Club of which she was president in 1931 and 1932. With their son Marvan, the Chases moved to Gustavus in 1939.

Mrs. Chase was postmaster there for the past seven years, succeeding her daughter, Mrs. Albert F. Parker, who resigned after 18 years service. Even though nearly 71 years old, Mrs. Chase made the daily mile long hike from her home to the post office, never missing a day until her accident Sunday.

Besides her husband, Mrs. Chase is survived by her daughter, Mrs. (Jennie M.) Parker, and two sons, Marvan and Archie, all of Gustavus; five grandchildren-Eugene and Charles Chase, and Mrs. Fred (Alberta) Newburn, all of Gustavus; Jay Chase of Anchorage; and Mrs. Lowell Trump of Juneau. She also leaves four young great-grandchildren-Muriel and Bruce Newburn, and Chris and Baby Trump.

THE DAILY ALASKA EMPIRE, Oct. 13, 1950

J. E. CHILBERG

Mr. Chilberg is identified with the progressive development of Alaska. He owns properties in nearly every Northern mining district. Mr. Chilberg went to Dawson in 1899, to take charge of two river steamers. From Lake Bennett he voyaged down the Yukon in a Peterboro canoe. In 1900 and 1901 he held the contract for carrying United States mail between Juneau and Unalaska. Mr. Chilberg was elected secretary and trustee of the Pioneer Mining Company in 1903, and still holds these offices in that corporation. He is a director of the Miners and Merchants Bank of Nome, and vice-president of the Scandinavian-American Bank of Seattle.

ALASKA YUKON, May 1905

CHINA JOE (See Vol. 2)

The feature department of the Seattle Sunday P-I gives our China Joe the following write up: "There is just one Chinaman in Juneau, and the story of his presence is a good example of the fair play spirit that ruled in the old frontier days, and which now has its survival in the Alaskan mining camps. When Juneau was a young camp, China Joe happened along and started a bakery. One winter the miners' provisions gave out, and it looked like the promising claims would have to be abandoned on account of the scarcity of food. The Chinaman had a big stock of flour on hand, and he volunteered to stake the boys so they could continue their work, and agreement being that he should be paid back when they made their clean-up in the spring. Joe had to shut down his bakery, but he did not lose anything. He was paid back with big interest.

Years afterwards, when the famous Treadwell mine was opened up, several hundred Chinese laborers were imported. Their presence was objected to by both whites and Indians, and at a big indignation meeting it was decided to round up all the Chinamen in the camp, load them on a boat and ship them out. The old timers did not forget the service China Joe had rendered them when their flour game out, so when the posse got to Joe's place a determined crowd of prospectors were ahead of them, who said Joe shouldn't be run out. Their word was law, and he was allowed to remain. Joe is one Chinaman who never had a rock thrown through the windows of his house. The mischief-loving kids of Juneau never molest him with their pranks. If they bothered him, and it became known at home, their fathers would spank them so soundly that they would never want to go near him again, and if their parents failed to chastise them, some of the old guard among the miners would take it on. China Joe is king of the roost of Juneau.

DAILY ALASKA DISPATCH, Sept. 18, 1903

NELLIE CHOQUETTE

Mrs. Nellie Choquette, 65, resident of Wrangell all her life until going to Petersburg a year or more ago, died last Sunday [July 28] at the home of her daughter, Mrs. Fred Porter in Petersburg.

Brought here by her father from Telegraph Creek at the age of three, Mrs. Choquette had made Wrangell her home through the years, attending the old mission school here in the early days as a girl and growing to womanhood in this community.

Besides her daughter, Mrs. Porter, she is survived by a son, Fred who is in the veteran's hospital in Walla Walla.

WRANGELL SENTINEL, Aug. 2, 1940

LEONARD M. CHURCHILL

Life closed Wednesday morning for Leonard M. Churchill, who as a young man of 28 came to Wrangell in April 1887 to take a brief look at this new country of which so little information was available in the states. He stayed on for 51 years.

Born at St. Johnsill, New York, Mr. Churchill went west to Minnesota as a boy of thirteen, then later struck out for the Pacific coast. He journeyed to Alaska in the old sidewheeler, Ancon. He worked on the steamers plying out from Wrangell, and in the 1890s, with the late William Taylor, owned and operated the steamer Baranof. They engaged in hauling lumber from the old sawmill at Shakan, and had a mail contract for the west coast of Prince of Wales island going down as far as

Hunter's Bay just north of Point Chacon, where one of the early day canneries was located, and did general transportation work.

Mr. Churchill was a member of the first city council organized after the incorporation of Wrangell. He served for many years in various city offices.

For the past 20 years his services have been in demand as administrator of estates and custodian and agent of properties for absentee owners.

Though lacking but two months of being 80 years old, he was possessed of unusual powers of memory and was apparently in good health until this spring.

Besides his wife whose death occurred in 1915, he is survived by four sons: Frank, Roy, David and Howard of Wrangell, and a daughter, Elizabeth in Seattle.

WRANGELL SENTINEL, Aug. 5, 1938

FRANK WILLIAM CLANCY

Frank William Clancy was born at East Machias, Maine. He removed to Seattle in 1882 and there entered into business. When the story of the great gold strike came from the northland he joined the stampede. On arriving at Skagway he was immediately impressed with the advantages of this location and resolved to locate here. As a pioneer of Skagway, he has ever been loyal to her interests, liberal toward all enterprises that help to up build here a great and progressive city. The Skagway Oyster Parlors of which he is a manager, is one of the most popular establishments in the city and is patronized by the elite of Skagway. At the late election for councilmen he received an immense vote which carried him to a seat in that body where his service and endeavors for the good of the public are appreciated by an admiring constituency.

DAILY ALASKAN, Feb. 19, 1899

GUS P. CLARY

Gus P. Clary, Aged 26, a miner in the employ of the

Treadwell company, was killed instantly Friday night about 10:30 when several tons of rock fell on him.

A brother and sister of deceased living at Reed, Kentucky, were communicated with and they ordered the body forwarded to that place.

Clary had been working at the mine since last September and was a young man of good habits, being much esteemed by those who knew him best. He was a native of the state of Illinois and was unmarried.

THE DOUGLAS ISLAND NEWS, April 5, 1916

FRANK CLEARY

Frank Cleary, in company with Dan McCarthy, made the trip from Valdez to Fairbanks in the winter of 1901-2 with a dog team, to the spot where Captain E. T. Barnette had cached supplied taken up the fall before. Cleary ran the Barnette Trading Post, staked the town site and trading post site, grubstaked the first man to find pay in the district, and until 1919 was one of the best known citizens of the famous camp.

He grubstaked Felix Pedro in 1902 and in May of that year Pedro discovered placer gold on the creek that bears his name. Mr. Cleary was a member of the first council of Fairbanks, and owned various valuable mining claims.

Cleary Creek, possibly one of the biggest producers in the camp, was named after him. He owned an interest on One, Two and Three below Discovery, and at one time owned a half interest in the Fairbanks Evening News.

Mr. Cleary has been employed in his capacity of a civil engineer on the Government Railroad in Alaska, with the Latouche mines at Latouche, Alaska, and has spent much time in Mexico, Bolivia, Argentine and other South American countries. At present he is interested, together with his brother-in-law, Captain E. T. Barnette in a big dredging property on the Chuta River, in the state of Michoacan, Mexico.

ALASKA WEEKLY, Jan. 2, 1931

F. W. CLINGER

Captain F.W. Clinger, master of the Alaska Steamship Company's liner Alameda, died at his home in Seattle yesterday.

Captain Clinger was a native of Washington and has sailed Puget Sound and Alaskan waters for over thirty five years, starting out as a mere boy. For the past fifteen years, Capt. Clinger was in the employ of the Alaska S.S. Co. and has been master of many of its best boats among which were the Dolphin, Edith, Olympia, Victoria ,and lastly, the Alameda.

His first trip to Alaska was in 1897and as master of the big tug Holyoke when he towed the stern wheeler, "W.R. Merwin," the barge "Politofsky," and the schooner, "W.J. Bryan" through the inside passage and then to St. Michaels. He has been running to Alaska ever since.

THE DAILY ALASKAN, Mar., 11, 1919

JOHN NATHAN COBB

John N. Cobb, dean of the College of Fisheries at the University of Washington, passed away at La Jolla, California Monday of this week. He was born at Oxford Furnace, N. J. on Feb. 20, 1868, sone of Samuel Spencer and Louise Catherine (Richards) Cobb; grandson of David and Kitty (Spencer) Cobb, and a descendant of Henry Cobb of Kent county, England

Cobb came to Seattle as Editor of a publication devoted to the fisheries interests. He had previously been a newspaper man; had been the Alaska representative of the U.S. Bureau of fisheries, and for some years was with the Union Fish Company in San Francisco and Alaska.

For a period of two years he was with the Alaska Packers Association, Alaska's largest fish packing concern, and finally joined the Washington University to organize and direct the College of fisheries in 1919, which has grown into an important school for the study of food fish.

Dean Cobb was a member of the scientific advisory board

of the international fisheries commission in which Canada and the United States are seeking to solve the problem of regulating halibut fishing.

Since 1898 he has been engaged by the United States and a number of states, in economic investigations of fisheries along the Atlantic Coast, in the Great Lakes, and along the Pacific. His investigations along the Atlantic extended from the lobster fisheries of Maine to sponge fisheries in Florida. Cobb's investigations at Hawaiian fisheries were the first made in the islands and attracted wide attention. The University of Washington fisheries school which Dean Cobb organized, is the only one of its kind in the United States.

He is survived by a widow, Mrs. Harriet B. Cobb, and a daughter, Harriet, a biological instructor in the University of Arizona.

ALASKA WEEKLY, Jan. 17, 1930
THE NATIONAL CYCLOPAEDIA, Vol. 26, 1937

TEX COBB

Tex Cobb, at 87, is physically and mentally healthy. He has lived in Alaska continuously since 1908, and in the Matanuska Valley since 1909

He came to Ketchikan in the spring of 1907, bought a boat and prospected along the streams of Southeastern Alaska. In 1908, he went back to his former home in Texas, about 125 miles from San Antonio, but the call of Alaska was so strong that he returned in January 1909, landing at Seward. After only a short stay in Seward, he came to the Susitna Valley and staked a claim on Cash Creek, which did not pay out. He floated down the Susitna on a raft to Susitna Station, and from there with three other men, he came by boat to Knik.

At Knik, he went into business buying and selling horses to prospectors and miners going into the Talkeetna Range. The business prospered during the summer, but when it came winter, Tex had to be sold out or kill his merchandise, for there was no feed for his horses. The result was that he packed his outfit and grub on the backs of two of them and traveled over the mountains to Willow Creek, where he found gold quartz and worked a claim until it played out.

In 1910 he brought Pete Murray the first white homesteader in the Valley, to the mouth of Wasilla Creek by boat from Knik. The trip took him across Knik Arm, up Palmer Slough, and into Wasilla Creek. There Murray bought an Indian shanty and homesteaded.

One of his longest periods away from the Valley was spent in the Idotarod-Georgetown area as a Deputy U. S. Marshal driving a dog team for the U.S. Marshal. It was while driving this dog-team one day that he came upon a prospector who had just made a rich gold strike. He asked the man if everything around him was staked and when told that everything below him was, but that there was a small area above him that wasn't. Tex laid claim to it. He took rich samples from it, but without working it, sold it for $20,000. When the Marshal was relieved in the district, and a trader came along short on dogs, Tex put his dogs in with him and came back to the Valley.

Tex bought a fishing site on Kalgin Island, south of Anchorage, in Cook Inlet, and has been fishing there for some years with set nets. The last few years he has worked only a part of his site and rented the rest. He says, "It has been a good thing, but it got too much for me."

In the Alaskan Range he has found gold deposits where he has taken $250.00 to $350.00 daily, and around the rim of the Matanuska Valley he knows places where one can still make from $10.00 to $25.00 a day. "Not worth the work," he says.

In recent years, Tex has hit upon a new, odd, but profitable source of income. Before the fishing season opens in the spring, he takes his big Labrador dogs to the lower rivers and shough of the Kenai Peninsula and hunts for hair seals. The seal sows bring their young into the slough and hide them in the tall grass. Tex rows his boat up the center of the Slough turning his

dogs loose on each side and waiting results. The dogs find the pups, bring them squirming to the boat, where Tex knocks them in the head. The seals are worth $3.00 per head for bounty, and the pelts of the larger ones are worth from $5.00 to $6.50 apiece. Tex has taken as high as 100 a day, and 50 in an ordinary catch.
ALASKA CALL, Nov. 1959

ORVILLE D. COCHRAN   (See Vol. 1)
Chairman of the Senate's Committee on Judiciary and Federal Relations, which processed sixty-five Senate and thirty-four House measures during this session, was Senator Orville D. Cochran, whose legislative career began in 1921 in the House of Representatives. Born in Missouri, Senator Cochran is a graduate of the University of Oregon School of Law and first went to Nome in the summer of 1900. He has had a part in the history of that town almost since its founding and can tell many stories of its gaudier days and of the famous people who helped make it, including Rex Beach, Key Pittman, Tex Richard, Jimmie Doolittle and many others. President of the Senate in 1943, Senator Cochran has been a member of that body continuously for the past ten years and for the past eight years has also been a member of the Board of Regents of the University of Alaska, a position to which he was reappointed by Governor Gruening during the Eighteenth Session.
ALASKA LIFE, June 1947

SAMUEL B. COCHRAN
A full and active life came to an end at Cordova with the death of Samuel B. "Tom" Cochran, sailor, adventurer, gold miner, precision machinist, and minister, at age 86.

He was born in St. Johns, New Brunswick, and left his native home after acquiring an academic education. He became an ordained minister but decided not to follow it. He left home for a life at sea. He first went to Sitka as an officer on a sailing vessel in 1876. After that he made three trips around the globe on windjammers.

In 1904, he went over the pass at Skagway to Dawson. When Fairbanks became the foremost gold camp in Alaska, he was among the advance guard there. In 1907 he went to the Katalla oil fields. and later took up his residence there.

THE ALASKA WEEKLY, Mar. 29, 1935.

EDWARD W. COFFEY

Dean of the Third Division's delegation to this Legislature was Senator Edward D. Coffey, born in Oklahoma and a resident of Alaska since the early 1920's. Having worked in some of Alaska's most famous mines–The Alaska Juneau, Chichagoff and Kennecott–and in the Bristol Bay salmon fishery, Senator Coffey is aware of the practical application of many of the bills that come up for consideration. He was first elected to the House in 1937 and to the Senate in 1941 and served as its President in the 1945 regular session and the 1946 special session. He now operates a real estate and insurance business in Anchorage.

ALASKA LIFE, June 1947

CASH COLE   (See Vol. 3)

Cash Cole has been a resident of the Territory from the time he was brought here by his parents in 1894, when he was but a youngster three years old. He was educated in our public schools and later attended the University of Minnesota.

Seven years ago he was married and has two bright boys for whom he sets an example of industry and good citizenship. He is engaged in the contracting, traming, and transfer business, in connection with his agency for the American Express Company. In fact, Cash Cole is generally recognized as one of the reliable young business men in Juneau.

THE JUNEAU SUNDAY CAPITAL, April 16, 1922

MAY KIMBALL COLLINS

May Kimball Collins, wife of Mayor E. B. Collins and

teacher in Alaskan schools for more than 20 years, died in St. Joseph's hospital here early this morning. Mrs. Collins was 52 years old.

Mrs. Collins, a past president of the pioneer women of Alaska, came here from California with her husband in 1906, and was one of the first white women in Goldstream. She helped to organize the first school at Fox, near here, and taught there until 1918.

Later she taught in the Fairbanks school. Her husband, a former assistant district attorney, her daughter, Mrs. Margaret Cooper of Oil Hill, Kansas, and a sister, Mrs. E. M. Hill of Hoquiam, Washington, survive.

KETCHIKAN ALASKA CHRONICLE, Nov. 2, 1934

WILLIAM MARTIN CONLEY

Valdez residents were shocked when it was told that William M. Conley, one of the oldest and most respected of pioneer citizens had passed away, following an illness of several months.

William Martin Conley was born in St. Paul, Minnesota, June 19, 1862, where he lived and attended school until he left at an early age to take up railroading, which he followed for a number of years.

He first came to Alaska in 1892, but went out that same year, going to Sacramento, California. Here he met the lady who was to become his wife, and January 7, 1897, he was married and returned to Alaska in 1898. Since that date Mr. Conley had never been outside, nor did he care to go, insisting that Alaska was his home and "good enough for him."

ALASKA WEEKLY, Dec. 13, 1935

THOMAS CONNIFF

Thomas Conniff, an old time Klondiker, committed suicide in Ruby March 28, 1912. He was here in the early days and afterward went to Nome.

He leaves a wife in Seattle, where, is understood, she is a nurse in one of the hospitals. He first came North with the Klondike rush in 1897, remaining some time in Dawson, and then went to Nome, where he lived for about three years. He then went outside, and acted in a clerical capacity in a logging camp until he came North to Iditarod last July, accompanied by a sister, who is at present cooking on Flat creek.

A sudden fit of despondence is thought to be the reason for the suicide. He was about 46 years old.

The coroners's jury found that Thomas Conniff came to his death on or about 4 p.m. on March 28, 1912, by a gunshot wound fired from a 30.30 Winchester rifle by himself.

DAWSON DAILY NEWS, May 29, 1912

JACK CONNOLLY

Jack Connolly, a well known old-timer of this and other camps of the North, breathed his last, his death being attributed to pneumonia.

The deceased is stated to have been about 33 [?] years of age. He was born in Ireland, coming to the United States as a boy and to Dawson during the early days of that camp. He had always followed mining. He has a sister living in Spokane, and funeral arrangements will not be made until she is appraised of the death.

A strange coincidence in the death of Connolly is the fact that he is the last of five partners all of whom have died natural deaths or have been killed within the last 12 months. On April 3rd, 1913, he was working with Joseph Waffler, Michael Twohey, Michael Layden, and Patrick Casey on No. 4 Goldstream, when the lives of Weffler and Twohey were crushed out in a cave-in. On May 24th, 1913, another partner, Layden, who was then mining on Dome creek, died at St. Joseph's hospital, while Patrick Casey, probably the best known of the five, died on October 25th, last.

FAIRBANKS DAILY NEWS-MINER, April 29, 1914

ARTHUR B. CONOVER

Captain Arthur B. Conover, a resident of Alaska for over 42 years, died on June 6. Conover was born on September 9, 1866 in Buffalo, New York. Before he came to Alaska he was an attorney for the Great Lakes Transportation Company.

He had his captain's papers and was entitled to take any vessel on any sea. In 1898 he first came to Alaska seeking specimens for the Smithsonian Institute.

He took up his residence on Telegraph Creek, and until 1925 he continued to live there, doing trapping, guiding, and mining.

In 1925 he came to Petersburg where he lived. In 1935 he moved to Long Island, and he stayed until his death with Mr. and Mrs. A. W. Zuver.

PETERSBURG PRESS, June 13, 1941

GEORGE COOK

George Cook, a pioneer resident of Valdez, and known in nearly every camp on the coast, was instantly killed last evening when a large rock fell on him, while working at Mile 16, Keystone Canyon, for the Alaska Road Commission.

Mr. Cook was working on a steep rock face, barring down following a blast. He had about finished on his work and was preparing to go into camp when a huge mass of rock a short piece up the cliff fell directly upon him carrying him down into the roadway, about ten feet down.

George Cook was born in California about 1864, near Sonora, and for many years was at "Angel's Camp." He came to Alaska in 1896, living at Juneau for several years. He resided in Valdez for the last 15 years and had many friends here. He was a man of good appearances and fine education.

His brother, Fred Cook, was frozen in death on Shoup glacier in May, 1911. Another brother, Delante Cook, resides in this city, and is at the present time working on his mining property.

DOUGLAS ISLAND NEWS, Sept. 17, 1920

N. H. COOMBS   (See Vol. 3)

Mr. Combs was married in 1909 to Miss Olive Storey of Nome. Their son, Nathan Coombs, was born beneath the midnight sun, March 4, 1911, and his brother, Allison Sheldon Coombs, was born at Council City, Alaska Nov. 7, 1905 [?].

ALASKA MAGAZINE, May 1917

JAMES COONEY

James Cooney, a well known native of Wrangell died, September 25, 1928. He was one of Wrangell's oldest citizens. He was converted to Christianity by Dr. S. Hall Young and from the time of his conversion on, he tried to exemplify his new faith to the other Indians. His last words was a blessing of peace on his fellow citizens.

He saw the first American flag raised in Wrangell and asked what it meant. When it was explained to him the significance of the flag, he became an ardent supporter of the government. He obtained a flag and displayed it in his house, a treasured possession. During Word War I, he contributed money to support the war effort, often expressing the wish that he was a younger man so he could serve his country. James Cooney's age cannot be definitely determined, but he was at least eighty-five years old. (Wrangell Sentinel)

STROLLER'S WEEKLY, Oct. 13, 1928.

PATRICK CORCORAN

Mr. Corcoran was born in Ireland. He came to this Territory on the John L. Stephens in the fall of 1867, being on the staff of the U. S. Quartermaster. He resigned this position, and was then appointed an officer of customs for this Territory in which capacity he acted for several years. Upon the discovery of gold in the Cassiar district, he threw up this position and engaged there in mining at which he made a success for a short period, when he returned to Sitka and went into the mercantile business. Upon the discovery of gold in this district, he closed out his business in Sitka and opened up again in Juneau, at which place, by his honest and integrity, he won a host of friends, and was fairly successful in his business.

Patrick Corcoran died in Juneau on February 3rd, 1887, aged 51 years.

THE ALASKA FREE PRESS, Feb. 12, 1887

HARRY PROSPER CORSER   (See Vol. 2)

H. P. Corser, retired Episcopal clergyman died at Bishop Howe General Hospital following a stroke the previous day.

Harry Prosper Corser was born at Portageville, New York on April 13, 1864. The family moved to Towanda, Pennsylvania, when he was a small child. He graduated from Lafayette college with a Ph. B degree and three years later received an M.S. degree from the same institution. He taught in private schools from 1885 until 1893, and in 1896 was graduated from Union Theological Seminary at which time he was ordained in the Presbyterian ministry. His first pastorate was at Flagstaff, Arizona, which he served two years before coming to Wrangell as a missionary. After four years of service here he withdrew from the Presbyterian Church.

The people of Wrangell built a church for him which during the first year was called the People's Church until Bishop Rowe, upon request of the congregation, made it a part of the Alaska missions of the Episcopal Church. Here Mr Corser served for 30 years until he was retired on pension in November 1934, after failing health prevented his continuing active service.

Mr. Corser was deeply interested in all that pertained to the welfare and development of the community. He was especially interested in school and served a number of years as president of the school board. He served on the executive board of the Red Cross from the time of its organization in Wrangell until his death. He was active in the Chamber of Commerce and other community organizations but was never affiliated with a fraternal body.

As a lecturer and the author of Totem Lore and Through the Ten Thousand Islands of Alaska, which brought him national recognition. Mr. Corser had a wide acquaintance throughout the States. He was one of the few Alaskans who gained listing in "Who's Who in America" from literary achievement.

WRANGELL SENTINEL, Feb. 7, 1936

A. D. COULTER

A. D. Coulter, widely known Seattle and Alaska mining man, died Sunday in Providence Hospital.

Mr. Coulter, founder and managing director of the Cornucopia Gold Mining Company in Eastern Oregon, retired from active business a year ago because of poor health.

Born in Peoria, Ill, sixty-eight years ago, he came West and in 1897 went to Alaska. Prior to that he was secretary of the Chicago bureau of charities, and for a time taught school in Durango, Colo.

Mr. Coulter had resided in Seattle since 1906. He was one of the founders of the Arctic Club and served as a news correspondent belonging to the Penman's Club of Chicago and the Masonic Lodge.

Surviving are his wife, Mrs. Margaret Ramsey Coulter, 2322 31st Ave., So.; two daughters, Mrs. Page M. Gilbert of Tacoma and Mrs. M. Cayley Smith, Jr. of Cleveland; and a brother, Charles C. Coulter of Denver.

ALASKA WEEKLY, Sept. 1, 1939

ROBERT M. COURTNEY

Robert M. Courtney, widely known Alaskan pioneer, died suddenly at Anchorage after a short illness.

Mr. Courtney was about 60 years of aga and had been in the North since the turn of the century. He first was employed as a bookkeeper for the North American Transportation and Trading Co. and later became its agent, about 1902.

Later, in 1904, Mr. Courtney became associated with Mr. Shonbeck in the operation of a general merchandise store at Cleary City and following several years in that business was associated with Mr. Griffin for some time. He went to Anchorage as an express and steamship agent and later established an accounting service. He has resided in Anchorage since 1914 and more recently has been associated with the Anchorage offices of the James C. Cooper accountancy firm which has headquarters in Juneau.

The pioneer is survived by his wife, two sons and a daughter. Mrs. Courtney and the daughter are now in Seattle. The sons are in Anchorage.

THE ALASKA WEEKLY, June 10, 1938

BETSY CUNNINGHAM

A recent issue of the Dawson News received here on the last boat conveys the sad news of the death in St. Mary's Hospital July 3 of Mrs. Betsy Cunningham, long-time resident of Dawson and pioneer mother of the Mayo district.

Many old-timers in this district still remember the late-departed pioneer woman when she arrived in Mayo as the vivacious bride of George Cunningham. For many years the Cunninghams were located in various part of this district during the earliest days of the camp. Their eldest daughter Elizabeth Gordon Stewart was the first white girl to be born in the Mayo district. That was in 1903 at a point on the Stewart river 40 miles above Mayo. Just last year Elizabeth was married to J. W. Gellatly, tea plantation owner of India, where they now reside.

A native of Scotland, the late Betsy Cunningham never quite lost her broad Scottish brogue and was renowned through out the Northland for her sparkling wit and hearty good-humor and laughter.

Mr. Cunningham died quite a number of years ago while

her beloved, little son "Jock," only eight, passed suddenly from a strange and sudden stomach ailment. Mrs. Cunningham never recovered from the sudden shock and tragedy of her small son's death.

Other remaining relatives include another daughter in Scotland, Florence in California, Mary and Margaret in B.C.

THE MAYO MINER, July 16, 1937

CLARENCE CUNNINGHAM

Clarence Cunningham died suddenly at his home in Alamo, B.C. on January 14 at the age of 76.

Mr. Cunningham was one of the outstanding figures in the development of Alaska and in 1903-05 was the center of a controversy over patents in coal claims at Katalla. This controversy with the Department of the Interior eventually reached the United States Supreme Court, which decided to favor of the Cunningham claims and vindicated Clarence Cunningham of all charges of dishonesty. This decision brought about the withdrawal of all similar accusations against prominent Seattle residents, among whom were Jacob Furth, noted banker; Charles F. Munday, attorney at law; and A. B. Frost, who was developing the Matanuska coal field. These coal lands are still undeveloped, supposedly due to powerful Eastern influences.

Prior to coming to Seattle, Mr. Cunningham had operated mines in the Coeur D'Alenes in Idaho. During the past 26 years he headed the Cunningham Mines, Ltd in the Sloan district of British Columbia, owners of one of the richest group of mines ever discovered in this province.

Mr. Cunningham is survived by his brother, Dr. John C. Cunningham of Spokane; and five sisters, Mrs. Rose O'Conner and Mrs. Alice Keilly of Chicago, Miss Mary Cunningham of St. Paul, Minn., Mrs. Nellie Cunningham of Seattle and Mrs. Simon Hellenthal of Juneau, Alaska.

ALASKA WEEKLY, Jan. 20, 1939

J. W. CURLEE

A service of almost thirty years in the U. S. Army including some twenty years in Alaska as a member of the Signal Corps, has been terminated by Master Sergeant J. W. Curlee by retirement to private life.

Curlee enlisted at Jefferson barracks, St. Louis, Mo., in the fall of 1908, and went to Alaska the following year, taking up the duties at old Fort Gibbon. He was transferred to the old Nenana station in 1910 and thence to Fairbanks and Little Delta, remaining about a year in that region. He returned to the States in 1911 and was assigned to duty in Alaska in 1915, going to Melozi. He was again ordered to the States in 1917 for overseas service and did not get beyond Fort Gibbons, subsequent orders having held him at the Yukon River post until 1921. He then proceeded to Seattle for duty in the headquarters office there.

Curlee returned to Fort Gibbon in 1922 to take charge of the abandoned post and later took over the radio station also, doing double duty there until relieved by Sergeant Charles Toback and Staff Sergeant Jimmy Campbell. The next shift took Curlee to Fort Yukon in 1923, where he officiated as operator in charge until 1934. He returned to the States that year and remained on duty there until his retirement.

Sargent and Mrs. Curlee were married in Seattle in September 1921.

ALASKA WEEKLY, April 2, 1937

JAMES CUSICK

James Cusick, 65 years old, of Latouche, died at 6:10 a.m. today from heart disease.

Born at Edwards, Ill., on June 11, 1868, Mr. Cusick came to the North country many years ago and thereafter made Alaska his permanent home. A man of enviable reputation, he had long been an exceptionally prominent worker in civic and territorial affairs. In 1928 Mr. Cusick was the Democratic party choice for Representative from this the Third Division to the Alaska House

of Representatives.
SEWARD DAILY GATEWAY, Sept. 13, 1933

WALDO CURTIS

Waldo Curtis is the oldest old-timer in Fort Yukon. In the fall of 1897 he boarded a down-river boat at Dawson and stayed with it until it landed at the town of Fort Yukon. Here he has made his headquarters for the past 44 years.

Waldo Curtis is and has been for the most of his mature life a trapper. He is a tall, deep-chested, soft-spoken member of the rugged individualist's fraternity. These men are the ones who have pushed their way in poling boats, with dogs and on foot into the remoter sections of Alaska depending upon their hands and ingenuity to carve out a living and open up a country for the push of civilization behind them.
JESSEN'S WEEKLY, July 18, 1947

A. ROSS CUTHBERT

The Royal Northwest Mounted Police announced the death in Regina in September 1916 of A. Ross Cuthbert. Cuthbert was stationed at Dawson for several years, during which he was commander in charge of the Dawson division of the mounted police. He entered the force many years ago, and steadily won his way forward. He was appointed inspector in 1896, and promoted to superintendent in 1902, and to assistant commissioner in 1913. He served in the South African war with the Canadian Mounted Rifles in 1900 for one year with rank of major.

Major Cuthbert leaves two sons, the elder Cuthbert being a lieutenant in the Royal Horse artillery, and the younger, Stuart, serving as a lieutenant in the Tenth Canadian Rifles. Both are at the front in Europe. The major also is survived by Mrs. Cuthbert and their daughter, Margaret, both living in Regina.

Major Cuthbert served in the Yukon from 1902 to 1908.
DAWSON DAILY NEWS, Sept. 21, 1916

JACK DALTON

Jack Dalton, noted Alaska trail blazer, died at San Francisco December 16 at the age of 89. Requiem mass was held at St. James Cathedral, Seattle last Saturday.

Dalton went to Alaska in 1880 and established a trading post at Haines and laid out the trail from that point to the Yukon River of Selkirk and Five Fingers. He took the first cattle and horses to the Interior for Circle and other camps and was in many other part of the Interior before the Klondike gold rush. He also is said to have taken the first coal out of the Chickaloon district. For the last several years he made his home Outside, and before going to San Francisco, about a year ago, was at Seaside, Oregon.

Surviving are his daughter Mrs. U. S. Grant, San Francisco now in Seattle; two sons, Ensign James Dalton, U.S.N., and Jack Dalton Jr., Los Angeles.

ALASKA WEEKLY, Dec. 29, 1944

FRANK DANDY

Frank Dandy passed away Monday morning [Nov. 3] after a short illness. He was almost 59 years of age. Little is known of his early life. William E. Lloyd, who was formerly in partnership with Mr. Dandy, says he thinks Dandy was born in London and partly raised there. Mr. Dandy first came to Wrangell during the rush of 1898, and has resided in this region ever since. Before coming to Wrangell, he spent three years on the Skeena river, and prior to that time he was located in Seattle.

The only surviving relative of which anything is known is a stepson, Charles Morse, who left Wrangell last year for Portland.

WRANGELL SENTINEL, Nov. 6, 1919

CHARLES E. DAVIDSON

Charles E. Davidson, Surveyor-General and Secretary of the Territory, was drowned across from Annex creek about 10 o'clock last night when he slipped from the deck of the Ja-Ka-Dah, on which he was making an outing trip with Mrs. Davidson, Dr. Robert Simpson and Mrs. Simpson. No trace was found of him and after searching for some time, they crossed to Annex creek and called up U.S. Marshal J. M. Tanner in Juneau about midnight.

Charles E. Davison is a pioneer of Juneau, coming to this city more than twenty years ago from California, where he was born and reared. From here he went to Fairbanks, where he resided until President Wilson appointed him Surveyor General in 1913. Mr. Davidson has been prominent in Democratic politics ever since his arrival in Alaska, and he was chairman of the Territorial Central Committee at the time of his appointment to office.

Mr. Davidson is survived by his widow and three children, Ethel Bella, Charles and James, who are in Juneau.

THE ALASKA DAILY EMPIRE August 9, 1919

J. H. (JACK) DAVIES

J. H. Davies, 60, former mayor of Ketchikan, died in the Ketchikan General Hospital earlier today.

He was born in Plymouth, Pennsylvania, February 8, 1875, the son of T. B. Davies. As a young man he came to Tacoma, Washington. Despite the fact that he had not had a great deal of schooling, he demonstrated his ability and became an employee in the office of Hugh Wallace, a lawyer, who is 1919 became ambassador to France.

Subsequently, Mr. Davies became mail clerk on boats running from Seattle to Neah Bay and Port Angeles. He also made a trip to Dawson in 1900. Later he joined the Puget Sound Towboat company and served as mate on several of the company boats.

In 1903 he came to Alaska as purser on the Georgia, remaining with that boat on her regular run between Juneau and Sitka.

In 1910 he became deputy United States marshal and was stationed in Ketchikan until 1916. He left that post in 1918, joining J. R. Beegle in organizing the insurance firm that bore Mr. Beegle's name. When the Beegle Packing company first was organized, Mr. Davies was active in that organization and for a time served as its manager. In 1919 he went to Juneau as a representative in the territorial legislature. He served only one term, elected by the people of the First division.

In 1931 he was elected to the city council. Little more than a year later the council elected him to serve as mayor, filling the unexpired term of F. R. Mitsch, who had resigned.

November 10, 1910, Mr. Davies and Ann Museth of Douglas were married in Douglas. They had two children, Jack and Tom.

Besides the widow and children, Mr. Davies is survived by his mother, Mrs. T. B. Davies, and a sister, Mrs. Margaret Martinetti. Both the latter arrived in Ketchikan aboard the steamer Alaska yesterday from their home in Tacoma, called north by the serious illness of Mr. Davies.

KETCHIKAN ALASKA CHRONICLE, April 30, 1935

HAROLD F. DAWES

Mr. Dawes was born and educated in Wisconsin. When he graduated from high school he went west and finally settled at Wrangell, Alaska, as proprietor of a weekly newspaper.

Later he sold his newspaper and attended Valparaiso University Law school, finishing the course in 1915.

As a member of the artillery park unit of the first army, Mr. Dawes served in France. After his discharge from the army he returned to Alaska and entered the practice of law at Juneau. He is a charter member of Alford John Bradford Post No. 4 of the Legion, and commander of the department of Alaska.

DOUGLAS ISLAND NEWS, April 29, 1921

LEONARD P. DAWES

Senator Leonard P. Dawes, one of Alaska's best-known physicians and surgeons and a resident of the Territory since 1910, was a newcomer to the Legislature this year. Born in Wisconsin, he took his medical course at the University of Illinois, where he studied surgery under Dr. Albert J. Ochsner. Following his graduation and internship, he taught for five years at the Chicago College of Medicine. Like many another, Dr. Dawes first came to Alaska only for a vacation trip, but he liked the looks of the town of Wrangell and decided to spend the summer there. The summer lengthened into a stay of five years, after which he moved to Juneau where he carried on an active practice until two years ago. He is the only Alaskan physician to hold a fellowship in the American College of Surgeons.

ALASKA LIFE, June 1947

CORA A. COCKERHAM DAY

Mrs. Jack Day, wife of one of the best known and most prominent mining operators of the camp, fell dead at noon today.

Mrs. Day's maiden name was Cora A Cockerham. She was born in Tennessee 34 years ago. Beside her parents she has three brothers and three sisters living. One brother is in the Klondike. Mrs. Day came here from Seattle in 1900 to join her husband who came here in 1898. John S. Day, the husband, is a native of Bowentur county, Quebec. He is a large operator on Last Chance and Bonanza.

DAWSON DAILY NEWS, June 3, 1905

HUGH DAY

Hugh Day died in Douglas, Alaska on Dec. 31st, 1916, a native of St. Hyacinthe, Quebec, aged 53 years. He came to Alaska when about 21 years of age and settled in Killisnoo. He afterwards carried mail from Juneau to the interior by way of the Taku. He went to the Klondike with the big rush, located a rich claim but lost it through speculation. He returned to Douglas, suffered lost of his property in the big fire of 1911, but rebuilt and a few years ago moved to Tenakee springs.

Wednesday he entered the hospital for treatment of a head injury he received in a street fight when he was 17 and in late years gave him considerable trouble. On Thursday he went into convulsion and died. He is survived by a son, Joseph, and a nephew, John L. Day.

DOUGLAS ISLAND NEWS, June 6, 1905

ED O. DECKER

When about 19 years of age, E. O. Decker left his home at Roxbury (Delaware), to seek his fortune in the west.

After spending many years in various sections of the west, including five years in the Black Hills of Dakota, Mr. Decker finally settled in Juneau, Alaska. There together with his brother, Jay Decker, he established a small trading store. So rapidly did their business increase, however, that they found it necessary to considerably extend their facilities, and recently they have completed an elegant store, 60x80 feet in dimensions, with plate glass front, from plans and specifications furnished by their uncle of Kingston. A big warehouse was also built.

Mr. Decker came east, not only to visit his old friends and relatives, but also to purchase a large stock of goods and to dispose of a large number of fine furs in New York city, and besides to have some fine fur garments made for both Mr. Decker and himself. Among those he showed a magnificent otter cape made for Mrs. Decker, and an elegant long sealskin coat made for himself. Mr. Decker wore a curious watch chain. It was made of a string of gold nuggets, deftly secured together. The nuggets were worth from $3 to $8 a piece, and like all Alaskan gold, pale and mildly lustrous.

Decker and his wife, a charming women, are now guests at the resident of his uncle, Roadmaster John Decker, of the Ulster & Delaware railroad, on O'Neil street, Kingston.

THE ALASKA MINING RECORD (Juneau), Feb. 3, 1897

ROSE ROSS DECKER

Mrs. Rose Ross Decker, former resident of Juneau, died March 6, at Oneonta, N.Y. She was the widow of Jason Decker, an early pioneer merchant who went to Juneau in 1888. The next year he organized the Decker Mercantile Company, which did a flourishing business for many years. It operated two boats, the Sea Lion and the Polar Bear, piloted by Captains York and Patterson. Goods were delivered to all points along the southeast coast of Alaska.

The Deckers were married in 1902 in Juneau. They retired in 1917 and went to Oneonta, where he died in 1921. Two daughters and one son survive, all born in Juneau and attending high school there. Mrs. Decker was a sister of the late Mrs. "Billy" Huson.

THE ALASKA WEEKLY, April 15, 1955

CLARA S. DEDMAN

Mrs. Clara S. Dedman, prominent pioneer hotel manager and owner of the Golden North Hotel, passed away at Skagway Friday night Feb. 21.

Mrs. Dedman came to Alaska during the gold rush days with her husband George Dedman and located at Skagway. They built the Golden North Hotel which became one of the leading institutions of the kind in the north. Mr. Dedman died several years ago and Mrs. Dedman continued to operate the hotel. She was known to Thousands of tourists and travelers.

Mrs. Dedman is survived by her son, Henry, who is residing in Skagway.

WRANGELL SENTINEL, Feb. 28, 1936

GEORGE R. DEDMAN   (See Vol. 1)

George R. Dedman, proprietor of the Golden North Hotel and pioneer of Skagway, where he had been engaged in the hotel business for more than a quarter of a century, died at the White Pass hospital yesterday, June 28, 1925. He is survived by his widow and son and the latter's family.

Mr. Dedman came to Skagway in the early days of the Klondike rush, and shortly thereafter engaged in the hotel business, associating himself after a year or two with Ed Foreman in the Golden North Hotel. He has been with that hostelry ever since, buying out the interest of Mr. Foreman a few years ago.

Before coming to Alaska, Mr. Dedman resided at Portland, Oregon.

DAWSON NEWS, July 4, 1925; ALASKA WEEKLY, JULY 10, 1925

CHARLES H. DEWITT

Charles H. DeWitt died at Willard Parker hospital in New York city on the evening of April 14, 1903 of smallpox.

Charles H. DeWitt was a pioneer of this city, having arrived here early in the rush to the Klondike with a large number of mules and horses. He engaged in the packing business until the completion of the railroad and was always one of the largest and most successful packers on the old Skagway trail. After the completion of the railroad, Mr. DeWitt became interested in Atlin mines, and was one of the heaviest owners of hydraulic properties in the camp. His interests were mostly on Spruce creek. He leaves property that will give his wife and children a competency. Mr. DeWitt was not in Skagway long until he was followed by his family and since the earliest days of this place they have been among the most popular of those in the city.

The deceased was a native of Ohio and was 54 years of age. He lived most of his life on the frontier and numbered friends by the thousands from Texas on the south to Alaska on the north. He was one of those big souled men, typical of the West, who made friends and kept them. He is survived by his wife and sons, Hugh and Lawrence, and other children [unnamed in obit].

DAILY ALASKAN (Skagway), April 18, 1903

ANDREW M. DIERINGER

Andrew Dieringer was born in Dieringer, Washington June 12, 1887, and would have been 47 years of age on his next birthday. He first came to Alaska in 1903 and after remaining for a time returned to Dieringer. He returned to Valdez again in 1906 and had resided in Valdez ever since. In June 1912 he wedded Miss Buelah Fogg of Valdez.

During his residence in Valdez, Mr. Dieringer was prominently identified with the business and civic affairs of the community. He organized and built up the Valdez Dock Company and the Valdez Transportation companies and was president of both corporations. With the growth of tourist traffic over the Richardson Highway, he built and operated the Tonsina Lodge at Tonsina, the finest roadhouse on the highway. He was for many years a member of the City Council of Valdez and devoted much of his time to the upbuilding of the community. He was also connected with the First Bank of Valdez, being a director of that institution.

Andrew Dieringer died in Seattle, Washington Jan. 30, 1933. Mr. Dieringer is survived by his widow, three sons, James Roy and Joseph, and two daughters, Anne and Betty, and his father, J. C. Dieringer, of Valdez, and two sisters, Mrs. I. W. Brundage of San Francisco, and Mrs. J. M. Lathrop of La Jolla, Calif.

THE VALDEZ MINER, Jan. 4, 1933; CORDOVA DAILY TIMES, Jan. 31, 1933

HENRY C. DOHRMANN

Henry C. Dohrmann, Sr., pioneer of the Northland, for some sixteen years a resident of Seward, Knik, Anchorage and the Cook Inlet country, and who came outside some eight years ago, taking up a residence in Persia, Iowa, passed away recently at the advanced age of 84.

Henry Dohrmann first went to Alaska 16 years ago, making his home in Seward. While living there a son, Albert, was drowned in Resurrection bay. Later he moved with his family to Knik, and still later went to Susitna Station, where he operated a saw mill. Again he returned to Knik for a time, and then went to Anchorage, when that town was put on the map by the government railroad.

He is survived by a daughter, Mrs. Oscar Gill of Anchorage, and a son, Henry C. Dohrmann, Jr., now resides in La Habra, California. He married the daughter of Reverend Howard, formerly of Knik, Alaska. Another daughter lives in Persia, Iowa.

ALASKA WEEKLY, Sept. 17, 1926

JERRY DOODY

On the first day of December 1897, Jerry Doody landed in Dyea and from that time to this the farthest south he has been is Skagway and now he is going to Vancouver and points south for a vacation and perhaps to engage in business until the war is over.

Born in old Essex country, Massachusetts, Jerry, early in life went west and after a time in Kansas located in Arizona where he joined Uncle Sam's army in the Quartermaster department and after serving several years, during which time he took part in the capture of Geronimo, the famous Indian chief, he went to California and from there to Alaska and the Yukon.

During his twenty one years in the north Mr. Doody has been one of the most successful and skillful photographers, with headquarters at Dawson, and has a large collection of views and negatives of the country in almost every part contiguous to the mighty Yukon river.

THE DAILY ALASKAN, Oct. 1, 1918

ANTONIO DORTERO

Antonio Dortero, who has been engaged in business in Skagway ever since the town first came into existence in 1897, passed away in the White Pass hospital there at 7 o'clock in the morning of Tuesday, January 6, 1920. He had been in poor health for many months previous, and the loss of his youngest son, Vincent, by influenza 18 months ago while in the U.S. army training camp at Fort Dodge, Iowa, so preyed on his mind that it materially hastened the end. The deceased was between 60 and 70 years of age, and left his wife, and stepdaughter, Mrs. D. L. Stevenson of Skagway, and son John of Seattle to mourn his loss.

Tony Dortero was a violinist of exceptional ability, although in the later years of his life, only his most intimate associated were aware of his accomplishment. When a young man he was a professional musician and in the boom mining days in Colorado and Wyoming his services were in constant demand in the gilded places that flourished throughout the middle western states and wherein the Goddess of Chance held undisputed sway and fortunes were gained or lost by the turn of a card of the dropping of the ivory ball.

On coming to the Pacific coast he located at Astoria, Oregon where he entered into the business he afterward followed until the time of his death. From Astoria he came north to Skagway.

THE WEEKLY STAR (Whitehorse), Jan. 9, 1920

PAUL DOVIDOVICS

Paul Dovidovics of Kotzebue, an Alaska pioneer since 1898, was a visitor in Juneau last week, and sailed October 21ST for Seattle. It is his first trip to the States since 1900.

Mr. Dovidovics operates a roadhouse in Kotzebue, where he formerly had a trading post. He was in Nome during the glamorous gold rush days of 1899 and 1900 when Nome had the impressive population of 30,000. For four years, from 1910 to 1914, Mr. Dovidovics carried mail by dog team from Kotzebue to Point Barrow, a distance of 50 miles. The only shelter available at the time for the entire route was in the schoolhouses at Kivilina, Point Hope, and Cape Lisurne. At present shelter cabins are provided every 35 or 40 miles from Kotzebue to Barrow.

Besides carrying mail to Barrow, Mr. Dovidovics for 16 years traveled by dog team over that section of Alaska and bought furs.

ALASKA CATHOLIC, Nov. 6, 1937

WILLIAM DRURY

The last stampeder has made the home port. The last member of that famous, colorful band of gold seekers who crossed the Chilkoot Trail of '98 headed for the Klondike has checked in.

Thirty-eight years after. Just a few weeks before Dawson celebrated its 40th anniversary of the finding of gold on Bonanza, along come 'Big Bill' Drury to claim the startling, unique distinction of being the last of the stampeders to arrive.

It all happened this way. Bill Drury young, husky, adventuresome, started for the Klondike. He came by Ashcroft Trail in the fall but instead of continuing on to the Klondike drifted into Atlin. There he and his present day partner Isaac Taylor started the firm of Taylor & Drury. The partners grew with the country. Today that firm is the largest individual mercantile firm in the Yukon Territory with branches and trading posts in every corner of the country.

The partnership thrived, business expanded. Partner Drury had no time to look for gold in the Klondike creeks. The gold of the North was closer to home for the big-and-easy-going slow spoken Bill and his partner.

For the past quarter of a century he has played an active and prominent part in the destinies of the Yukon's greatest trading firm.

It used to be that Bill Drury made his fur-buying expeditions into the Yukon outposts by dog team. But those days are gone forever. He still makes those long trips but all by air now.

Outside his business interests he had many others. The town of Whitehorse would be lost without its 'Big Bill' Drury. He has taken an active part in the growth of the Yukon's solid

He has taken an active part in the growth of the Yukon's solid little Gateway town. He is one of the chief stockholders of the newspaper, he has served on many committees, has lent his support to many worthwhile enterprises.

[An accompanying photo lists his children: William l, William S, Mary Alice and Thomas E.]

WHITEHORSE STAR, August 21, 1936

CALIXTE AIME DUGAS

His Honor Calixte Aime Dugas was born at St. Remi, Quebec, February 11, 1845. He was the son of Adolphe A. Dugas, "a patriot of 1837," and Clotilde Olginy. He was educated in St. Sulpice college; was admitted to the bar and practiced law in Montreal; was police magistrate; Judge of the sessions of peace; and chairman of the quarters sessions of Montreal.

He was a major in the Sixty-fifth regiment and commanded the corps in the Northwest rebellion. He retired with rank in 1889 and made judge of the Yukon court in 1898. He served in the Yukon as senior judge during the years the territory was provided with three territorial judges, and during which time there was a Yukon appeals court. He also served several terms on the Yukon Council. He left Dawson in the fall of 1911.

Judge Dugas was married twice, first to Susan Harkin, who died in 1907 and second to Matilda Kirkpatrick. Mr. Justice Dugas, the pioneer judge of the Yukon, died suddenly in his old home city of Montreal, August 25, 1914. He is survived by his wife and a son, Aime Dugas, formerly in the gold commissioner's office in Dawson, now in Portland, Oregon.

DAWSON DAILY NEWS, Aug, 27, 1914.

WILLIAM, DUNCAN (See Vol. 3)

One of the most famous characters of Alaska passed away at Metlakahtla on August 31, when Rev. William Duncan died at that place of apoplexy. He was 86 years old and was born in Beverly, England.

Converted to militant Christianity in 1857, he decided to work among "the heathen." His first work was in Northern British Columbia among the Tsimpsean Indians. He learned the language of the natives and founded a colony, but difficulty with the Hudson's Bay Company led him to take his converts into American territory. He obtained permission from the United States to settle on Annette island, in southeastern Alaska.

The new colony prospered from 1887 on and ten years ago was considered one of the most important settlements in the North.

It contained 130 houses, a number of public buildings, all Indian-built; the largest church in Alaska; the largest library in the territory; a cannery employing 150 men and packing 10,000 cases of salmon yearly; and a store carrying a stock valued at $25,000. The Metlakahtla brass band, which toured the country a few years ago, was one of the most famous organizations of native musicians ever formed among the Indians.

Duncan's government was strictly a one-man rule. He considered his converts as children and refused to allow them that measure of self-government which they saw natives enjoying in other Indian colonies established under patronage of the United States Bureau of Education. Controversies regarding control of the school and business affairs of the colony marred the later years of his life, but the great outstanding feature of his work of civilizing the Tsimpseans survived in the records of the church and in articles printed far and wide.

DOUGLAS ISLAND NEWS, Sept. 13, 1918

SAM C. DUNHAM

The real old-time Yukon and Alaska pioneers still remember Sam C. Dunham, who, as a poet, antedated Robert W. Service, but Dunham is practically forgotten. Yet he wrote some mighty good human interest stuff, which was embodied in a book of verse which he first published more than twenty years ago. His most pretentious effort was called the "Goldsmith of Nome."

Other popular poems were called "Alaska to Uncle Sam," and "The Lament of the Old Sourdough." Numbers of shorter poems were published, and every one of them had a peculiarly northern appeal. Dunham first went to Circle City, spending his first winter there, and it was there that he wrote his first Northern verse. Going into the Yukon, he accompanied Joaquin Miller, the Poet of the Sierras, over the Chilkoot pass in the fall of 1897, and both Miller and Dunham celebrated the event in verse. In 1900 Mr. Dunham was appointed supervisor of the census for Alaska, a trust which he discharged with great credit to himself and the census bureau. Leaving Alaska in 1902, he went to Tonopah, Nevada, then a brand new mining camp, where he commenced the publication of a newspaper. It was a success and he made a good deal of money in the venture only to lose it later in mining speculation. Mr. Dunham died in New York city a year or more ago. [Re-printed from the Alaska Weekly]

THE DAWSON NEWS, July 21, 1925

JOHN W. DUNN

John W. Dunn, 61, died in Juneau on March 19. He was the junior senator Fourth division and veteran legislator, lawyer, and miner of Ruby. He was born in Ohio, June 28, 1869, and was educated in the public and private schools of Denver, Colorado. He graduated in 1897 from the Denver Law School and served with the Colorado volunteers during the Spanish-American war in 1898-99.

In 1905 Dunn came to Alaska and was connected with E.R. Peoples of Fairbanks until the following year when the Iditarod strike took place. He joined the stampede and later went to Ruby where he resided many years.

The senator served his first term as a lawmaker in the House in 1919, was returned to the Senate in 1923.

ALASKA WEEKLY, March 20, 1931.

S. B. DUNN

S. B. Dunn lived on his ranch just north of Roseburg and engaged in poultry, fruit, and broccoli farming. Dr. Dunn with his three brothers left Iowa in February 1898 for the Klondike. While packing their outfit over the Chilcoot Pass, one of the brothers became seriously ill and was accompanied home by another brother, leaving only two to pack their outfit of 7,200 pounds over the Pass, and down to lake Bennett, where they built two scows on which they transported their outfit to Dawson without mishap, arriving there July 21, 1898.

ALASKA WEEKLY, SEPT 13, 1929.

WELDON LAMAR DURHAM

Weldon Lamar Durham died last night of a heart attack in his room in the Alaska railroad dormitory shortly before nine o'clock..

Weldon Lamar Durham who was familiarly known to his host of friends throughout the railbelt a "Bull" Durham was an oldtimer in the service of the Alaska Railroad, having been attached to the Anchorage headquarters offices since early construction days. For a number of years he held a position as assistant roadmaster, and had responsibility of looking after the requirements of camps and sections and other out of town units, a task which necessitated long hours and constant contact with all points along the railroad. He was born at Newton, Mississippi, Sept. 21, 1871.

ALASKA WEEKLY, Sept. 7, 1928

ALVAH EAMES

Alvah Eames came to Alaska May 5, 1900, from Portland, Oregon. He was in Valdez from 1900 to 1910 and at Cordova from 1910 to 1922. He was president of Cordova Igloo No. 19 in 1920-1931, and is in the United States mail service.

ALASKA DISPATCH, May 5, 1922

MILDRED EDDY

Mildred Eddy, wife of William Eddy formerly of Nome and later Deputy United States Marshall at Douglas, died at the county poor farm hospital here Thursday night. Her Father and ex judge of Hawaii, was reputed to be a millionaire at the time of his death. Until a few years ago she had been fairly well supplied with money, but poor financial investments following closely on one another reduced her to straitened circumstances. She lived at expensive hotels and apartments, friends say, until the money from her late husband's insurance was exhausted.
KUSKO TIMES, Nov. 24, 1928.

WILLIAM EGAN

Wm. Egan was killed and three companions were buried Sunday morning, March 27, by a huge snowslide which swept down from the mountain side behind the property of the Valdez Gold Mining company, about seven miles back from the waterfront, on Shoup glacier.

Mr. Egan in company with Gus Kring, Fred Johnson, Fred Erickson, and Ed Stone, was engaged in shoveling out the tram cable which is used to haul supplies from the lower camp to the upper. The slide, which came without warning, buried the four men, Gus Kring being saved by the slide breaking across the canyon, about 300 feet above him.

Mr. Kring, who was the sole witness of the disaster, states that he was engaged in shoveling when he heard the roar of the approaching avalanche, and when he looked saw the crest of the snow wave strike Mr. Egan and Mr. Stone, who were several hundred feet above him. It had already buried Johnson and Erickson, farther up the mountain side. Mr. Kring hastened to the spot where he had last seen Messrs. Egan and Stone and started digging them out, being joined later by Johnson and Erickson who had worked their way out of the loosely packed snow over them. Jack Cook, who is chef for the party, also rendered valuable aid.

Mr. Stone was found first, a few feet below where the slide engulfed him. He was nearly dead from suffocation and the pressure of the ice pack. After he was revived, the work of searching for Mr. Egan was taken up, and his body was found a few yards above the spot where Stone was rescued. He was dead when uncovered, as first aid administered by the quartette failed to indicate any signs of life. Death apparently was instantaneous and painless as there were no indications of a struggle.

The body was placed on a hand sled and pulled the seven miles to the beach, the party being augmented by Ed Held, E.E. MacDonald, Gilbert Lee, Alex Smart and Ernest Johnson. The trip was a most difficult one the men being practically exhausted from breaking trail.

William Egan was born at Sumner, Iowa, January 29, 1867, and was 53 years old at the time of his death. He was united in marriage at Lewistown, Montana, in 1894 to Miss Cora Allen, who survives him. Seven children were born to them, Clinton, Emmet and Ethel, who have attained their majority, and Alaska, Alive, William and Francis, who are yet under age. In 1902 the call of the North lured Mr. Egan to Alaska and he first landed at Douglas where he worked for a time as a miner. He came to Valdez in 1903.

THE VALDEZ MINER, April 2, 1921

ALBERT R. ELDRIDGE

That Albert R. Eldridge, better known to his hosts of friends as "Bert," pioneer merchant of McGrath, had died in airplane while being transported by Pilot Blunt to Anchorage was the sad, shocking and most unexpected news. Mr. Eldridge was on his way to Anchorage hospital, and accompanying him in the plane was Jack Morris, of McGrath.

Albert R. Eldridge was born in Illinois about 62 years ago. Little is known of his early life, except that as a young man he moved to the Dakotas, and probably lived in other parts of the West. He arrived at Nome with the stampede, to that camp, where he spent some years. He arrived about 1910 at McGrath, where he later opened up a mercantile establishment and where he continued to reside and thrive up to the time of his passing. He was an excellent business man, one of the highest integrity, one always willing to help. To mourn his loss he leaves one brother, probably two, somewhere in Illinois, a son somewhere in Washington State, as well as other relatives residing in Yakima, Wash, and other parts.

THE KUSKO TIMES, Apr. 16,1932

JOHN B. ELLENBACHER

John B. Ellenbacher, a native of Germany, aged 60 years, died at St. Ann's Hospital on Douglas Island on Saturday, July 21. The funeral was held at the Evergreen cemetery, Juneau, on Monday July 23rd.

John Ellenbacher came to the United States at an early age and located in the state of Michigan. He learned the machinist's trade, in which he was quite proficient, as evidenced by the fact that he climbed to the position of head mechanic of the Calumet and Hecla Copper Co., which position he held until coming to Alaska about 15 years ago. He has twice held a similar position at Treadwell, once for a term of 4 years and again for 2 years–up until 2 years ago. He leaves a wife and daughter in Salt Lake City, a daughter in Montana, a sister in Paris and a sister in Germany to mourn his loss.

DOUGLAS ISLAND NEWS, July 25, 1900

ALBERT D. ELLIOTT

The Clerk of the District Court and ex-officio Secretary of State is Hon. Albert D. Elliott. He was born in the year 1859 in the state of Pennsylvania. He is a graduate of Harvard in the class of 1889 in the collegiate course. He also graduated from the law department of the University of Michigan. He came to Alaska during the summer of 1897 and was appointed Clerk of the District Court, which position he has since held. During the absence of the Governor, he is by law made the acting governor.

Mr. Elliott is not a tall man, weights about 160 pounds, wears a mustache and has dark brown hair.

DOUGLAS ISLAND NEWS, Jan. 1899

THOMAS. S. ELSEMORE

Thomas S. Elsemore died May 29, 1940 at the Maynard Hospital in Seattle.

Since the time he first came to Peterburg in 1912, Mr. Elsemore took an active part in civic affairs and was constantly concerned with the sound growth of the town.

He was born February 1, 1884 in Maine and came to Petersburg as U. S. Deputy Marshal in 1912. On April 28, 1917 he became Assistant Cashier of the Bank of Petersburg and on July 5 of the same year was appointed Cashier, the office he held at the time of his death.

Mr. Elsemore also served on the City Council and was first elected Mayor in 1920. He served in the latter office for several terms after that. He also served as U. S. Commissioner and City Clerk.

In addition to his wife and two children, Jerry and Thomasine, Mr. Elsemore is survived by his parents and a number of brothers and sisters in Maine.

PETERSBURG PRESS, May 31, 1940

CHARLES ENGQUIST

Charlie Engquist, a resident Alaskan since 1909 passed away in Seward Sunday evening following an illness that brought him to Seward about two weeks ago.

Mr. Engquist, who was born in Sweden 67 years ago, mined at Willow some years ago. He was known to many of the old-timers in the Interior districts and his poolroom at Flat was a popular home-like resort.

His health condition become serious, Mrs. Engquist was notified Saturday and in response to the call arrived here Monday on a Bowman Airways plane, 24 hours after her husband had passed away.

Mrs. Alfred Johnson of Selah, Wash., is a surviving sister, and it is through her request that the body will be taken to the Eastern Washington town by the bereaved wife for burial. A brother Frank Engquist, lives at Yakima. Mrs. Engquist's people live in California.

SEWARD GATEWAY, October 15, 1935

ISAAC EVANS

Frank H. Richards, recently appointed United States marshal of Nome, has announced his appointments. Mr. Richards has selected Isaac Evans of this city [Dawson] to be chief deputy.

Isaac Evans, who is to be the officer deputy at Teller City, is a resident of Tacoma. He was at one time deputy sheriff of Pierce county and was for a number of years on the detective force of the Tacoma police department.

THE DAILY KLONDIKE NUGGET, May 16, 1901

AIDA MAY EVEREST

One of the most, if not the most pleasant social event ever to take place in the city of Skaguay since its organization, was the marriage of Miss Aida May Everest, eldest daughter of Mr. and Mrs. C.W. Everest, to Mr. Herman Hogland which was solemnized at the family residence last Saturday evening, February 18,th1899. Miss. Maude Everest was maid of honor.

SKAGWAY NEWS, Feb. 24, 1899

EMMA G. FEERO

Mrs. Emma G. Feero, mother of Deputy U. S. Marshal William E. Feero of Douglas, died at her home in Skagway recently from complications arising from heart trouble. She was a native of Maine, having been born at Hamden, that state June 20, 1859. Mrs. Feero was one of the pioneer settlers of Skagway, having gone there October 27, 1897, and had since made that place her home. She is survived by two daughters and two sons: Mrs. J. N. Hanson and Mrs. Karl Larson, both of Skagway; and William E. of Douglas; an adopted son, Phillip Olson, who was taken by her when only seven weeks old; seventeen grandchildren, all born in Alaska; and a sister, Mrs. A. B. Scott of Tacoma. Her husband, John E. Feero, died in Skagway December 8, 1898, slightly more than a year after bringing his wife and then small children to that place.

VALDEZ MINER, March 30, 1929

JOHN FREDERICK FEITNER

About two o'clock Monday morning the city was startled by the rapidly spreading report of the suicide by hanging of John Frederick Feitner, a baker, who, except to one of two witnesses was known as John Schmitt. Feitner had for more than a year been in the employ of M. F. Fremmer, working faithfully and well in the bakery owned by the latter on Frank street. Nearly two months ago Feitner, with the assistance of his late employer, established for himself a small bakery on Franklin street, just below Third, but business was slow, and his passion for gaming kept him in poverty, if not in actual want. He was seen about town on Saturday evening, but his failure to deliver bread at Fremmer's store on Monday morning started an investigation with the result that his corpse was found suspended by a strap from the ceiling of his shop, with one foot barely touching the floor, the other still upon the chair from which he had stepped into eternity.

The deceased was a native of Grunstadt, Rhine Ptalz, Germany, where relatives survive him, was about 40 years of age and a member of the order of Odd Fellows.

ALASKA MINING RECORD, Dec. 30, 1896

WILLIAM CLARK ("SKAGWAY BILL") FONDA

Gray-haired Alaska Yukon Pioneers, garbed in fur-lined parkas, hold their right arms aloft over the casket of William

Clark "Skagway Bill" Fonda this week. They passed his prospecting pan and "divvied in" as part of their ritual for a departed brother.

Several hundred former Alaskans who had assembled at the Johnson & Hamilton Mortuary heard speakers pay tribute to "Skagway Bill"'s life, and declare that in death he only had "mushed on" to a new claim; that he was prospecting for more glorious gold and pioneering in a new land.

But there were hearty sobs, nonetheless, as the pioneers passed by his bier and filed out of the chapel.

A.J. Goddard, recorder of the Pioneers read a poem of the North that "Skagway Bill" had written and that he wanted read at his funeral. A soloist sang Alaskan songs. Then the pioneers gathered up "Skagway Bill"'s prospecting pan and left.

So ended the saga of "Skagway Bill" Fonda who had roamed from the tip of South America to the edge of the Arctic Circle in seeking his fortune. At the age of 7 he drove mules on the Erie Canal; at 9 he helped paint the Brooklyn bridge; at 21 he was captain of his own 500-ton steamer on the Hudson River. Then he came west on a 110 day sea voyage to Seattle. In 1896 he went to Alaska.

"I spent twenty years up there," Fonda often said. "I built the first cabin in Skagway. I built the first bridge. I laid out the city of Skagway in 1897." He helped build the railroad from Anchorage to Indian River.

A familiar figure in miner's clothes, carrying a gold pick, pan and shovel at local Sourdough parades, he was the model for Alonzo Victor Lewis' statue of the Sourdough. He died August 31 [1938] at the age of 80.

THE ALASKA WEEKLY, Sept. 9, 1938

W. R. FORREST

Frank H. Richards, recently appointed United States marshal of Nome, has announced his appointments. Mr. Richards has selected W. R. Forrest of this city [Dawson] to his chief deputy.

Chief Deputy Forrest is well known in this city. He served as state senator from King county in the first legislature after the territory became a state. Subsequently he served one term as county auditor. He has been prominent in newspaper work, being at one time connected with the Seattle Press Times and afterward with the Post Intelligencer in an editorial capacity.

DAILY KLONDIKE NUGGET (Dawson), May 16, 1901

FRANK H. FOSTER

Frank H. Foster, 72, member of a pioneer Seattle family who lived many years in Alaska and was prominent in Territorial legal and legislative circles, died last week in Olympia, following a long illness. He was the son of George Foster and Nettie Low. His mother was the first white child born at Alki Point. Mr. Foster was a member of the Mayflower Society; Sons of the American Revolution

Mr. Foster practiced law in Cordova and Juneau, Alaska, for 33 years. He served in the Alaska Legislature several terms and at one time was U.S. District Attorney for the 3rd Division of Alaska. He moved to Olympia in 1944. He was in the State Attorney General's office and also practiced law in Olympia.

Surviving are his wife, Claire; three daughters, Mrs. Ernest Schroeder, Olympia; and Mrs. J. Ed. Richey and Mrs. Loren Schuster, Seattle; two sisters, Mrs. Ethel McCarthy and Mrs. Roderic Crandall, both in New Mexico; two brothers, Ray Foster, Omak; and Arthur Foster, Spokane; nine grandchildren and two great-grandchildren.

ALASKA WEEKLY, Feb. 29, 1952

Z. E. FOSTER

Mrs. Foster is the wife of a prominent mining operator in the Inmachuk section is in town from Deering, accompanied by her two children. She will shortly be joined by her husband, and they will spend the winter at their home in Southern California.

Mrs. Foster is a pioneer of the northern country, having as early as 1897 being engaged in missionary work at the Friends' Mission, Point Blossom. The Fosters left Nome in 1901 and have lived continuously since in the north. Their eldest child was born in Nome in 1900 and, a second one was born in Deering last year.
NOME SEMI-WEEKLY NUGGET, Sept, 19, 1903

ARTHUR FRAME

Arthur Frame was born in Sheldon, Iowa in 1880, where he remained until 1895, when with his parents moved to South Dakota. There he entered Yankton College, which he attended until 1899, leaving that college in his junior year. From 1898 until 1901 he was a law student in the office of Judge Bartlett, at Yankton, reading law for one year in connection with his school work. He practiced law in South Dakota from 1901 to 1903, and in Seattle in 1904. He went to Skagway in 1905, where he remained a year, removing to Fairbanks in the summer of 1907, and is at present associated with the law firm of McGinn & Sullivan.
ALASKA YUKON MAGAZINE, Jan. 1909

GROVER C. FRAME

Grover C. Frame, 41, an Alaskan Sourdough, son of Mrs. J. W. Frame of this city and J. W. Frame, of Ketchikan, Alaska, and Pioneer Alaskan newspaperman, passed away at Sedro-Woodley, Washington, last Sunday and was buried in the family plot at Everett last Sunday afternoon.

There were few better known figures in Alaska mining camps than Grover Frame. He accompanied his father north in 1898 during the Klondike excitement and followed the fortunes of his father who was in the newspaper business. He was on almost all of the stampedes for years and in recent years was extensively engaged in the automobile business operating lines of autos in the various cities in western Alaska. He was really

Alaska's pioneer automobile man running his cars over roads into the interior Alaska where cars had never been before.

A little less than three years ago he took some cars to Hyder, southeastern Alaska to operate a jitney line. Finding that the development of the camp did not at that time warrant the establishment of the line, he went to Ketchikan where his father was operating a newspaper. It was there he was taken sick with his last illness. He was there for many months and several weeks ago went to Sedro-Woodley for treatment. His mother accompanied him and nursed him until the last, and she and his brother Ira, accompanied the remains to the last resting place at Everett. Rev. George W. Frame, head of the Methodist missions in this section, an uncle and his wife were also at the funeral. His father John W. Frame had been called to Washington, D. C. for an important conference.

Grover C. Frame was born at Hillsdale, Michigan, April 20, 1884. He came west with his parents when he was two years of age and lived at Snohomish until 1898 when he went to Alaska and lived there practically all the time from then on, except for occasional visits to this city to visit his mother.

He is survived by his mother and father and three brothers: Ira of Port Angeles; Park of Hollywood, California; and William Jr. of Hyder, Alaska.

STROLLER'S WEEKLY (Douglas), Feb. 28, 1925

DONALD FRAZER :

Donald Frazer, a native of Cape Breton, Nova Scotia, died in this city on Monday, May 23, 1904, aged 68 years. He was born on the bleak shores of Cape Breton Island, Nova Scotia, and chose at an early age the vocation of seaman. For many years he sailed on a merchantman in the East India trade. During the civil war in the United States he was connected with the service, although not as a soldier. He came to Alaska in 1887. Here he has lived and here he died. A man of more than ordinary intelligence, he has won friends in the northern land.

Of his relatives, we have been able to learn but little, more than that a nephew and a niece live in Nova Scotia.
DOUGLAS ISLAND NEWS 25, 1904

ROBERT A. FRIEDRICH

General Robert A. Friedrich died in his apartments in Juneau at 11:35 o'clock this forenoon. He was a native of Kentucky and was fifty eight years of age.

Friedrich was born in the state of Kentucky. His father was for years an officer in the Prussian army. He removed from his native land to the state of Kentucky, where he married a lady who belonged to one of the first families of the state. His son, Robert was educated in the native state and graduated from the law department of the State University. He removed to Topeka, Kansas, where he entered upon the practice of law in 1872 and remained at that place until 1880.

He first practiced law under the firm name of Case & Friedrich at Topeka, Kansas, in 1887 and in the early nineties came to San Francisco and became a member of the law firm of Ackerman, Friedrich & Colin, and in the spring of 1898 was appointed by President McKinley as District Attorney for Alaska, and was District Attorney for the third Judicial District of Alaska at the time of his death.

He married the daughter of ex-State Senators Geo. W. Proebstel of Umatilla county of Oregon. His wife and one daughter, the only child, who is 17 years of age, live in their house at Alameda, California.

THE ALASKAN, Jan. 10, 1903; MINING JOURNAL, Jan. 3, 1903

C. W. FRIES

C. W. Fries died at San Diego, Calif., at 9:05 p.m. Tuesday, [May 1922]. News of the death of Mr. Fries was not unexpected, as he has been very ill for some time. He had been visiting with relatives in St. Louis and was on his way to Juneau when his heart condition became so serious that he was unable to complete his journey.

Mr. Fries was prominent in civic affairs, having served on the city council for several terms. He resigned shortly before his departure for the States.

He was born in Bavaria 70 years ago and came to the United States when he was four years old, and spent most of his life in St. Louis. In 1905 he came to Alaska because of his health and was first at Windham bay, engaging in mining. Later he moved to Juneau where he maintained his residence until his death. Though interested in other ventures, he was essentially a mining man, and in 1918, together with several others, he secured an option on the Hirst-Chichagof property on Chichagof island and was successful in putting the mine on an operating basis.

He is survived by four sisters and one brother: Mrs. Josephine Overstreet of Seattle; Mrs. Sophie Korman, Mrs. Louis Dankenbring and Mrs. Louise Bronkhorst, all of St. Louis; and Martin Fries of Denver. Mrs. Fries died about five years ago.

JOHN PHILLIP FRISBY

John P. Frisby, better known as "Jack" Frisby, a widely known old-time mining man, died in his cabin in the Susitna district in the latter part of November. Frisby and Charles Smith have been trapping in the Susitna district, with headquarters in a cabin on Alexander creek, about 12 miles from Susitna station and about 30 miles from the Alaska railroad.

John Philip Frisby was born at Rochester, Minn., December 2, 1860, and he had been a resident of the North for many years, engaged for the most part, in prospecting and mining in the various camps. He was among the first stampeders to invade the Koyukuk district nearly 39 years ago, and in more recent years he devoted considerable time to prospecting the Willow creek district where he was interested in a number of properties at the time of his death.

ALASKA WEEKLY, Dec16, 1927; STROLLER'S WEEKLY

LOUIS GAGNER

Louis Gagner died in Wrangell last Friday morning [July 15]. He was about 58 years of age. He owned the gas-boat, Viola, on which he made his home.

Louis Gagner was born near the City of Quebec. When about 30 years of age he came West, stopping for a short time with friends in Kamloops, B.C. From there he went to Tacoma, and for about 20 years was a resident of the State of Washington. About eight years ago he came to Wrangell and from that time until his death he followed the life of a fisherman.

Just before his death Mr. Gagner was asked concerning his relatives and he gave the name of a half brother whom he said he had not seen in more than 20 years and who resides in Holyoke, Mass. Mr. Gagner left brothers and sisters and numerous relatives in the Province of Quebec. He is a first cousin of General Boulanger. His only known relative in the West is a cousin residing in Kamloops, B.C. His silence concerning his other relatives suggests the possibility of an estrangement from them.

WRANGELL SENTINEL, July 21, 1921

CON GALLAGHER (See Vols. 2 & 4)

Capt. Con Gallagher, pioneer resident and cannery man of Southeastern Alaska, who died at the home of a daughter in Seattle recently, was 76 years of age. He was born in County Donegal, Ireland. When he was 21 years of age he came to the United States and located at Beaver Island, Mich. About 25 years ago, he came to Southeastern Alaska with the Alaska packers and from that time made his home in that district.

Captain Gallagher drove the first trap piles in Southeastern Alaska, about 1900, at Excursion Inlet, for the Alaska Packers, the trap being known as "the river trap." He continued with that company and with the Alaska Fisheries Union for a number of years as outside man at their various plants and in 1923 he was outside foreman for the Sanborn-Cutting plant at Kake.

In 1910 he went into the fishing business for himself, locating a trap at White Rock, Chatham Straits, and in 1915 he put in another trap at Penter Cove, operating until 1917, when he sold out to the Ivy Straits Packing Company.

Captain Gallagher is survived by three sons: Philip, Neil and Con, who all reside in Juneau, and three daughters: Mrs. Rose Malloy of Juneau; Mrs. Mary Joyce of Seattle; and Mrs. Lila Whalen of Point Robert, Wash.; and five grandchildren. Rose and Donald Gallagher children of Neil, who reside in Juneau, and a son and daughter of Mrs. Whalen and a daughter of Mrs. Joyce.

ALASKA WEEKLY, April 13, 1923

JANE GAMBLE

Jane Gamble, wife of Samuel Gamble, was born 41 years ago in Australia where she grew to womanhood, coming with her husband to America in 1898 and to Whitehorse in 1901.

The Gambles own a home in Whitehorse but both have been in the Kluane, principally on Burwash, for the past several years. Mr. Gamble spent the winter on the creek and his wife stayed in town, joining him late in March. She suffered almost continuously with stomach trouble, but as it was no worse on the creeks than while she was in town, she decided to spend the summer with her husband on the creek. Almost from the date of her arrival on Burwash she steadily grew worse until death ended her sufferings. They had no children.

Jane Gamble died on Burwash creek, where they own several mining claims, on the 14th of August after an illness extending over several months.

WHITEHORSE STAR, Sept. 3, 1909

CHARLES D. GARFIELD

Charles Garfield first came to Alaska from the State of Washington 26 years ago and mushed over the trail to the Klondike strike and later was in Atlin for a time.

Nearly 19 years ago accompanied by his wife, he became

deputy collector and inspector at the Port of Juneau. After a year he was sent to Nome and worked there for five years and transferred to Juneau where he was chief deputy collector until he resigned in 1922.

He is a member and secretary of the Territorial Fish commission and was a candidate for the office of Collector of Customs.

WRANGELL SENTINEL, Jan. 21, 1933

ALFRED GAUVIN

Alfred Gauvin was born at St. Simon, Romonesque County, Province of Quebec, May 22, 1860. While still a very young man he left his native home, and went to Fall River, Mass there he found work in a cotton mill. From there to Grand Rapids, Mich. Then for several years he worked as a cook on boats on Lake Superior. During the boom days of the great Northwest, Alfred drifted to Seattle where he worked for the Stimpson Mill Co. for three years until he left for the Yukon in 1895, and along with his brother, Wilfred and Frank Pinchon located some of the richest gravel in the Klondike.

KLONDIKE NEWS, Apr. 1. 1898

JIM. GAY

It is only fair to mention "Sourdough Jim" Gay, as he was familiarly known in Roseburg, for he has departed on his last long stampede, and passed on beyond the shimmering aurora borealis since the following sketch was penned about him.

"Sourdough Jim" Gay participated in the Alaska gold rush and followed that adventure by several years of service with the department of the interior. Bear hunting, however, proved his greatest thrill and he still talks about the hunting afforded in that country.

"'I landed in Juneau the night before Thanksgiving. The town was wide open and celebrating in great style. When I got off the boat I had just 65 cents to my name. I gave an Indian 50 cents to carry my luggage to a hotel and then went down to the bar to watch the fun. I ordered a Tom and Jerry and sat down to drink it slowly. When I got through I went up to the bar and laid my 15 cents on the bar. Tom and Jerry was 10 cents in the states, but it was 25 cents up there. I told the barkeeper that was all I had. He looked at me hard. 'Is that the truth?' he said. 'Yes,' I replied, 'Then keep your money and have another on the house,' he said. I went to work in the Treadwell mine. Where I worked it was 440 feet below the ocean bed. After I prospected and hunted, and for a time was special agent for the department of the interior.'"

ALASKA WEEKLY, Sept. 13, 1929

ARNOLD F. GEORGE

Arnold George, Dawson newspaper editor from 1898 to 1908, dropped dead recently in Medicine Hat.

For the ten years he resided in Dawson he was one of the best known citizens in the Yukon. He was editor of the Dawson Nugget for two years and then for several years he was editor of the Dawson News.

Some years ago he moved to California and bought a farm, but soon tired of it and returned to Dawson and journalism. In 1908 he accepted a position with the Canadian Immigration Department. In 1909 he was in charge of the publicity in the Canadian building at the Alaska-Yukon-Pacific Exposition at Seattle and lectured there daily.

At the time of his death Prof. George was a resident of Calgary, where his widow and daughter live. Another daughter, who is married, and is the mother of several children, resides in New York.

THE ALASKA WEEKLY, May 8, 1925

ALFRED P. J. GHEZZI

Alfred P. J. Ghezzi was born at Malora, Auckland, New Zealand, July 1, 1881. Coming to the United States in 1904, he hit the trail for Alaska the same year, arriving at Ketchikan. The following spring found him at Dawson, and in 1906 he moved to Chatanika, where he lived until 1917; during that year he moved to Nenana, where he now resides and is engaged in the mercantile business. Ghezzi is married and has three children. He was elected Grand Secretary at the last Grand Igloo meeting, having acted in that capacity during the session, in the absence of Past Grand Secretary P. B. Charles.

PATHFINDER OF ALASKA, July 23, 1913

ANNA MAY EISENBERG GIBSON

Mrs. Thomas H. Gibson first came to the Interior Alaskan mining town [Fairbanks] as a bride in 1910.

The history of Fairbanks and the lives of Tom and Anna Gibson were inseparably bound together. Tom died last year. When Mrs. Gibson went Outside recently to make her home, she took a bit of the Golden Heart of Alaska with her.

Tom and his mother, and a brother, Elmer, came to Fairbanks in 1904, from Dawson. They built their home on the banks of the Chena Slough where the Wendell Street bridge has since been constructed.

Tom and Elmer Gibson were professional meat hunters for minding camps, restaurants, and markets. Since they had to transport their meat to their customers, it was a natural step to transport mining supplies as well as food to the creeks.

In 1909 Tom met Anna May Eisenberg in Seattle while visiting his mother, who had gone there from Fairbanks, and they were married on Jan. 14, 1910. Tom returned to Fairbanks with the 22-year old Anna the following April.

Gibson already had become something of a real estate holder in Fairbanks and the young couple moved into a small cabin at 220 1st Avenue. Although it was to undergo many changes and additions, it remained their home for 48 years, until Tom's death last year.

Tom and Anna shared such interests as baseball, auto racing, hunting and fishing. A bad accident put him in the hospital three years ago, then he became a spectator instead of a participant in car racing events.

Gibson was a river boat captain, hauling supplied by barge, he owned an auto stage line which operated between Fairbanks and Valdez. The roads became quagmires in the spring and dust ribbons in summer, and drifted with snow in the fall. Tom alternately drove the baggage-laden cars or with the passengers pushed them over the "tough" spots. The stages managed to get through.

Tom owned and operated a modern garage which he built himself. In fact, he built many buildings in Fairbanks, including the present Copper Hardware building.

Mrs. Gibson, herself, was active in community affairs. She devoted much time to the American Red Cross during World War I, and during World War II interested herself in the welfare of Jewish soldiers and their families at Ladd Air Force Base.

Now Mrs. Gibson is residing with a sister in the East, her address being: c/o Mrs. Louis Pollock, Norwich, Conn. She plans to visit with her four sisters and one brother all in the East.

FAIRBANKS NEWS-MINER (Golden Days), July 17, 1959

GEORGE KNUTE GILBERT

George Knute Gilbert, 57, who after spending an hour talking over business matters in the office of Davis & Gilbert on Frank Street was on his way home, when he dropped dead at 10:00 a.m. as the result of cerebral hemorrhage.

The deceased was born in Osakis, Minn., December 13 1866. He was named after Senator Knute Nelson, who was a very close friend of the family. He was one of the adventurous spirits who came to Alaska in the gold rush of 1897 and spent some time in the Dawson country. He is well known in Fairbanks, Cordova, and Juneau where he resided before going to Ketchikan in July of the year 1918.

After going to Ketchikan, Mr. Gilbert became a partner of the firm of Davis & Gilbert, and has recently been considering selling out to Mr. Davis as he wished to go to California where he thought two or three months of sunshine would put him in good shape.

A wife, Mrs. Dorothy Gilbert, and a brother, C. C. Gilbert of Malaban, Philippine Islands, are left to mourn his loss.

PETERSBURG WEEKLY REPORT, Sept. 14, 1923

THOMAS W. GILMORE

Tom Gilmore, with Felix Pedro, were responsible for the discovery of the Fairbanks gold fields. He was the original discoverer of Vault and Gilmore Creeks, which he located on September 30, 1902. He owned many claims on the creek named after him, some of which he opened up and mined in partnership with Jimmy McPike.

About twenty years ago Tom Gilmore took unto himself a life's partner, a Mrs. Devens of Fairbanks. For many years they operated a roadhouse on Pedro Creek at the mouth of Gilmore, where the weary musher received unbounded hospitality.

Gilmore spent a fortune in the development of quartz properties in the Fairbanks district, and to the time he left Alaska, had great faith in the future of Fairbanks as a quartz camp. Almost a year ago Tom Gilmore disposed of his placer interests to the Fairbanks Exploration Co., and was enjoying the fruit of his long years of labor in the Northland when death claimed him. Gilmore died at his home in Chula Vista, California on Friday last.

ALASKA WEEKLY, Dec. 30, 1932

WILLIAM A. GILMORE (See Vol.1)

The following is a sketch of William A. Gilmore, Republican candidate for delegate to congress: Born in Oakland, California, January 19th, 1870, and Scotch- Irish ancestry. Before a year old moved to Portland, Oregon and thence to Vancouver, Washington. Educated in public schools and colleges of Oregon and Washington. Studied law in Chicago; graduated in 1897, and in 1898 began to practice in Seattle. Arrived in Nome June 14,

1900. Married in 1901. Has four children, all born in Nome. Elected mayor of Nome in April, 1911, receiving 90 per cent of total vote cast. In 1899 was secretary Republican State Committee of Washington, and also was city committeeman in fifth ward, Seattle. Member of many lodges and organizations. At present time president of Nome Bar Association and practicing at Nome.

William A. Gilmore arrived in Nome June 14, 1900, and the following year was married and is the proud father of four children, all born in Nome. He was elected mayor of Nome in April 1911, and re-elected to that office last month, carrying both elections.

ALASKA PIONEER, May 1912 ; THE DOUGLAS ISLAND NEWS, May 8, 1912

F. E. GINGRASS

F. E. Gingrass who has been an inmate of the Pioneers Home at Sitka for the past three years, died February 25, 1934.

Mr. Gingrass was a little past 66 years of age, according to his sister, Mrs. Mare Pepin of Escanaba, Michigan. He was born in Canada, but his parents moved to the United States when he was a small child. He went from Michigan to New Mexico when a young man and after living at various mining camps came to Alaska in early days.

He came to Wrangell about thirty years ago. He was in the machine shop business here and later in the shrimp business. He served several terms on the city council and took an active interest in the Redman's lodge.

WRANGELL SENTINEL, March 9, 1934

HAFTOR GJERDE

Gjerde was born in Kristiansung, Norway in 1887. Since 1912 he has been well known as a member of the local halibut fleet in Petersburg. He first came to Petersburg with his brother Andrew and they operated a small halibut boat. In 1917 he and his brother bought the Happy which they operated together a number of years until Haftor bought the Rambler. A few years later he sold the Rambler and built the Midway which he owned and operated until his death. Oscar Otness has been operating the Midway since last March.

He was a member of the Sons of Norway Lodge, was a stockholder in the Trading Union and was a member of the Lutheran Church.

Gjerde died in Seattle November 23, 1940. He is survived by his widow and one son, Andrew, both of whom have been in Seattle with him; a sister in Seattle; and a brother, Andrew, in Petersburg.

PETERSBURG PRESS, Nov. 29, 1940

CHARLES GOLDSTEIN

Pioneer Alaskan Charles Goldstein, who first came to Juneau as a boy of 15, today celebrated his 90th birthday in the city he has done so much to build.

Still holding an active interest in his business affairs, Goldstein today marked his birthday by going as he does daily to his office, now located in his own building in the heart of the city he helped to found.

Born in London in 1869, Goldstein lived in Canada and San Francisco until his family came to Alaska in 1885. Four years later, Goldstein returned to San Francisco to marry Laura Goldberg, and to remain until the Klondike Gold Rush brought him back to Alaska for good.

This time he started in the fur trading business, later had a store in Juneau for many years. In 1906 he bought the building on the site of the present Goldstein Building, rebuilding it in 1914.

In 1939, the second building was destroyed by fire, but Goldstein rebuilt, putting up the present building in the early 1940s. In addition to owning the Goldstein building, the man who embodies the growth of Juneau today holds many other business interests here.

Except for the few years he spent in the 1890s in California, Goldstein has watched Juneau and Alaska grow for 75 years. Today, he said, the most important thing is to "see some industry come in here."

JUNEAU EMPIRE, Aug. 18, 1959

ISADORE GOLDSTEIN

When he closed his general store on Front Street a few weeks ago, Mr. Goldstein ended a business that he had been operated for 50 years.

Mr. and Mrs. Goldstein will spend their winters in San Francisco, where they have relatives.

Isadore Goldstein came to Alaska first in 1886. His father, Robert Goldstein started the third store in Juneau, and the Goldstein family moved here from San Francisco where Isadore. was born.

When Robert Goldstein passed away, his son, Isadore took over the store which he has operated for the last 50 years–with the exception of two years, 1910 and 1911 when he went into Iditarod–a real gold rush town. After his return to Juneau in 1913, he remained here until he joined the army, during the World War I and went overseas in 1918. He returned here in 1919 after service in Europe.

During the last thirty years Goldstein has served six terms as mayor of Juneau, and two terms in the city council. When President Harding–the only president ever to have visited Alaska–was in Juneau, Mayor Goldstein's was host.

In 1926, Isadore Goldstein and Miss Carol Kahn of San Francisco were married. Their son, Robert finished high school in Juneau and is now a senior in San Jose State University in California.Mr. and Mrs. Goldstein will spend their winters in San Francisco, where they have relatives. Isadore Goldstein died in San Francisco on June 19, 1959.

ALASKA STATE HISTORICAL LIBRARY, Biography File (Undated)

JOHN GOODELL

The news comes of the passing of John Goodell, one of the old sourdough residents of the southern coast of Alaska. Death came by his own hand at his home at Sitka. The manner of his passing calls for a degree of charity on the part of the old-time friends of this sturdy sourdough, because he was long a sufferer from an incurable disease, had recently lost a federal position which sufficed to give him a living, and too proud to ask aid of friends or take refuge in the home for aged people at Sitka and physically unable to earn a livelihood by manual labor, he elected to end it all.

John Goodell was a lawyer by profession. His gift of oratory was exceeded by few attorneys in the west. He started to practice law in a little Oregon town, where his fame as a pleader spread throughout the state. In the days of '98 he came to Alaska. In '99 he opened a law office at Valdez, and remained there for several years. He was then appointed United States commissioner with headquarters at Knik, where he resided for many years, and was known and beloved by all the old-timers of this district.

John Goodell had his faults and failings. None of us are immune in this respect, although some of us may be too hypocritical to admit them. But John Goodell had a big heart and a good-natured disposition that won his friends that were numbered by his acquaintances.

A few months prior to his demise, Goodell was deputy United States marshal at Sitka. Being a consistent republican in politics, he was removed to make room for a democrat. He had reached an advanced age, and bereft of a position that gave him a living, it is probable that life for him had ceased to have a sufficient attraction to longer wish to continue the struggle for existence. While the manner of his death is regrettable, in that it is naturally repugnant to the canons of society, in view of all the circumstances the mantle of charity may be spread over this old sourdough, whose end from whatever cause, is deeply mourned

in this part of Alaska, where he so long was a well known figure.
ANCHORAGE DAILY TIMES, July 25, 1916

J. LOOMIS GOULD

One of the pioneer missionaries of Alaska, Rev. J. Loomis Gould, died at Fort Myers, Fla., on August 8 [?], [1921] at the age of 84 [?] Years. He lived in the territory for 30 years as a Presbyterian minister to the Hydeh Indians. He was born in Lewis Co., Va., and was a veteran of the Civil War. He was one of the organizers of the public school system of West Virginia, and was superintendent of schools of his home county, and was one of the organizers of the Presbytery of Alaska.
THE VALDEZ MINER, Oct. 15, 1921

LAVINA JAMES GRANT

Funeral services were held Sunday afternoon at Redman's hall for Mrs. W. D. Grant, pioneer Wrangell resident whose death occurred Friday, July 7, at her home on Church street.

Lavina James was born on November 11, 1857 at Paris, Illinois. She was married at Kansas City, Missouri on May 7, 1882, to William D. Grant, a young man from New Jersey whom she had met when living with a married sister at Junction City, Kansas, where she was attending school. After their marriage the young couple later moved to Idaho Falls, Idaho, where Mr. Grant for 14 years was United States deputy marshal.

Mrs. Grant is survived by her husband, three children: Mrs Katherine Gazal of Juneau; S. D. Grant and B. Y. Grant of Wrangell; one child having died in infancy; three grandchildren; Miss Jean Grant and Billy Grant of Wrangell, Jerry Neilson of Aberdeen, Wash., and numerous relatives in the states.
WRANGELL SENTINEL, July 14, 1933

JOE GREEN

The other First Division holdover, Senator Joe Green, is a native of Iowa and came to Alaska in 1907 to engage in mining in the Interior. He has covered most of the Territory at one time and another and has lived in many parts of it. First elected to the House of Representatives in 1933, he served as Speaker in 1937 and has been in the Senate for the past two sessions and the 1946 special session.

ALASKA LIFE, June 1947

JOE J. GREENE

Joe J. Greene of Ketchikan is a pioneer in newspaper work in the Northland. He first went to Juneau in 1896 as the representative of a cylinder press company, and installed the first cylinder press ever put up in Alaska. That was on the now defunct Alaska Miner. Then the Klondike discovery was made, and Joe headed for the new Eldorado. He worked on the Dawson newspapers until 1899, when the Nome camp was brought in. In 1899 he joined the rush and with some associates got a lease on No. 10 Dexter creek, one of the rich streams of the camp.

In 1903 he left Nome, came outside, but was soon headed for Dawson where he bought an equity in the Dawson News. His partners were Settlemeir and Devers. They bought the News from Roediger and McIntyre. In 1914, when the WWI came on, Greene sold his interest to Settlemeir and Devers, and came outside.

But after being in the Northland for so many years, Greene returned to Ketchikan where he has charge of the mechanical department of the Chronicle. Green says that his old partner, Settlemeir, has struck it rich in a mine in the Mayo camp. He lately heard that some of the ore goes as high as $500 in silver to the ton.

Devers, who left Dawson because of ill health, is now located in Texas and is fast recovering. He has bought a fine place down there.

ALASKA WEEKLY, November 13, 1925

BRUNO GREIF

Bruno Greif died in Tacoma, Wash. in September 1924. He was born 78 years ago in Saxony, Germany. He was a widely traveled man, and a brewer by occupation. He was located for a time in Juneau in the early days of that city. In February 1898, he came to Wrangell and entered the brewery business here. He remained in Wrangell for 14 years until 1910, when his physician recommended a change of climate.

WRANGELL SENTINEL, Sept. 18, 1924

ANDREW JACKSON GRIFFIN

Judge Griffin died in Fairbanks. Andrew Jackson Griffin was born in Shellbark, Wis. April 26, 1865. He went to Fairbanks in the early days, and at one time was city clerk. Going to Richardson at the time of the Tenderfoot gold strike, he had made his home there every since.

With the exception of one year, Judge Griffin served as United States Commissioner at Richardson from 1909 until 1932, when the Tanana district was combined with the Fairbanks precinct. For a number of years past he has been postmaster at Richardson.

He has a niece residing in California.

ALASKA WEEKLY, Jan 15, 1932

W. D. GROSS

W.D. Gross is a pioneer of the Northland. Indeed, he was a mere youth when he joined the stampede in the Klondike. He was in the store business at times, and did quite well, both in Dawson, Yukon Territory, and Fairbanks, Alaska. But he hit the strike when he came out to the coast towns of Juneau and Ketchikan and established theatres. He owns and operates the Coliseum theatre in Juneau and the Coliseum theatre in Ketchikan. His theatres are housed in the buildings, each built for the purpose. At this time in order to be right up to date, he is installing the "talkies" as they are called. His business has prospered because he has sought and succeeded in providing his patrons with worthwhile entertainment. But the outstanding achievement in the life of W.D. Gross is the fact that it was he who originated the idea of raising a Christmas fund for the old pioneer occupants of the Pioneers' Home at Sitka, a cash fund to be distributed to each occupant on Christmas Day, thus giving the fine old boys a little silver to jingle in their pockets. The first cash fund was raised for the 1927 Christmas. About $1,400 was raised, the greater part being contributed by Mr. Gross himself, as he gave the gross receipts of his two theatres for one day's run to the purpose.

ALASKA WEEKLY, May 10, 1929

E. C. GUERIN

Mr. E. C. Guerin was born in Oregon on August 11, 1882, and came to this country as a young man going into the Yukon country where he engaged in placer mining for several years. Later he was offered a position in the U.S. Land Office which he has held for many years.

Guerin is survived by his widow, a daughter and a son who live in Juneau. In addition a brother and a sister who reside in Oregon and another brother who lives in Los Angeles. [The only daughter named was a Mrs. Malcolm Morrison of Seattle.]

PETERSBURG PRESS, June 23, 1933

W. T. HALE

W. T, Hale, secretary-treasurer of the Wrangell Packing Company died shortly before 2 o'clock this morning from a heart seizure.

Mr. Hale was born in Liverpool, California 67 years ago. For nearly fifty years he has been connected with salmon packing in Alaska, his first experience being gained in Bristol Bay and Bering Sea..

He was superintendent of the North Pacific Trading and Packing Co. at Kluwock from 1912- 1917.The next two years he was interested in a plant in Monterey, California. In 1929 the Wrangell Packing was formed with F. C. Barnes as president and Mr. Hale as secretary-treasurer.

Mr. Hale is survived by his wife to whom he was married 24 years ago: two sisters in Oakland, California, and his nephew Elwyn Hale of San Francisco, son of Mr. Hale's brother C. P. Hale, Bristol Bay cannery man who died a few years ago.

WRANGELL SENTINEL, Aug 11, 1939

M. E. HANDY

M. E. Handy, pioneer resident of Alaska, who first went north in the gold rush of '98, died May 21 in Ketchikan at the home of his daughter, Mrs. W. D. Pickering. Mr. Handy was 75 years old.

He was born in Wisconsin March 4, 1858. After going to Alaska in the gold rush days he remained in the Interior for many years before coming to Southeastern Alaska. He came to Ketchikan about 12 years ago from Haines, after his son Fred E. Handy had been appointed deputy United States marshal.

Mr. Handy had been residing with his daughter for the past eight months. He had been in ill health for some time.

Mr. Handy is survived by a son, daughter and four grandchildren in Alaska and a son and daughter in the States. The son in the Territory is Fred Handy, now residing at Fairbanks, and the daughter is Mrs. Pickering of Ketchikan. The four grandchildren are Mrs. G. L. Rich, daughter of Mrs. Pickering; Gene and Theron Handy, all of Ketchikan; and Everett Handy of Fairbanks.

ALASKA WEEKLY, June 2, 1933

PETER HANS HANSON

Peter Hans Hanson, old time Petersburg resident, died at the local hospital early Tuesday morning [March 12] at the age of 75. He was born February 1, 1865.

Mr. Hanson first came to Alaska in May, 1886, and

engaged in mining. He was in the Gold Rush of 1896, going over the Dyea Trail at the time of the Colorado wreck in Wrangell Narrows. Colorado Reef is named after this wreck. Mr. Hanson was sent down from Juneau to unload ore from the Colorado.

Mr. Hanson worked as foreman under Mr. Harvey at Hattie Camps in the lower part of Duncan Canal. This was in 1905-1906.

Next he went to Wrangell from which point he was dispatched to look over property in the Mill Creek area on the mainland. Following this he was sent to the States and was working on properties, when he was involved in a blast accident, causing him to lose his memory for quite a number of years.

He returned again to Alaska in 1927 and made his home here up to the time of his death, living at his home at Skog's Creek across from Scow Bay.

Survivors are Henry Hanson of Astoria, Wn., Andrew and Johnnie of Petersburg, a daughter Katherine of Portland, Ore., two nephews, James and Robert Concannon of Petersburg, and other nephews and nieces who reside at Portland, Chicago, and Clyde, Kansas, and a brother in Denver, Colorado.

Mr. Hanson was a partner of John Olens, who had lived with him since about 1897.

PETERSBURG PRESS, March 15, 1940

ARTHUR HARPER

The death of Arthur Harper in November last removed from the Yukon one of its old landmarks.

Fully a quarter of a century ago Mr. Harper first arrived on the Yukon, and it was his home continuously up to the time of his death.

When he first reached the country the Indians were hostile and treacherous and had just burned several of the posts of the Hudson Bay Company. One of these are situated near the site of what is now known as Fort Selkirk, and where Mr. Harper resided for so many years of his life.

By kindness and fair dealing he won the everlasting regard of the Indian tribes, until they came to look upon him as a father, and flocked to him for advice.

Very little is know of Mr. Harper's early life, but the latter twenty-five years is an open book, upon whose pages there can be found nothing that ever-sullied his fair name. He was a kind-hearted man, greatly admired by his white neighbors and worshiped by his darker friends, and there will be mourning among the Children of the Forests when the news off his departure to the Great Spirit becomes known.

Mr. Harper's residence at Fort Selkirk had probably more to do with placating the hostile Indians, and thus allowing the white man to develop the country than any other factor in the history of the interior.

He was sixty-three years of age at the time of his death, and had long been suffering from that dread disease consumption. It is hoped by his family and friends that a journey to the warm and dry climates of Arizona and New Mexico would benefit the sufferer and prolong his useful life. But the trip was too much for his enfeebled system, and his gentle spirit passed away from Yuma, on November 24, 1897. Although he died far from the northern home he loved so well, his good deeds there live after him and will ever be a monument to his memory.

KLONDIKE NEWS, April 1, 1898

MARTIN HARRAIS

Martin Harrais is a self-made man. He was born in Russia, of German parentage, and became a sailor, coming to America when he was 20 years old. He worked in the shipyard in San Francisco. Later he removed to Seattle and lived there nine years. He attended night school and worked his way and graduated from the Washington State University in 1897. In the spring of the same year he joined the rush to Dawson, where he engaged in mining, and in 1903 stampeded to the Tanana. He settled in Chena, and has been the mayor of the town practically ever since his arrival. He is now a mining operator and owner of a stamp mill.

ALASKA PIONEER, May 1912

MARTIN HARRIS

Martin Harris, a pioneer of the upper Copper river and Tanana country, froze his feet while going to the head of the White river with some Nabesna Indians, for whom he was going to build a mission building. Being 200 miles from the surgical assistance which would have saved his life, Harris died before his last message reached the telegraph station at Tanana crossing.

"Shusana" Harris, as he was generally called, was a native of Tennessee, about 70 years of age. His wife and a married daughter are said to reside in Seattle, and two daughters are at Nez Perce, Idaho. He has been in Alaska since 1898, acting for a while as agent of the North American Trading company, exploring the Copper river and White river countries for copper. He is believed to own some mines for which he and his partners were offered $150,000 some time ago.

DOUGLAS ISLAND NEWS, March 16, 1909

RICHARD T. HARRIS

Richard T. Harris, discoverer of Juneau's placer fields and founder of that thriving little city, is an interesting visitor to Skagway. Mr. Harris is one of Alaska's oldest pioneers having spent more than twenty years in the district. He has seen Alaska grow from a wild uninhabited region, visited only by trappers and fur traders, into one of the greatest gold producing sections of the world, with its coast dotted by modern cities.

It was twenty years ago last August, that Mr. Harris and Joseph Juneau, a French Canadian discovered Silver Bow basin four miles back of Juneau and located the town site where that city now stands. The town was named Harrisburg and retained that name four years. The mining district was called Harris, which name it still bears. Mr. Harris says he named the city for the capital of Pennsylvania in which state he was raised, but to everybody else the name stood for old Dick Harris. Silver Bow basin was named for a similar basin of that name in Montana, one of the greatest producing camps in the nation and one upon which Butte depends for its existence. Mr. Harris was in the great stampede to the Silver Bow basin in Montana. In fact, he recorded the first mining claim in Montana in July, 1862, being with the first miners who discovered gold at East Bannock in what was then Montana territory. He was also one of the first discoverers of gold in Colorado in 1859. Mr. Harris has only been away from Alaska once in the more than two decades since he first located in this district.

Although he has been a frontier miner throughout his eventful life, Mr. Harris is a college graduate and presents the appearance of an educated gentleman. He is a cousin of John Dalsell, the famous Pittsburgh congressman who is one of the leaders of the house, being a prominent member of the ways and means committee. He is 67 years of age, but is still active and as greatly interested in mining affairs as he was when he started his career in Colorado over forty years ago.

This is Mr. Harris' first visit to Skagway, though he was on Skagway bay 14 yrs ago. At that time there was no one here.
DAILY ALASKA DISPATCH, Sept. 15, 1900

SMITH HARRIS
Dr. Smith Harris, pioneer of the Northland, passed away one day last week at the advanced age of 83 years, at the Pioneers' Home in Sitka where he had been living for some years past. Mr. Harris had pioneered in the Northland since he went there in the prime of life. He settled in Ketchikan in 1900 at the time the town was a mere village. He always identified with the town's affairs and was active in welfare work. In 1914 he was elected mayor of the city. He is survived by a niece, Mrs. Baldwin, who lives in Portland, Oregon.
ALASKA WEEKLY, May 14, 1926

CHARLES HARRISON

As a young man, Charles Harrison took orders in the church and became a deacon and an enthusiastic worker in the city of London and had charge of St. Thomas, one of the important churches of that great city. Becoming overworked in 1882, he came to the United States for the benefit of his health. He married before leaving London and he and his wife after leaving the United States finally located on Graham island, having charge of Massett, the Haida settlement. This village has about 400 inhabitants who have progressed rapidly in civilization during the last quarter of a century. Mr. Harrison made a study of their language, wrote a grammar of it and also a dictionary. He translated the gospel of St. Matthew and the prayer book into this language. These have all been printed by the Royal society of Canada and are now being used in missionary work among the Indians. He spent ten years as a missionary and then became a representative of the government of British Columbia and Ottawa and has made himself generally useful in that way for the last fourteen years. He is now returning from a trip to Victoria where he secured a steamship to make regular weekly trips between Prince Rupert and Massett, commending the first week in March.

MINING JOURNAL, Feb. 9, 1907

E. W. HASKETT

The Salem (Iowa) *News,* published at the former home of the late district attorney of Alaska, has the following in regard to him:

"Mr. Haskett, though young, had by his energy and perseverance in his profession, risen to a position creditable to himself, and that opened up a future for higher honors. He was at one time a resident here, a student at Whittier, and afterwards taught school. He joined the Congregational church March 29, 1868; studied law in the office of Scott, Howell, of Keokuk, Iowa, and was admitted to the bar in 1872. In 1874 he was married to Miss Jennie Lester, and who, with a little daughter,

Hattie, still survives him. He was born in Wabash county, Indiana, October 23, 1848. In 1884 he was appointed by President Arthur as U. S. District Attorney of Alaska."

THE ALASKAN, Dec. 19, 1885

CHARLES WESLEY HAWKESWORTH

Charles W. Hawkesworth, 62, an Alaskan for the past 33 years, died suddenly but peacefully at his home in Juneau Monday night.

Hawkesworth spent all his years in Alaska as a teacher and official of the Office of Indian Affairs, formerly the Bureau of Education. His last position was that of Assistant to the General Superintendent of the Office of Indian Affairs, Alaska Division.

Charles Wesley Hawkesworth was born April 18, 1878 at Port George, Nova Scotia. He was educated in the Massachusetts public schools, and graduated from Bowdoin College in Maine with a B.A. Degree.

After nine years teaching experience, some of it at Arlington, Washington, Hawkesworth came to Alaska in 1907. Mrs. Hawkesworth came with him, on what was their honeymoon trip. They went to Point Barrow, most northerly point on this North American continent where the young Presbyterian theological student had obtained appointment as a teacher for the old Bureau of Education of the Department of Interior.

Hawkesworth remained at the far north at Barrow, Nome and Kotzebue until 1911 when he was transferred to Hydaburg in Southeast Alaska. At Hydaburg he started the first Native store. He also served in Klukwan during this period. By this time Hawkesworth had decided to enter the ministry and devote his life in missionary work in Alaska.

PETERSBURG PRESS, Nov. 8, 1940

ERASTUS CORNING HAWKINS

Erastus Corning Hawkins had recently undergone an operation at a hospital in New York and his death soon followed.

It was last Fall when Mr. Hawkins took his final adieu from the people of this section, and they turned out in public meeting to give some expression of the kindly feeling that was in the hearts of every man, woman, and child who knew him.

His great work here had practically been completed. He had built the Copper River & Northwestern Railway and had turned it over to the operating department. He spent several months in Seattle preparing reports and completing routine details. In the meantime he declined the offer of Mr. Morgan to go to China and take charge of large railway construction there.

Mr. Hawkins had attained the age of about fifty years and had reared a family of five children: two daughters, Misses Gilberta and Clarissa; and three sons: Mason, Howard and Tad. During the past summer the family spent several weeks in Cordova, with the completion of the railroad.

The White Pass & Yukon and the Copper River & Northwestern Railways are two monuments that will ever be pointed to in Alaska as the achievements of a master mind.

THE CHITNA LEADER, April 13, 1912

JOHN J. HEALY

Captain John J. Healy, founder and former manager at Dawson of the N.A.T. & T. Co., dropped dead on the 17th inst. of heart failure, at Los Angeles, California.

Captain J. J. Healy was a pioneer of Alaska and the Yukon and no man was better known in the north. He had a remarkable career as a frontiersman. He was known in every mining camp in the west years ago and came to Alaska after a sensational career as deputy marshall and sheriff in Montana. He established a trading post at Dyea about 1893, and there, through the migration of prospectors, became acquainted with the possibilities of the interior. He went to Chicago and secured the aid of the Cudahye and founded the N.A.T. & T. company, which soon became an active and powerful competitor of the Alaska Commercial company, before that time the sole commercial invader of the great north. Captain Healy was at Circle when the Klondike strike was made and became a large figure in the early and strenuous days of that historic camp. A quarrel with the Cudahye caused him to sever his connection with the company and for several years he has been heard of chiefly as the moving figure in the Alaska-Siberia railroad enterprise.

DOUGLAS ISLAND NEWS, Sept. 23, 1908

JAMES ROBERT HECKMAN (See Vol. 2)

Mr. Heckman was born in Chester county, Nova Scotia, Canada, Oct. 17, 1865. His parents moved to Ferndale, Humboldt County, California. At the age of 20 Mr. Heckman came to Alaska in the employ of the Arctic Packing company, afterwards merged with the Alaska Packers' Association. He owns the principal merchantile store in Ketchikan and has substantial interests in the Alaska Fisheries company, operating three canneries: the Sunny Point Packing company; the Pure Food Fish company; and the Beagle Packing company. He is a vice-president of the Miners' and Merchants' Bank. Mr. Heckman has made his home in Ketchikan and vicinity since 1888.

In 1893 he married Miss Marie C. Capp, of London, England. He was elected a member of the House for the 1915 Territorial session, and elected a member of the 1917 Senate

ALASKA MAGAZINE; May 1917; KETCHIKAN CHRONICLE, Aug. 21, 1939

E. A. HEGG

E.A. Hegg, official photographer for the Copper River and Northwestern railway, is known throughout the country by his pictures of Alaska. He went to Alaska from Bellingham in 1897, spending the winter at the White Pass where he made the first photographs of the stampede over the pass.

The following spring he went to Dawson and was the first photographer to establish himself. In 1900 he came to Nome and later returned to Southeastern Alaska. He landed in Cordova and

established a photographic business, making that part of Alaska familiar to magazine and newspaper readers every where. The magnificent beauties of the Copper River valley have found an appreciative interpreter in Mr. Hegg's camera.
ALASKA-YUKON MAGAZINE, Dec. 1910

JOHN HEITMANN

Capt. John Heitmann, 47 years of age, died at 8:30 o'clock last night at St. Ann Hospital, from a hemorrhage of the stump of his right arm, which was amputated at the shoulder February 21.

The amputation of Captain Heitmann's arm was necessitated by an injury which he received February 20 aboard the fishing schooner Alaska, of which he was master, when he slipped and caught his arm in the winch in which it was torn almost entirely from the shoulder. He was brought to Juneau immediately, the trip being 13 hours, and taken to St. Anns Hospital.

Mrs. Heitmann accompanied by her son Earl, came to Juneau from Seattle at once, after receiving word of the accident of her husband. She and her son will leave tonight on the Admiral Rogers, accompanying the body to Seattle for burial..

Captain Heitmann was a native of Norway, born in that country August 20, 1875. For a number of years he had been engaged in the fishing business on the Pacific Coast and with his family had made his home in Seattle. He was a member of Doris Lodge, F and A.M., and of the Chapter of York Rite, both of Seattle.

He is survived by his wife, three children Beatrice Jean, Katherine Eleanor, in Seattle; a son Earl; a brother, E. Erickson in Alpine, Cal.; and a sister, Mrs. W. S. Sargent in New Hazeltine, B.C.

Capt. A. Nilsen, superintendent of the Northwestern Fisheries plant at Dundas, is a brother of Mrs. Heitmann.
ALASKA WEEKLY, March 23, 1923

ARTHUR W. HENNING

Arthur W. Henning, failed to rally after an operation at the Mayor Clinic at Rochester on September 21 [1938].

"Art" as he was almost universally known to thousands in Juneau, went North in 1907 and was associated with Charles Goldstein in business for several years, later coming Outside for some time and returning in 1917 to join The Empire as office manager, a position he held until 1922 when he again returned to Seattle as secretary treasurer of the Hardy Metal Corporation. In 1931 he returned to The Empire and with the election of J. Goldstein as mayor he became city clerk, a position he filled during the Goldstein regime of five years. Two years ago he again became associated with the Charles Goldstein Co. where he had been until his more recent illness.

Art was 53 years of age, having been born in St. Paul, Minn., on May 14, 1885.

Mr. Henning leaves his son, Robert of Juneau, and four brothers: Fred of Juneau; Hanford of Ketchikan; and Iver and Edward of Seattle. Mrs. Henning died about 20 years ago during the influenza epidemic.

ALASKA WEEKLY, Oct. 7, 1938

JOHN HERBERGER

John Herberger died last Saturday evening [Jan. 23], and his long and useful life was at an end.

He was born 73 years ago at Issney, Wurtenburg, Germany, and came to this country with his parents in 1850, and nine years later braved the perils of the trip by wagon train across mountain and plain to the Pacific Coast. After a few years spent in the Sunset State he came north as far as what is now Canyon City, Oregon, where he resided until 1897 when he came to Skagway. Mr. Herberger was well known and respected by every citizen of our little city, and the heartfelt sympathy of our people is extended his daughter, Mrs. M. H. McLeilan.

THE INTERLOPER (Skagway), Jan. 30, 1909

ROBERT HICKS

Robert Hicks passed away at Long City, June 29, at 8 o'clock in the morning.

Robert Hicks, a native of Southland, New Zealand, was 35 years of age, and leaves an aged father, one brother, and four sisters living in Southland, N.Z. In October, 1897 Hicks joined in the rush to the Klondike, going in over the trail, remaining there until 1910, when he went to the Iditarod, engaged in mining and was very successful. In the Fall of 1912 he left Iditarod, bound for Rudy, and has since his arrive here been engaged in prospecting and mining on Glen gulch and other creeks continuously until May 24 when he was taken down with typhoid fever. Hicks had considerable money and some mining machinery on Long creek.

RUBY RECORD-CITIZEN, July 5, 1918

SALEM TOWNE HINCKLEY

Salem Towne Hinckley, born Jan. 8, 1850 at Ellsworth, Maine, died at the Home March 3. He had resided at the Home for the past 9 months. Hinckley was a woodsman for the Alaska Road Commission in Anchorage, and had been in the territory for 32 years.

THE ARROWHEAD (Sitka), March 16, 1935

JOHN HISLOP

John Hislop, assistant chief engineer for the White Pass and Yukon railroad, being at present the Mayor of the city as well as President of the City Council, is prominent in the affairs of Skagway and the development of the northland. He received his early education in the schools of his native county, Waterloo, Ontario. After teaching school three years he took a full course in the science department of McGill university, Montreal, graduating in 1884, and received the degree of Bachelor of Applied Sciences or civil engineer. He has been at different times connected with the Canadian Pacific, Burlington, Santa Fe,

Union Pacific, etc. He was elected at the recent city election for councilmen by the largest majority of any candidate on the ticket. At the organization of the new council he was unanimously chosen as chairman.

DAILY ALASKAN, Feb. 19, 1899

WILFORD BACON HOGGATT

Born at Paoli, Indiana, Sept. 11, 1865, the son of William M. and Isabelle (Bacon) Hoggatt, he is of remote Scotch-English descent, his ancestors coming to America during the seventeenth century and settling in North Carolina. At the conclusion of his training in the public schools of his native town, he was appointed to the United States Naval Academy at Annapolis, where he was graduated in 1884 with third honors, the youngest member in a class of forty-eight.

He later attended the Columbian University Law School, graduating in the class of 1893, and afterwards completed a year's study in the Columbia School of Mines. On January 12, 1893, he was married to Miss Marie Hayden, of Washington.

He served eighteen years in the navy, with the rank of lieutenant, and during the recent Spanish-American war was honored by President McKinley by being placed at the Naval Board of Strategy.

At the conclusion of this war he resigned the commission to engage in mining in Alaska. Here, with his brother, Mr. H. E. Hoggatt, he developed and operated the Julian Mines at Berner's Bay, sixty miles from Juneau, and at the time of his appointment by President Roosevelt to his present office as governor, was generally recognized as one of the representative and successful men of affairs of Southeastern Alaska. This appointment was received March 21, 1906, and the oath of office was taken May 1 of the same year, the management of his mining properties having meanwhile been turned over to his brother.

ALASKA-YUKON MAGAZINE, Sept. 1907

JOHN HOLMGREN

John Holmgren was born in Sweden 73 years ago [1860], and never was married. Coming to America as a child with his parents, he resided in the states until the Alaska gold rush days. He was in Fairbanks shortly after the strike, and was the first man in company with his partner to put down a deep shaft and strike pay on Dome creek. Afterward he was in the Koyukuk and Iditarod. In Fairbanks he bought in on Crew [Crow?] creek properties in 1921.

After leaving the Fairbanks camp in 1911, he mined rich property on the Wild Cat group on Flat creek in the Iditarod; later owned the Greenstone group in the Ruby camp, which he sold to the Guggenheims.

John Holmgren passed away Saturday night at the Columbus hospital, Seattle. He is survived by two sisters living in Sweden and a niece in California.

ANCHORAGE WEEKLY TIMES, March 2, 1933

JOHN C. HOWARD

John C. Howard was born June 4, 1827 in Jefferson county, Ohio. When the civil war broke out he enlisted in Company B of the Twelfth regiment of Kansas volunteer infantry and served until the war closed, being mustered out of service June 20, 1865. In 1871 he moved to Colorado and for several years was editor and proprietor of the San Juan Prospector of Del Norte. He afterwards resided at Ouray Telluride and Delta until 1886 when he left Colorado to come to Alaska. Howard has been a resident of Juneau since 1886 and founded the Alaska Free Press, Juneau's first paper.

John Howard died in Juneau, Alaska in July 1897. He leaves a wife and three sons, Frank C. is a well known newspaper man and prospector and Arthur is at present on the staff of the Alaska Miner. Mr. Howard has always been a prominent member of Seward Post, No. 36, G. A. R.

ALASKA SEARCHLIGHT, July 10, 1897

MARGARET BRUCE MCLAIN HUGHES

[Sarasota, Fla.] After fighting off a pack of snarling dogs to reach her body, police discovered this week that Mrs. Margaret Bruce McLain Hughes, 72-year old relief client and reputedly the first woman to reach the Yukon during the Klondike gold rush, possessed thousands of dollars in jewels.

Mrs. Hughes died in a one-room cabin in which she had lived as a poverty-stricken women with several dogs her only companions.

Police were forced to kill one of the dogs before they could reach her body. They found diamonds rubies, pearls and newspaper clippings disclosed that she had once lead a glamorous life in Alaska and had been an extensive property owner.

ALASKA WEEKLY, Jan. 15, 1937

WILLIAM R. HULBERT

William R. Hulbert, the aged gardener for the B.Y.N. company was stricken with paralysis Tuesday evening about 5 o'clock and died that night.

Hulbert had been in Whitehorse since 1903, having charge of the company's gardens in which work he had not an equal in the country. He was a native of England and at one time was a wealthy resident of London. He lost his property in an enterprise which embraced shipping mutton in cold storage from Australia to London. His wife died several years ago in London where several grown children continue to reside and where he visited two years ago. One daughter lives near Victoria, B.C., and a son in Seattle. Friends say he was about 66 years old.

THE WEEKLY STAR (Whitehorse), Sept. 23, 1910

FRANK W. HUMFREY

Frank Humfrey died of acute appendicitis at the Dawes Hospital at eleven o'clock last night. He was 31 years old, a veteran of the World War.

Frank Washington Humfrey came North in 1909 and was

employed in the Treadwell Market. He lived on the Island [Douglas] for a number of years and moved to Juneau where he worked for the Alaska Meat Company.

Mr. Humfrey was born in Gloucester, Gloucestershire, England. He is survived by his mother, Mrs. M. Humfrey; his father, B.C Humfrey ; a brother, R. Humfrey, all of Vancouver, B.C.; and a brother, A.A. (Max) Humfrey of Juneau.
THE ALASKA DAILY EMPIRE, Aug. 24, 1921

DALE WARD HUNT

Dale Ward Hunt died of typhoid fever. Hunt, former mayor of Ketchikan and son of Senator and Mrs. Forest J. Hunt passed away on Wednesday at Ketchikan.

Surviving Mr. Hunt is his wife, his father and mother, three sisters, Mrs. J. A.. Talbot, Jr., Mrs. G. M. Wells, Mrs. A. A. Sharpe, and a niece, Mrs. C. L. Cloudy, all of Ketchikan.

Dale Hunt was born at Artondale [?], Puget Sound, Wash., December 16, 1885. He came to Alaska with his parents in 1898. Fraternally and socially he was well known and prominent. He was twice mayor of Ketchikan. He was manager of the Sunny Point Packing Company, in which he owned stock, and was also stockholder in other canneries in the Ketchikan district.
PETERSBURG WEEKLY REPORT, Dec. 21, 1923

HARRIET FROST HUNT (MRS. FOREST J.)

Mrs. Forest J. Hunt, 69-year-old pioneer Ketchikan woman, died at 8:00 last night at the Ketchikan General hospital after a confinement there since Sunday morning.

Mrs. Hunt was the mother of three daughters: Amie, Elaine, and Bertha, all married and living in Ketchikan. Two boys born to her, Dale and Elmer, preceded her in death. Mr. Hunt, well known in this city as well as throughout Alaska as a pioneer merchant and legislator, is at present proprietor of the Hunt Bookstore in the city.

Their daughter, Elaine, is now Mrs. J. A. Talbot, wife of the Ketchikan businessman and city councilman, and the mother of two children, Jane and John.

Amie, married to A. A. Sharpe, local United States post office employee, is the mother of two children, Ward and Harriet. Mrs. Bertha Wells, the former Bertha Hunt, is the mother of two children, Elmer and Mrs. Charles Cloudy, and the grandmother of three children, Joan, Elaine, and Charles Cloudy, Jr.

Two sisters, Mrs. Anna Morgan and Mrs. Amelia Stewart, and one brother, Robert Emmet Frost, all residing in and near Tacoma, Washington, survive Mrs. Hunt in the states. Other survivors in Ketchikan are Mrs. Hunt's brother-in-law, A. W. Morgan and his son, Clyde, and family.

Mrs. Hunt was the daughter of a pioneer family of Pierce county, Washington, her father and grandfather having crossed the western plains to settle in Tumwater, Washington in 1844. She was born Harriet Frost and married Mr. Hunt in 1880, living for a time before coming north in 1898, on a farm near Gig Harbor, Washington.

Mr. Hunt preceded her here but a few months, interested in an enterprise in Wrangell which was at the time the proposed terminus of a route to interior Canadian gold fields via the Stikine River. Mrs. Hunt herself entered an enterprising field at that time, operating a restaurant and bakery.

The family moved to Ketchikan in 1900, when interest in the route to the interior through Wrangell declined. Here she entered actively the civic and social life of the then thriving mining center, serving on the first municipal school board and being chairman of the first library association here. She also affiliated herself in her husband's business. As mentioned, in 1900, the year of Ketchikan's incorporation, Mrs. Hunt organized and became chairman of the Library association. Until her death she served continuously as a member of the board. The Ketchikan library today may be said to stand as a testimonial to her diligent and, at times, individual efforts.

She was an active member of auxiliary number 7, Pioneers of Alaska of Ketchikan, and of the Women's Chamber of Commerce of which she was the principal founder.

She was appointed national republican committeewoman for Alaska by the organization's (Order of Eastern Star) convention in Kansas City, the first woman in Alaska to be recognized as such.

KETCHIKAN ALASKA CHRONICLE, June 13, 1934

NICHOLAS HURLAVITCH (NICK HURLEY)

The old time Dawson boxer, Nick Hurley, recently died on the coast. The Sporting editor of the Tacoma News writes of Nick as follows:

"Nick Hurley was one of the best known boxers in the Northwest. He was born in San Jose, California of Slavonic parents. His father conducted a large grocery store in that city and was well to do. Hurley is not his correct name. Before he entered the ring he was known as Nicholas Hurlavitch.

"Hurley came North from California in 1898, settling in Portland. Later he went to Seattle and boxed a big fellow by the name of Tom Costello, who had appeared in a contest here in Tacoma with 'Denver Ed' Smith at the old Phoenix theater. Hurley whipped Costello in a hurry and was later matched with a Bellingham Negro named Dan Godfrey. Nick disposed of Godfrey at the Seattle Athletic club, when the club's gymnasium was on first avenue, and became a big favorite in Seattle. He was a showy boxer, and a good hitter.

"The following year 1899, Hurley went to Alaska, where he was known as 'champion of the Yukon.' He met and defeated all the big men in the far North and was such a strong favorite that the Dawson Amateur Athletic Association, of which Joe Boyle was matchmaker, sent to Chicago and imported Joe Choyinski to meet Nick. They boxed twice, Hurley winning one bout and Choyinski the other. The last important contest Hurley had in Yukon was his bout with Billy Woods six years ago. Woods whipped Nick in 18 rounds, the contest being one of the prettiest ever pulled off in that country.

"Hurley first came into prominence in San Francisco by attempting to stay four rounds with Peter Maher at the old Grand Opera house. Nick was too small to tackle the Irish champion, and was beaten in a round or two, but he made a good showing which established him. He toured the East two years later under the management of Billy Pierce, then editor of the Boston Police News. Pierce afterward managed Joe Walcott when the Barbadosa Demon split with Tom O'Rourke. Under Pierce's management Hurley met all the best middle and light heavyweights in the East at that time, including Paddy Purtell, Kid McCoy, and others.

"Hurley was in Tacoma about three weeks ago. Nick wasn't looking any too prosperous then and things evidently were not breaking right for him. He told the writer he intended to return to Alaska this spring but his trip North of course is canceled. Nick was a nifty looking fellow when he was at his best. He was a neat dresser and well built and had a rugged constitution. In the past three years he has aged a lot and at the time of his death, his hair was almost white."

DAWSON NEWS, April 3, 1911

JOSEPH H. HUTCHINSON

Born at Black Hawk in Gilpin country, Colo., Hutchinson was raised in a mining atmosphere. His father, James Hutchison, was a mining operator and Joe followed that career. He was superintendent of the Silver Dollar mine at Silver City, Idaho, when a young man. Entering politics, he was elected lieutenant governor of Idaho during the term of Governor Stuenenberg, who was assassinated at his home at Caldwell after his term expired.

Joseph Hutchinson went to Nome, Alaska in the rush to the Northland. He went to Cripple Creek in the boom days of that famous camp and was caller on the mining stock exchange at Colorado Springs. He went to Goldfield in the early days of the camp and played an important part in mining and politics for a decade. Since leaving Goldfield he has resided in Reno.

Joseph Hutchinson, widely known in mining camps from Nome to Mexico and a resident of Nevada for more than twenty-five years, is ill in a San Francisco hospital and no hope is held for his recovery. He has been attended since by his brother, Charles J. Hutchinson of Seattle.

ALASKA WEEKLY, Sept. 5, 1930

H. B. INGRAM

H. B Ingram of Portland, Oregon died March 17 from a heart attack. Mr. Ingram, 60, was in the wholesale grocery business in Portland for 28 years. Mr. Ingram was born in Belfont, Pa., April 27, 1867. He went to Alaska during the gold rush and was a member of the first Alaskans territorial legislature. He was 12 years in Valdez.

He is survived by his widow and a daughter, Mrs. Marion Chandlee, both of Portland.

THE VALDEZ MINER, Mar. 18, 1927

JOHN IRVING (See Vol. 2)

Capt. John Irving was the founder and, for many years, principal owner, President and Manager of the old Canadian Pacific Navigation company, operating steamships to Alaska and in British Columbia waters. He was master of the flagship of the fleet, the Islander, which was built on plans prepared by him for the coast trade. In addition to his steamship business, in which a score of ships, large and small, were used, he owned and operated wharves in various British Columbia ports and owned mines and other properties. He sold the Canadian Pacific Navigation Company to the Canadian Pacific Railroad company a score of years or more ago.

For many years "Captain John" never permitted lack of money for his fare to deprive a man of traveling up or down the coast when it was necessary for him to make a trip. It has been said that on many trips there were more passengers holding trip passes he had issued than there were with tickets purchased at his office.

Capt. Irving represented the Atlin District in the British Columbia Legislature for many years.

Capt. Irving's home at the present time is in Victoria, and he spends most of his time there and Vancouver, and in American cities of the Northwest.

DAILY ALASKA EMPIRE, June 25, 1930

EGBERT WYCLIFFE JACKSON

E.W. Jackson was born at Hampton Village, New Brunswick, on October 21, 1860, coming to the Yukon in the great rush of 97-98 and locating on Indian River where he followed mining and for a number of years was mail carrier for the district lying between Dawson and Indian River. He died November 29, 1934 at St Mary's Hospital in Dawson.

Mr. Jackson is survived by his widow and three sons, a daughter, and two sisters. Mrs, E.W. Jackson now resides in Santa Clara, California with her son, Joseph Egbert Jackson; Mrs. C.T., Ross, the only daughter, born at Indian River, resides at Livermore, California; Ramsey J. Jackson, a son, also born at Indian River, lives in San Jose, California; the third son, William A. Jackson, resides at Bear Creek with his wife and family. The two sisters, Mrs. I. Freeze and Mrs. Lottie Chamberlain [Chamberland?] are residents of Hampton Village, King County, New Brunswick.

THE ALASKA WEEKLY, Dec. 21, 1934

JAMES JACKSON

The late famous chief Anahoots' nephew, known here as James Jackson, died October 18 at his home. Jackson was 85, had been a fisherman. He was born at Hoonah.

Also a chief, Jackson was an impressive figure of a man, 6 feet 6 inches tall, with a shock of snow-white hair. For the past

several years he has been blind, and he suffered a stroke some time ago. He is said to be the last of the chiefs.
ARROWHEAD (Sitka), Nov. 3, 1934

JOHN JACKSON
Died, at Treadwell, Alaska, on Wednesday, May 11th, John Jackson, a native of Wasa, Finland, aged 32 years. The deceased came to his death by a fall in the 700 mine.
DOUGLAS ISLAND NEWS, May 21, 1902

T. W. JACKSON
Judge T. W. Jackson, 84, "The Old Canadian," is dead. Judge Jackson spent many years in the Yukon, mostly at White Horse. He was born in Kent County, Ontario, came west in 1880, and after visiting the Yellowhead, settled near Indian Head, Saskatchewan.
VANCOUVER SUN, Feb. 17, 1932

GEORGE JAMES
George James was born in Davenport. Iowa., and saw one week of '59. His early life was spent on the farm, receiving his "little learning" in the common schools of Iowa. At the age of 19 he started westward, finally landing in Puget Sound in the spring of 1882 and was employed in the engineering department of the N.P.R.R.

He remained there for two years and then moved to Snohomish county Washington, engaged in civil engineering and surveying. In 1897 he joined the rush to the Klondike. In 1900 he went to Nome where he became the principal owner and manager of No. 14 Ophir creek in the Council city district. Bulletin No. 203 of the geological report speaks highly of Mr. James' work on No. 14. One thing sure, Mr. James goes to the Outside this fall probably the best paid man on the Seward Peninsula.

He was elected a delegate to the Alaskan convention.
NOME SEMI-WEEKLY MINING EDITION, Oct 13, 1905

D. H. JARVIS   (See Vol. 3)

Captain Jarvis was born in Berlin, Worcester county, Maryland, August 24, 1862. He graduated from the cadet school into the revenue service at New Bedford, Mass., in 1883. As lieutenant in command of the revenue cutter Bear, he organized and led the overland relief expedition to the starving whalers at Point Barrow in 1897-1898. After sailing as far north as the ice would permit, Lieutenant Jarvis organized a land expedition to the six imprisoned vessels. The expedition traveled 1,800 miles into a wild and unknown country, bringing aide to the suffering men. In recognition of his bravery, Congress voted Captain Jarvis a gold medal, bear profile in bas relief. In April 2, 1896, Captain Jarvis was married to Miss Ethel Tabor.

ALASKA DAILY DISPATCH, Jan. 7, 1911.

R. H. JEFFRIES

Mr. Jeffries in early days helped survey the route for a proposed railroad up the Stikine river and thoroughly enjoys the present day method of travel on the river.

Mr. Jeffries and two other men returned last week from a trip in Copper Mountain near Sulzer on the west coast of Prince of Wales island, where Jeffries located copper claims which he worked during 1898 and 1899. He found the crumbling remains of the log cabin which he helped to build and the 100-foot tunnel on which he labored with might and main before abandoning it for other fields.

WRANGELL SENTINEL, Aug. 17, 1934

THOMAS JENKINS   (See Vol. 3)

Rev. Thomas Jenkins was born at Shenley in Buckinghamshire, England, is an alumnus of Kenyon college, Gambler, Ohio, and Bexley Hall, the church divinity school in Ohio. He was ordained deacon and priest in the diocese of southern Ohio, spent three years in mission work in Ohio and was a member of the Associate mission in Cincinnati two years.

In August 1902, he was sent to Ketchikan to supervise the remodeling and addition to the St. John mission. He has made the church and all it stands for a power of good in this community.

KETCHIKAN MINING JOURNAL, Jan. 1907

C. P. JENNE

Dr. C. P. Jennie died of a heart attack in his sleep. Dr. Jenne was a resident of Juneau for more than a quarter of a century where he was active in all civic affairs and has hundreds of friends who mourn his passing at the age of fifty.

He is survived by his widow, Crystal Snow Jenne; two daughters, Corrine and Phyllis; and one son, Charles. Corrine was en route to Mills College and Charles to Fairbanks to continue his studies at the University of Alaska when they received news of their father's sudden death. Residing at the Jenne home is Mrs. Anna Snow, mother of Mrs. Jenne, and Lyman Snow, a nephew.

ALASKA WEEKLY, Sept. 23, 1938

CRYSTAL SNOW JENNE

Crystal Snow Jenne was born in California, and with her parents, Mr. and Mrs. George T. Snow, arrived at Juneau, Alaska in April 1887. In the year 1894, three years before the famous gold rush, with her parents, she crossed the Chilcoot Pass on foot and spent four real pioneer years in the Yukon Valley.

Educated in Alaskan schools, she was the sole member of the second class to graduate in an Alaskan High School. She later taught several years in the public schools of Alaska and was teaching in the Juneau school from which she graduated at the time she married Dr. Jenne, well known dentist of Juneau.

Mrs. Jenne is the mother of three Alaskan-born children who are being raised in Alaska and educated in her old home school.

WRANGELL SENTINEL, April 13, 1934

WILLIAM JENSEN

Capt. William Jensen, aged 72 years, veteran Alaska Steamship Company skipper, died yesterday evening here. He retired four years ago, and was a painter of clipper ship canvasses, achieving wide recognition for authentic pictures of sea life. Capt. Jensen is survived by his widow and a brother, both in Seattle, and three sisters in Norway.

It was in 1895 that Capt. Jensen landed in San Francisco, a comparatively forlorn, unknown Norwegian seaman from the decks of a sailing ship. He decided to stay on the Pacific Coast, and shortly afterwards came to Seattle. In 1901, after he had acquired a navigator's license, he joined the deck officers mess of one of the units of one of the predecessors of the present Alaska Steamship company, and remained in the service until four years ago. In the capacity of pilot and later master, Capt. Bill Jensen commanded every unit of the Alaska Steamship Company's fleet, but principally the steamers Northwestern and Alaska.

FAIRBANKS DAILY NEWS-MINER, Dec. 31, 1932

GUS A. JEPSON

Gus A. Jepson was born in Guttenburg, Sweden on June 21, 1871, and educated in public schools. When he was 14 years old he shipped out on a full-rigged sailing ship. For three years he served under the flags of five countries, finally reaching San Francisco. He worked as a rigger for the bridge gang of the Southern Pacific Railroad Company for a number of years. Tiring of the land, he returned to the sea and served for seven years.

Back to the railroad he went and worked on the Overland division of the railroad until 1890. Speaking of this he said, "I saw more snow in California that year than I ever saw in Alaska for twenty years." But in 1890, he shipped out on the USS Albatross and served until he was discharged at Mare Island. He planned to go to navigation school. While working on a pile driver gang to earn money for school he was hurt in an accident and was laid up in the company hospital for 13 months. The experience killed his ambition to go to sea.

Again he went back to the railroad, and later to the Mare Island navy yard where he worked for four years. Again he tried to enlist in the navy, but the accident had left him with poor hearing and could not pass the physical. For the next two years Gus worked for the Harbor Commission in San Francisco, later contracting work through Nevada, California, and Montana.

Then the sea called again and he shipped as ship's carpenter on the full-rigged ship Star of France. He also served carpenter on the four masted bark, Mangan Reever bound for Bristol Bay.

Then 20 years ago he sailed North as a passenger for Cordova to work on bridge construction. When the work was completed he lived in Chitina, Kennicott, Mother Lode, Ellamar, Latouche, and the Bearing Sea coal fields. Since those years Gus has spent most of his time in Cordova engaged in his trade as a carpenter.

But having drifted the seven seas, he likes Alaska the best of all. "As long as I have to scratch out a living," he said as he finished his story, "I'd a soon scratch in Alaska as any other place."

CORDOVA DAILY TIMES, June 2, 1928

JOHNSON (CHIEF)

Johnson, chief of the Eagle clan of the Taku, was drowned near Killisnoo on the 23rd inst. Chief Johnson was one of the thriftiest Indians in Southeastern Alaska. Several years ago he built a large house on an elevated bench above the Taku Indian village adjacent to Juneau. The house is one of the striking sights on Gastineau channel, as it is faced with the insignia of his clan and "Chief Johnson House" painted across the front in large letters. Johnson celebrated the erection of his house with a big potlach, as which he distributed hundreds of presents to the Indians who had gathered from far and near to take part in the dancing and revelry that lasted for several days. Johnson was

owner of a schooner and was a shrewd trader.
THE DAILY ALASKAN, January 26, 1904

CHARLES SUMNER JOHNSON (See Vol. 2)
Charles Sumner Johnson, the judge of the United States District Court, was born in Jones county, Iowa, in a log cabin on the Iowa prairies in the year 1854. At the age of thirteen he removed to Clarinda of that state, and graduated from the high school. He then learned the printer's trade after which he attended the Agricultural College at Ames, Iowa, but was not permitted to graduate from that school owing to the lack of means with which to finish his course. Some time after this he attended the law department of the Iowa State University, and graduated from that school in the class of 1877.

He then moved to Wahoo, Nebr., where he entered upon the practice of law. In 1879 he was elected city attorney and was elected a member of the Nebraska legislature in 1882. In 1885 he removed to Nelson, in the same state, and the year following was elected prosecuting the county attorney and was afterward reelected to that office.

During the year 1889 he was appointed U. S. District attorney for Alaska which position he held for four and one-half years after which he removed to Juneau and engaged in the practice of law with Mr. John G. Heid one of the leading lawyers of Alaska. In 1897 he received the appointment of U. S. District judge and was confirmed by the senate.

Judge Johnson attended three national conventions in 1884, 1888, and 1896, and was chairman of his delegation in the last convention and also a member of the committee appointed to notify President McKinley of his nomination and visited Canton, Ohio, when the committee met there for the performance of its duties. The Judge is at the present time the national committeeman for Alaska.
DOUGLAS ISLAND NEWS, Jan. 18, 1899

CHESTER A. JOHNSON

Funeral services were held yesterday afternoon at the local cemetery for Chester A. Johnson under the auspices of the local Post of the American Legion. Johnson died last Thursday in Ketchikan.

Chester Johnson was born January 8, 1898 in Bayfield, Wisconsin. He came to Petersburg in 1913 and has lived here almost continuously since that time.

He enlisted July 5, 1917 with Headquarters Company, 167th Infantry of the Rainbow Division in the United States Army. During the time he spent overseas during the World War he saw action in many of the major battles, including service in the Lorraine Sector from February 21 to March 21, 1918; Baccaret Sector, March 21 to June 18; Champagne-Marne, July 10; Alane-Marne, July 16 to July 27; St. Mihiel, Sept. 12 to Sept. 16; Meuse Argonne, October 10 to November 9. He was transferred into the Army of Occupation November 16, 1918.

After returning to the United States he received an honorable discharge from the Army at Fort D. A. Russell, Wyoming on May 12, 1919, shortly after which he returned to Petersburg.

Johnson is survived by his mother, Mrs. E. M. Johnson, two sons, William and Alfred, a sister, Mrs. J. B. Wanberg, and a brother, Ted, all of Petersburg.

Other surviving relatives are William B. Johnson, a brother, Moore, Montana; and five sisters, Mrs. Olaf Edwards and Mrs. Fred Hansen, Bayfield, Wisconsin; Mrs. A. R. Witlark and Mrs. Sidney Smith, Los Angeles, California; Mrs. C. D. Lawrence, Seattle, Washington.

PETERSBURG PRESS, Sept. 20, 1940.

GUS JOHNSON   (See Vol. 2)

Gus Johnson first came into the northern country in 1894, when the lure of the frontier first brought him to Juneau in a small sailing sloop manned by himself and two companions from Puget

Sound. From Juneau he explored Cook's inlet in 1896. He returned to Juneau and joined the gold rush to the Yukon, arriving here early in 1897. He mined with much success in the early days of the camp on Gold Hill, after which endeavor he came to Dawson, where he established himself in the laundry business.

His success as a gardener, who attained most phenomenal results in this, his pet hobby, is well known as he raised in his garden in his spare moments some of the best garden produce ever witnessed in Dawson. His hothouse and garden specimens have won him prizes at nearly every Discovery Day exhibition during the past number of years. He is an active partner in the Lone Star Mining Company's property.

Mr. Johnson was a prime mover in the Midnight Dome road project, and it was due mainly to his efforts and decision that the road was made feasible and construction began.

Mrs. Johnson and daughter, Virginia, left Dawson a few years ago for Seattle, where they have made their home and where Virginia is proceeding with her studies.

As a token of esteem and as a farewell gift, [moving to Seattle] many of the Gus Johnson, department sourdough, and co-workers in the Midnight Dome automobile road gathered at the Dawson Curling Clubs's rooms on Saturday night and presented the loyal pioneer with a gold-studded paper knife. The gift was a very handsome one, and was fittingly presented by Dr. J. O. Lachapelle on behalf of the Pioneer road construction committee.

THE DAWSON NEWS, Sept. 15, 1925

HATTIE JOHNSON

Mrs. Hattie Johnson, wife of Andy Johnson, and resident of Seldovia since 1906, passed away at the Seward hospital this morning, March 7.

Mrs. Johnson was born at Kodiak 41 years ago, the daughter of Captain Henry Bowen. Her father was a Boston skipper who came to Alaska in the early days and entered the service of the North American Commercial company. He conducted sea otter hunts, dealt in furs generally, was noted for his intrepid seamanship. In those days travel was mostly by sail and Captain Bowen as master of one of the company's schooners covered a lot of water. It was on a trip from Kodiak to the Cordova district that Captain Bowen and his entire crew were lost.

Mrs. Johnson is survived by her husband and three daughters: Mrs. Susan Haskins; Mrs. Hattie Fox; and Elsie, the youngest child. Two sisters: Mrs. Chas. Hamelbacher, and Mrs. Ernie Weik are local residents; as also a brother, Fred, at present engaged on a fox farm near Portlock. Another brother, Rufus, lived in Anchorage though for many years a resident of Seldovia. A half brother, Julian Smith and his sister Annie live in the states.

THE SELDOVIA HERALD, March 7, 1931

PETER JOHNSON

Peter Johnson is another long-time sourdough, having lived in Alaska and the Yukon territory for twenty-one years. He went to Roseburg, Oregon, two years ago with his son, R. M. Johnson, is engaged in the poultry business on a large scale on his ranch one mile south of Roseburg.

He and his wife went to Alaska in 1898 and worked at the Treadwell mines at Douglas for several years. He held a technical position and his work at different times made it necessary for him to visit nearly every mining district in Alaska and the Yukon. He was personally acquainted with most all of the old-timers in the Klondike and Alaska.

Mr. and Mrs. Johnson have six children, all born in Douglas, Alaska, and all of them grew up in that country. They remained in Alaska until 1919. A daughter, Mrs. Gertrude Hellgesen, who resides with her husband in Juneau, was a guest at the picnic and has departed for her Northern home.

ALASKA WEEKLY, Sept. 13, 1929

THEODORE JOHNSON

Theodore Johnson, pioneer merchant of the Northland, died suddenly at his home in Seattle on Monday evening last. Born in Sweden 64 years ago, Theodore Johnson struck out as a 15-year-old lad, and for five years made his home at New Britton [New Britain?], Conn. He came to Seattle in 1888, and ten years later joined the "Gold Rush." He entered into business at Skagway with E. R. Peoples. The firm later established at Fairbanks, where, for many years, they enjoyed an excellent patronage. In 1917 they disposed of their business holdings to the Northern Commercial Co., and two years later Mr. Johnson came back to settle down in Seattle.

ALASKA WEEKLY, March 18, 1932

WILL A. JOHNSON

Will A. Johnson came to Prince William Sound in 1906, "out to make my fortune in copper," as he says. He heard talk of a gold strike in the Cook Inlet district, and when the bottom dropped out of copper he started west.

From Seward he mushed over the Indian Creek pass and down Ship Creek, turning off some miles from the present site of Anchorage to cross Eagle River near its mouth. He continued around the head of Knik Arm to the town of Knik, and on from there across country to Susitna Station, supply point at that time for the Cache Creek mining area.

It was necessary to break trail all the way, and sometimes he made only eight or ten miles in a day.

That winter he traveled over a thousand miles by dog team, going north into the Cache Creek district to prospect. In May of 1909 he returned to the place now known as Talkeetna, and built the first cabin there. He also built his own boat to use in prospecting, and spent many strenuous years traveling up the rivers and through the wilderness by boat, with pack horses, or by dog team, looking for gold.

Making his way through the vast country beyond Cook

Inlet, he built several cabins as headquarters for his wandering. One which he constructed at Gold Creek, fifteen miles north of what is now Cutty, finally became his home.

As dear to him as human friends were the members of his dog teams, particularly a half-Chesapeake leader called Curley.

"He often stood between me and danger," says Mr. Johnson. "He was one the most outstanding characters who ever came to Alaska."

Before the construction of the Alaska Railroad in 1915, Mr. Johnson was called on to take survey parties through the proposed route to the Interior. His intimate knowledge of the terrain was also responsible for his being asked to act as guide for the Bennett-Rice expedition, headed by Hugh H. Bennett, for some years Chief of the Reclamation Service, Department of Agriculture. He spent the whole summer of 1915 with these men. "That meant packing on our backs through the wilderness," says Mr. Johnson, "and going through the country with a compass in my hand."

The party went up the Susitna River a hundred miles, and up the Yentna about forty, taking in an area ten to fifteen miles wide where tributaries cut the valley.

When the threat of war came to Alaska, Mr. Johnson turned from his mining operations to act as guard for the railroad bridge which crossed the Susitna River at Gold Creek. High flood waters later washed out his outfit and made it impossible for him to continue working his ground while the war lasted. He and his wife then moved to Anchorage. For two years during the war, he worked for the Northern Commercial Company there.

The inspiration of much of Mr. Johnson's poetry has been his wife, whom he met in the States and married in 1925. Mrs. Johnson is a native of Ireland, whose own spirit of adventure led her more than half way around the world before she came to Gold Creek to share her husband's cabin near "The Hills of Evermore." As loyal an Alaskan as he, she enjoyed the years they spent prospecting together and roughing it in their remote Alaskan home.

Now retired he spends most of his time writing. Though he has produced a large number of poems, and has given serious thought to their composition, he has written only for his own amusement and has never attempted to publish his work.

ALASKA LIFE, Jan. 1948

FRANCIS ALAIN JONES

Frank entered the world in Minneapolis, Minnesota on November 9, 1880. The first five years of his life was spent in traveling as his parents were in the theatrical business and rarely spent more than a month in any one place. Frank's early education was secured in the company of the Flat Head Indians in Montana. Later he went to the public schools at Port Townsend, Wash. and finished in St. Ignatius College in San Francisco.

At 18, Frank was the superintendent of the Youths's Directory, a boys' home in San Francisco. Frank worked at the home for number of years and took a job with Wells Fargo. Then he went into the laundry business. Ill health and a desire for a change of scene caused Frank to leave that business and to regain his health, he took up farming, raising chickens on a California ranch. While working on the ranch Frank essayed to teach a number of young ladies the graceful art of riding a bicycle. Among these students was there was one Miss Anna Doyle, and as he reports the events, he eventually rode up to the alter with her in 1906 in San Francisco.

Being anxious to make more money, he went into the painting business. Then he tried the grocery business. Hearing of the construction going on in Alaska, the couple sailed for Cordova, landing there April 13, 1909. The next day they went out on station work at Mile 104.

Station work being completed, Frank came back to Cordova as a straw boss over a steel gang, and had saved quite a stake and was planning on leaving for the states for the winter when his baggage and money was burned up in a fire which destroyed the Morrison Building .

Frank borrowed money and bought an interest in the Cordova Hand Laundry in the basement of the Lambert building. In 1917, he brought the laundry. In 1918, he joined the Tank Corps and went to New York and then received the news that the Armistice had been signed.

Coming back he help organized the American Legion and has been engaged in various civic affairs since.
CORDOVA DAILY TIMES, Dec. 10, 1927.

NATHANIEL CLINTON JONES

The funeral of Nathaniel Clinton Jones was held on Friday afternoon, May 10th, at the Congregational church. The deceased was 38 years of age. Nathaniel Jones was born at Pinckneywill, Ill., on July 1st 1891 he married at Burnett, Ind., to Miss Mattie J. Edwards. His wife died in 1894. Both of his parents are dead. Two brothers, one at Pinckneywill, Ill., and one at Nashville, Tenn., survive him. The burial was at the Douglas cemetery.
 DOUGLAS ISLAND NEWS, May 21, 1902

VICTOR JORY

Victor Jory was born in a road house on Bonanza Creek in Yukon Territory. His father and mother owned the roadhouse. They came to Dawson in 1899 and their son was born in 1901. Twenty thousand dollars richer the Jorys went outside after the boom days and while still in his 'teens the young Jory became an actor.

He wavered between the square ring and the footlights for a time but finally the theater won him in a very close race, because at the time, he became the wrestling and boxing champion of British Columbia.

Speaking of his education, Mr. Jory said: "I never finished a high school course, but I was able to get into the University of California because some of the boys in the fraternity to which I was pledged took the entrance exams for me. I was at the university for six or seven months, and I probably attended class as many as 15 or twenty times until they discovered someone else was answering roll call for me. Then the faculty decided I had better be an actor. I couldn't be as great a "flop" as an actor as I had been as a student."

Victor Jory had the leading male role in "The Mad Honey Moon." When the play opened in Minneapolis this winter, the paper devoted two columns to the actor.

Mr. and Mrs. Ed Jory came to came to Skagway early in 1898 from Oregon[?]. Ed engaged in the transfer business while he wife was a typesetter on the Skagway News. The woman went to Dawson late in '99 and her husband the following spring. They left the north about 1905.

STROLLER'S WEEKLY AND DOUGLAS ISLAND NEWS, Feb. 24, 1929.

FRANK JOSEPH

Frank Joseph, 60 year old pioneer native, died March 10th at his home. Joseph was born in Sitka in 1874 and had been a fisherman by trade. He was a member of the ANB, and the fire department. At the funeral, held from the Creek Orthodox Church, March 11th, the fire department conveyed the remains to the cemetery on the fire truck, as a last honor in memory of the missing member, who had been well liked by everyone.

He is survived by a daughter, Maisie Joseph of Kake, Alaska; and a son, John Joseph of Sitka. Other relatives are John Jacobs and Charles Joseph both of Sitka.

THE ARROWHEAD (Sitka), March 16, 1935

W. C. JOSLYN

W. C. Joslyn, one of the oldest sourdoughs of the camp, is dead. Word to this effect was brought to town on Sunday night by Donald McDonald who has been mining all winter on Bonanza, near Joslyn's residence. Yesterday morning Sergeant Daly and Constable Sonnie, of the R.C.M.P. proceeded to the cabin on 65 below on Bonanza, where the aged man had lived for years, and found the body lying on its left side on the floor of the cabin with a hand against the heart. Joslyn had not been seen since Saturday and it is thought that he passed away some time during the week end.

The first intimation that something was wrong with the old timer came on Sunday afternoon, when Louis Roal, who had brought provisions from town to Joslyn, knocked at his door and obtaining no reply, left the provisions in front of the door and immediately proceeded to the cabin of R. Smith Constans, a neighbor. Roal informed Constans that he had knocked at Joslyn's door and had received no reply whereat Constans immediately went over to the little cabin, which is situated on the tailing piles, and upon entering he found the old sourdough dead.

Upon making an inspection of the cabin Sergeant Daly found that there were plenty of provisions on hand and the miner had not been in want. It is thought he died of heart failure, but this will not be definitely ascertained until an autopsy is held.

Mr. Joslyn has lived on Bonanza creek for years. He came to this country in the early days and had remained here ever since. During the last number of years he had been given support by the government, but in return he had been in charge of a piece of the government road on Bonanza, which he had taken great pride in keeping in excellent condition.

Joslyn was about 70 years of age, and it is thought from a perusal of his correspondence, but he was born in Batavia, northern California. He was married; but he had not seen his wife for years. Letters of some years back give her address as Buffalo, New York, but it is not known whether she still resides there.

A newspaper clipping from a California paper of the date of 1908 tells of the death of Joslyn's mother in Batavia. It also reveals the fact that the deceased came from a family of nine children, eight of whom were living at that time in the United States.

DAWSON NEWS, Feb. 9, 1926

JOE JUNEAU

All of the old settlers in the vicinity of Thief River Falls know Joe Juneau, and in fact he is known all over the northwest, for he is one of those fearless, restless characters who push into the wilderness and made homes for themselves, among the aborigines. With others, equally as hardy and daring, they crowded the Red man a little further west or north and formed the entering wedge for the higher, if not more rugged civilization which was sure to follow.

Joe comes legitimately by his wandering pioneer instinct, the family for generation having been the forerunners of their race. From an article in the Milwaukee Sentinel of September 13, an extract is taken regarding a cousin and an uncle of Mr. Juneau, who have won more than a passing renown during their tempestuous careers. The Sentinel says:

"In 1880 a French Canadian named Juneau wandered up Silver Bow basin, the beautiful canyon back of the town which bears his name. He panned the first gold from a field which has enriched the world by many millions, and which will continue to contribute to its wealth for many years to come. Juneau was one of those fearless characters who helped to conquer the wilderness. He was a pathfinder in the full sense of the world, yet he died penniless. When the news came to Juneau the old man was dead in Dawson and it became known that his last wish was to be buried on the mountain overlooking the town that was named for him, the money was quickly subscribed to bring his body to the spot where he said he wanted to wait for the judgment. In a little park on the shore of lake Michigan there in an elegant bronze statue erected to the memory of Solomon Juneau, founder of Milwaukee, an uncle of the Joe of this story. How much we of today owe to those old fellows who wore themselves out in breaking a path for us to follow! Let us all take off our hats to the Joe Juneaus who have gone over as well as those who are still on this side."

COOKSTON DAILY TIMES (Minn.), October 3, 1903

PAUL KABLER

Paul Kabler, formerly of Juneau, was accidentally killed at the new town of Copper in the Tolstoi district by the discharge of a short gun. [pistol ?]

Mr. Kabler was well known in Juneau, having lived here for past seventeen years and during that time came in close touch with the public on account of his connection with the Frye-Bruhn market here, he being manager.

Mr. Kabler was married here in 1900. A wife and son, Paul, survive him, and a sister, Mrs. Peter McCormack lives at Wrangell. Mr. Kabler was a member of the local order of Moose. He was 45 years of age and was born in Beaver Dam, Wis.

ALASKA DAILY EMPIRE, May 17, 1916

NICHOLAS KASHEVAROFF

Rev. N. P. Kashevaroff, priest-in-charge of the Russian Orthodox Catholic church at Kodiak, is visiting his brother and sister-in-law, Father and Mrs. A. P. Kashevaroff in Juneau this week. He arrived on the steamship Yukon Tuesday morning from the Prince William Sound district. It is the first time in three years that the brothers have seen each other.

For the past twenty years, Father Nicholas Kashevaroff has been stationed at Kodiak and first started his work in lay-reader in 1876. In 1885 he was ordained at San Francisco and came north to take over the parish at Afognak. From there he transferred to the Bristol Bay country which parish included 27 chapels, some being as far as 200 miles apart.

During his long stay at Kodiak he has made several overland trips to Nushagak, and travels considerably each year whenever possible. His parish includes Kodiak Island and the adjacent country to the north, west and south, requiring trips from Kanatak to Perryville at definite intervals.

In a brief interview, Father A. P. Kashevaroff, curator of the Alaska Territorial Museum, revealed several interesting facts concerning his two brother and himself. His oldest brother, Rev.

Peter Kashevaroff, situated at St. George Island at the present, began missionary work under the Russian Catholic church in 1875 and since that time has been a missionary in the Yukon, the Aleutian chain of islands and at his present station. The Kashevaroff brothers are the oldest living missionaries of any denomination in the Alaskan territory.

When asked about the present situation of the Russian Catholic missionary work, Father Kashevaroff stated that although none of the 12 missionary priests now in the Territory have once quit their posts, many difficulties have been encountered since the Russian revolution in 1917 when connections with the home church were severed. However, he explained that conditions have much improved since the separation and are progressing favorably.

In reply to a query as to their attitude and experience during the Klondike rush, Father Kashevaroff said, "We didn't get excited over the rush. We were there before they came and are still carrying on our work now that it is all over."

Father Kashevaroff has taken his brother around the city and out the road to the Mendenhall Glacier, as it is his first visit to Juneau. The visitor says that he is very much impressed at the size and modernity of Juneau and marvels at the roads and many automobiles, for he still makes many trips in skin boats and dog sleds, although the advent of the gas boat makes some of his trips via this means possible.

Father Nicholas Kashevaroff will return to Kodiak on the Admiral Rogers which sails Sunday.

STROLLER'S WEEKLY AND DOUGLAS ISLAND NEWS, Nov. 23, 1929

NICHOLAS P. KASHEVAROFF

Rev. Nicholas P. Kashevaroff, aged patriarch of the Russian Orthodox church at Kodiak for 50 years and who passed through Seward last month en route to the Sitka Home, died December 5 according to word sent here.

Father Kashevaroff was born on Kodiak island and started

his religious work there. It is believed that the remains will be returned to Kodiak for burial.

He is survived by three daughters and two sons, and by a brother who is curator of the Alaska museum at Juneau.

SEWARD GATEWAY, Dec. 10, 1933

THOMAS E. P. KEEGAN

A mantle of sadness was cast over Juneau yesterday morning when a telegram was received by Mayor I Goldstein conveying the news of the death in Seattle Thursday of Chief of Police Thomas E. P. Keegan of Juneau.

Mr. Keegan came to Alaska with a cannery concern 22 years ago and followed that business for several years, sometimes for himself but mostly as an employee of others. He became chief of police of Juneau in 1920 and had filled the position continuously since and until going south on a vacation six weeks ago. He was a splendid officer and his standing and reputation in the community were enviable.

He was born and raised in Lewis county, Washington, and his entire life was spent on the Pacific coast. He leaves two sons, Melville and Edwin, 20 and 18 years of age. Both the sons left here for Seattle on the Alaska Wednesday morning to be with their father but he passed away before they arrived. Mr. Keegan was about 65 years of age. He stood over 6 feet and was a noble specimen of physical manhood.

STROLLER'S WEEKLY, Feb. 9, 1924

FRANK TRUMAN KEELAR

Frank Keelar was born in Waterford, New York. At an early age he left his home for New Orleans and after a time went to California to dig for gold. He traveled all over the gold fields of that state, sometimes as a miner, sometimes as a merchant, and sometimes combining the two. It was in 1861 when he first went to California. Some years later he established himself in business in San Francisco, and about fifteen years ago removed his business to Oakland. There he built himself a handsome home, and thought he was rich enough to retire from the merchant business. He was at that time a heavy speculator in farm lands, and is still paying taxes on many acres. He came to Skagway March 9th of last year, and started his present line of business. This has so prospered that he now has two large stores on Holly street. His confidence in the future of Skagway has never weakened since he first landed. He owns considerable real estate in the city, and is still a buyer–which is the most tangible proof of his confidence that can be given. Mr. Keelar has his wife with him.

DAILY ALASKAN, Feb. 19, 1899

W. K. KELLER

Undoubtedly, the most important event in connection with high school history in the past year was the retirement Feb. 15 of Mr. W. K. Keller as superintendent of Juneau public schools. He left the position to take the office of Territorial Commissioner of Education.

Mr. Keller was superintendent of Juneau public schools seven years and a half, having come here in 1923 from Fairbanks, where he had filled a similar position two years.

Mr. Keller raised the standard of study so that in 1927, the Juneau high school was the first in the Territory to become an accredited member of the Northwest Association of Secondary Schools and Colleges, thus enabling its graduates to enter any college or university on the same terms as the graduates of accredited high schools in the States.

W. K. Keller was born in Redmond, Washington. He was graduated from the high school at Kirkland, Washington. He attended the Washington State Normal School at Cheney, Washington, the University of Washington at Seattle, and the Washington State College at Pullman. He attended the Teachers' College, Columbia University, New York City, taking advanced work toward a degree of Doctor of Philosophy in Education. He holds Bachelor of Arts and Master of Arts degrees.

Before coming to Alaska, Mr. Keller had teaching experience in Washington, Idaho and Oregon. He assumed his duties as Alaska commissioner of Education March 1. Fortunately his ability and services are not lost entirely to the Juneau high school. From his work in the field, the institution here, like every other educational institution in the Territory, is sure to be affected to its advantage and thus will continue to benefit from his efforts.

TOTEM YEARBOOK, 1931 (Juneau High School)
WRANGELL SENTINEL, Oct. 7, 1932

MRS. MICHAEL DODSON KELLY

Mrs. Michael Kelly, a resident for 13 years of Dawson and vicinity and wife of one of the best known mining operators of Lovett gulch died suddenly at their home on Lovett yesterday.

Mrs. Kelly was about 50 years of age. She leaves a host of friends in Yukon who keenly mourn her departure. She was married to Mrs. Kelly five years ago. Prior to that she was Mrs. Dodson.

Mrs. Kelly leaves a daughter, Mrs. E. B. Judd, the wife of a prosperous merchant in the States. She is also survived by a brother living in Billings, Montana. Her father, a veteran of the American Civil war, died two months ago at the ripe age of 84 years.

DAWSON DAILY NEWS, April 27, 1911

PHIL M. KELLY

Philip Milton Kelly collapsed suddenly at the Dawson City curling rink on November 29, when he started to throw a stone. He was taken to the club house but passed away, coming out of the coma for only a few seconds.

Philip Kelly was a well known mining man and had served for many years as the chief mining recorder of the Territory. He was one of the earliest of the real early-day pioneers having come to this part of the Territory in the spring of 1896, when only 23 years of age, a year before the beginning of the great gold rush of

1897-98.

There are few other pioneers in the Territory that knew the country as well as Phil Kelly, as he has followed mining in practically every district of the Territory before his appointment to government office in 1912.

Philip M. Kelly was born in Seattle, Washington, 61 years ago. He is survived by his widow of this city, a widowed daughter, Mrs. H.A. McEwan of Vancouver, B.C., and two sons, Gerald and Brian, who are located in Carmacks, Y.T.

THE ALASKA WEEKLY, Dec.21, 1934.

J. J. KENNEDY

Between 11 and 12 o'clock Saturday night, J. J. Kennedy passed away at the Holy Cross Hospital. Mr. Kennedy was a prominent member of the Nome bar. He came to this city from San Francisco in connection with certain important litigations which was thought would come to trial this winter.

Mr Kennedy was a native of the state of California, and was 43 years of age. He was a member of the Nome bar.

NOME SEMI-WEEKLY NUGGET, Feb. 8, 1905

LAWRENCE KERR

Lawrence Kerr, 61, resident of the Territory since the turn of the century died early Wednesday morning at Juneau of a heart attack.

Born March 8, 1884, near Harrisville, Penn., Kerr went to Nome in company with his uncle around 1900. There he served as U. S. District Court reporter under William A. Holtzheimer, then District Judge for the Second Division, and participated actively in public affairs of the pioneer community. Esther Birdsall Darling, Alaskan writer, made him one of her characters in her adventurous novel of early Nome, "The Break-Up."

Coming to Juneau about 15 years ago, Kerr continued his association with Federal agencies, mostly in connection with the U.S. District court, being generally recognized as one of the most expert court reporters n the Territory.

During legislative sessions he had acted in various capacities, being clerk for the Senate Judiciary Committed during the last session.

During the height of war activity in Alaska, Mr. Kerr worked with the Army personnel near Sitka, as secretary to Post Commander Stribling, and accompanied him to a new station at Tillamook, Oregon where he stayed a year. At the time of his death he was chief clerk in the office of Attorney General Ralph J. Rivers.

Survivors are a sister, Mrs. Ollie Galbraith of Butler County, near Harrisville, Penn; and an aunt, Mrs. Violet Cassity of Pittsburg, Penn.

WRANGELL SENTINEL, June 15, 1915

WILLIAM KEUHM

Mr. Keuhm is a native of Maryland, having been born in that state on the 4th of March, 1876. He came to Alaska in 1900, landing first at Nome. Mr. Keuhm came to Anchorage early in its history and has remained here ever since. He is a miner by occupation and has visited many of the mining camps of the "Great Land."

ANCHORAGE WEEKLY TIMES, Nov. 22, 1917

NICKOLAS KING

Nicholas King, pioneer of Alaska, passed away at his home in Douglas Tuesday afternoon about five o'clock. His death was due to pneumonia.

Mr. King was born in Elsen, Germany, Oct. 24, 1863, being over 74 years of age. When he was 17 he came to the United States settling in California from whence he came to Douglas 43 years ago. He was an employee of the Treadwell Company for 33 years. Since the cave-in he worked at the Alaska Juneau company. For more than 20 years he served as a member of the Douglas school board.

Mr. King is survived by his widow, three daughters, Mrs. Tom Cashen, Mrs. W. P. Kirby of Douglas; and Mrs. Herbert Vander Wyer of Seattle; and one son, John King of Bellevue Midlakes, Washington, also thirteen grandchildren, nine of whom live in Douglas. Mr. and Mrs. King celebrated the 50th anniversary of their marriage two years ago this winter.

DOUGLAS ISLAND NEWS, Jan. 21, 1928

ROBERT L. KING

Robert L. King was born in Kentucky, and at the time of his death was thirty-eight years of age.

He taught ten years in various public scvhools and teachers colleges in the states, and entered the service of the Office of Indian Affairs at Haskell Institute, Lawrence, Kansas, in 1931. In 1937 he came to Alaska as Principal of the Industrial school at Eklutna, where he served for one and a half years.

In February 1940, he was appointed as teacher of the Pauloff Harbor Territorial School, to fill out the vacancy caused by the death of Howard Trueblood.

Sometime during the summer, we do not know the date, he was killed in a gasboat explosion somewhere around the Kodiak Islands.

ALASKA SCHOOL BULLETIN, Sept. 1940

THOMAS KING

When Charles Ross returned to his ranch on Hinchinbrook island the other day after having spent a month in Cordova, he found Thomas King, an Alaska Pioneer, who had been left in charge of the place, was dead, says the Cordova Times.

King was about 40 years of age and came to Alaska from Madison, Wisconsin. He spent a number of years in the Tanana valley and since 1913 has been a resident of Cordova, being employed most of the time as a fisherman. Last April he was badly burned aboard the Clark & Graham boat Ikaros, which caught fire while tied at the Cordova dock. King spent many months in the

Cordova hospital and never fully recovered from the burns received. He was badly crippled and had lived with Mr. Ross for some time.

ANCHORAGE WEEKLY TIMES, Feb. 14, 1918

JOHN KINKEAD

The first governor of Alaska, the Hon. John Kinkead died at Carson, Nev. On Aug. 15.

Kinkead was born in Fayette, Pa. In 1826. His father's family started West when he was yet a young boy, coming as far as Ohio, where Kinkead received his education.

In 1849, he crossed the plains to Salt Lake and became a member of the firm of Livingston & Kinkead. Three years later he moved to California, and was married at Marysville on January 1, 1856 to Miss Lizzie Fall, daughter of John C. Fall of Marysville.

He came soon afterwards, in 1859, to Carson and established a business with Mr. Fall.

He was a member of the two constitutional conventions held before the admission of the State. In 1878 he was elected governor to Nevada, in which office he served for four years.

He was appointed governor of Alaska by President Arthur, and held the office until his successor was appointed by President Cleveland.

DAILY ALASKA DISPATCH, Aug. 29, 1904

THOMAS KIRKPATRICK

Thomas Kirkpatrick is the resident superintendent of the immense interests of Harper and Ladue in the Dawson Town Site Company, in the sawmill, and in their immense mining interests. He is also a part owner in the property.

So excessively modest, however is Mr. Kirkpatrick, that we have been unable to obtain any particulars of his life upon which to base a biographical sketch.

Tom Kirkpatrick is a man of affairs; one who handles large transactions daily and with consummate ease. Nothing seems to worry him nor frustrate him, and he moves on in the even tenor of his way as calm as a Spring morning.

He is still young in years, possibly thirty-five, rather above the medium height, and a glossy dark mustache adorns his regular pleasant features. While he is perfectly at home in the office of the company, or while keeping the books of the store, he is also one of the Yukon's noted travelers, and may often be seen on the coldest winter days speeding behind a splendid dog team on a fifty or hundred mile journey. Every detail of the Company's immense business, from the value of a dump to the number of feet of lumber in a saw log, he is thoroughly familiar with, and might be termed an all-around business athlete.

KLONDIKE NEWS April 1, 1898

A. N. KITTELSEN

Dr. A. N. Kittelsen, pioneer of the Northland and one of the organizers of the first recorder of the Nome Recording district, Seward peninsula in 1898, died at Nome September 3, 1926, a victim of cancer of the stomach.

He resided on the Seward peninsula ever since the mining camp of Nome was discovered up to the time death called him, save for an occasional trip to the states. As a government doctor he located at Golovin Bay some two years before Nome gold discovery was made. The three original discoverers, Lindeberg, Bryntesen, and Lindbloom, who set out from Golovin Bay for what was afterward named the Nome district, found gold on Anvil Creek; returned to Golovin Bay, and made up a party of seven, themselves included, the number required to form a recording district. Dr. Kittelsen was chosen as a member of the party and consequently was among those who located on Anvil Creek.

Dr. Kittelsen came outside late last spring, and went to Mayo Brothers' Institute for an operation. Operating surgeons held out slight hope of his recovery. He insisted, however, that if he must die, he wished to pass over the Last Great Divide in the Bering Sea city that had so long been his home. He took passage on the last northbound trip of the steamer Victoria and had to be taken aboard ship in a stretcher. He stood the trip, but passed on soon after reaching Nome.

Dr. Kittelsen was clerk of the district court, as well as being concerned in mining operations, when taken by death. He was 57 years of age and is survived by a grieving widow.

ALASKA WEEKLY, Sept. 17, 1926

VICTOR KLEINSCHMIDT

Victor Kleinschmidt, one of the pioneer mining operators of this district, is dead, his charred remains having been discovered in his cabin of his cabin on the Niggerhead association, near Olnes, last Saturday.

Victor Kleinschmidt was an early arrival in Alaska, having resided in Valdez and other coastal town before prior to his coming to the interior in the very early days of the gold rush. He was engaged in the laundry business in Valdez and established in the same business here when he first arrived. He later entered mining, first establishing on Fairbanks creek. When Dome came into prominence as a producer he was successful in staking association on the flats, retaining large interests in the Niggerhead and other association which proved to be heavy producers. Royalties from his holding gave him a stake, but this was lost in subsequent years through personal working of the ground. He died virtually destitute save for properties that could not be mined profitably.

Ill health and approaching blindness had seriously hampered and worried him in recent years and may have led to suicide.

FAIRBANKS DAILY NEWS-MINER, Mar. 23, 1925

JOHN KLONOS

Klonos is from the sunny land of Greece. He was born on Aegean Islands, May 6, 1871. He first came to Alaska in 1896, landing in Juneau where he remained for some time. John is a miner by occupation and has been in almost all the camps in Alaska. He came to Anchorage in 1916 and still makes his home

there. Before joining the Igloo here he was a member in Iditarod and later went to Fairbanks.
ANCHORAGE WEEKLY TIMES, Jan. 31, 1918

SAM KOHN

Sam Kohn, a pioneer of Alaska since 1884, died Wednesday morning March 13 at St. Ann's Hospital.

He had lived in Alaska for the past 35 years and in Juneau, off and on, for the past 20 years. He had prospected in Cassiar, near Wrangell and Juneau, and other Alaskan towns. He represented the old school of prospectors and pioneers whose latchstring was always on the outside.

His sister, Mrs. Alice Foster, survives in Cody, WY.
WRANGELL SENTINEL, March 21, 1918

MARION KOSKEY

Mrs. Marion Koskey died at 6:20 o'clock last evening succumbing to an attack of acute intestinal indigestion that claimed her within fourteen hours after the disease asserted itself.

. She was the mother of four minor children: Sylvia aged 15; Axel aged 13; Harold aged 11; and Lulu aged 8 years. Mr. Koskey was killed by a rockslide in the Ebner mine during the fall of 1903. Besides the children, Mrs. Koskey is survived by a sister, Mrs. Manda Koskey, who resides in this city;.

Left penniless by the death of her husband, hers was one continual struggle–in which she succeeded in educating her loved ones and bringing them up to love and care for her.

Mrs. Koskey was born in Finland on December 27, 1873, and was 38 years, two months and two days old.
WEEKLY ALASKA DISPATCH, March 2, 1912

AXEL KRONQUIST

Alex Kronquist was born in Finland on September 3, 1870. When 17 years old, he came to America and was employed in the copper mines in Michigan. He came to Douglas 28 years ago and worked for the Treadwell Company. He served for two terms on the city council and was Chief of the fire department for several years Axel Kronquist died on Wednesday at St. Anns Hospital in Juneau. He was married in Douglas and his wife and seven children survive him. The children are Rangner, age 24, a student at Whitman College; Mrs. Lorena B. Morris of Ellensburg, Washington; Lily employed in Tacoma; Saimie, Arnie, Enne, and Glen at home. His father is still living in Finland, a brother Fred Kronquist, resides in Douglas and another brother, Eno, is in Michigan. Mrs. Arne Shudshift of Douglas is a cousin.

DOUGLAS ISLAND NEWS & STROLLER'S WEEKLY, June 29, 1929

FATHER B. LAFORTUNE

Father B. LaFortune, pioneer Catholic missionary among Eskimos in North Alaska, arrived   in Fairbanks recently by PAA [Pan American Airlines] from Nome for hospitalization at St. Joseph's.

It is Father LaFortune's first sickness and his first long trip away from Nome since he arrived in 1903. Kotzebue has hitherto been the extreme point of his travels. His main ministry in Alaska has been with the Eskimos and he has been associated with those of the Seward Peninsula area ever since his arrival in the Territory.

Father LaFortune was born 78 years ago in French Canada. He studied in both Canada and the United States, and holds a degree in mathematics from the Sorbonne in Paris. He is reputed to be the best Eskimo speaker of any white man in Alaska.

Father LaFortune led a rugged life in Alaska. He always drove his own dogs and holds the record for the run from Teller to Nome–95 miles in 9 hours. Since 1925 he has spent most of his time on King Island.

JESSEN'S WEEKLY, August 8, 1947

ARTHUR LANG   (See Vol. 2)

Mr. Lang was born in Ontario, Canada, September 24,

1859, and when about eighteen years of age went to the then Territory of Washington, where he resided until he came to Alaska. In 1908 he married Miss Pauline de Koslowski.

Mr. Lang first came North in 1897 when he visited Southeastern Alaska, where he remained for several months. He returned to Seattle and later joined the rush to Nome, where he remained for some time. Again returning to Seattle he accepted a position in the office of the City Comptroller, in which position he remained until he came to Valdez in 1904 to take the position of cashier in the banking department of the Valdez Bank &Mercantile Co. In 1913 he was appointed Clark of the District Court.

Arthur Lang died at his home in Valdez on March 10th, after an illness of several weeks. He is survived by his wife, and by a brother, William Lang of Vancouver, B. C., and a sister, Mrs. S. A. Hemple of Valdez and Seattle.

PATHFINDER, March 1924

JOHN PETER LAUMEISTER

John Peter Laumeister was elected to succeed himself at the last election for city councilmen. He is prominently known as the fighting member of the council. That is he is ever ready do so his best for the people and for the progress and development of Skagway. He and his brother conduct the largest butchering business in the north. He is ever found in the front rank of workers whenever Skagway's interests are to be served.

DAILY ALASKAN, Feb. 19, 1899

WALTER W. LIGGETT

Walter W. Liggett, who has been writing for Plain Talk magazine, has succeeded the late George Daniel Ehton as editor of the publication.

The new editor of Plain Talk began has career in journalism in Alaska. He was editor of the Skagway Daily Alaskan for about two years when he was just out of college. Later he was a member of a White Pass train crew at Skagway. He married Miss Norma

Ask in Juneau on December 2, 1900.

Mr. Liggett left Skagway for his old home State of Minnesota and became a reporter and then special writer on the St. Paul Dispatch. For a time he was publicity agent for the Nonpartisan League in Minnesota. For several years he has been writing special articles for magazines and newspaper syndicates.

THE DAILY ALASKA EMPIRE, July 19, 1930

FRED LILJEGREN

Fred Liljegren called "the father of the blue fox industry on Prince William Sound," passed away from a stroke of apoplexy. He was born in Gotland, Sweden, January 24, 1860 [?]. He first came to the United States in 1881, and settled in California. In 1889 he came to Alaska, and for five years was employed at Odiak, near the site of the present town of Cordova, as captain on a cannery tender. Mr. Liljegren saw the possibilities of blue fox ranching.

In 1895 he put blue fox on Story island, about fifty miles from Cordova, and had continuously resided there up to the time of his death. He had made a fine success of the fox raising business, and his success led others to follow his example.

Mr. Liljegren was a widower. He is survived by three children: Charles W. Liljegren of Cordova; Mrs. Amanda Bennett and John E. Liljegren, of Story Island.

ALASKA WEEKLY, May 15, 1925; THE PATHFINDER, June 17, 1925

DANIEL LINDEBORG

Daniel Lindeborg, pioneer settler of the Hyder district and the man who more than any other was responsible for the foundation of the town of Hyder, passed away in Vancouver Tuesday, according to telegraphic advices received by local business associates.

Mr. Lindeborg came to this country about the year 1885 at the age of 19 years and made his home in America continuously during the remaining years of his life. During the greater part of his career he was engaged in mining and it was this predilection which ultimately resulted in his becoming a settler in this district in 1903 or 1904.

After looking over the country, Mr. Lindeborg and his brother, the late Andrew Lindeborg, decided to settle here. Later he took up as a homestead the 79 acre tract of land which comprises the present Lindeborg addition to the Hyder townsite. This was subsequently taken over by the Hyder Townsite Improvements Company of which Mr. Lindeborg and Mrs. J. A. Hall were the founders. He was also interested in the foundation of the Hyder Radio and Telephone Company and the Bank of Hyder, two of the town's most important institutions. He also acquired by the location some of the district's most important mineral properties, including the famous Big Missouri, the Riverside mine, the Forty-Nine, and others of lesser note. These he later disposed of at figures which yielded him a substantial fortune.

Mr. Lindeborg resided here until 1922, when he moved to Vancouver, where he made his home up to the time of his untimely death.

HYDER WEEKLY HERALD, Jan 10, 1931

ED A. LINDMAN

E. A. Lindman, pioneer Wrangell resident, died last Sunday afternoon, July 2, in Wenatchee, according to word received here from his daughter, Mrs. Ken Talmage. The body will be brought north, probably on the Northland, for burial in Wrangell where he had been prominent since 1907.

Ed Lindman had been one of Wrangell's first citizens for many years, arriving here around 1907. During his long residence he had taken an active part in every civic movement, was instrumental in obtaining the establishment of an Elks lodge in Wrangell, and had been one of the wheel horses behind the volunteer fire department.

For years Lindman was Wrangell's undertaker as well as

being interested in various other enterprises. Alone, and in failing health, Ed went south last fall to be with his two daughters in Wenatchee and Seattle.

WRANGELL SENTINEL, July 7, 1944

THOMAS A. LIPPY

Lippy started his career as an iron molder in Pennsylvania. Mr. Lippy early in life became greatly interested in athletics and physical culture, an interest which led him to abandon his trade and 1894 move to Fargo, N.D. where he became associated with the physical development of the Y.M.C.A.

A few years later he was transferred to Seattle, where he was employed as physical director of the Y.M.C.A. In 1896 an injury to his knee forced his retirement from the gymnasium floor.

In 1897 he left Seattle and went to Klondike and was there when the gold rush started. A lucky staking resulted in his returning to Seattle with a small fortune, and he again became active in the industrial and realty development of the city.

On his return to Seattle for the Northland he built a stone house on a large lot at the corner of Boren Avenue and James Street. The home was known in the early days as one of the show places of the city. He lived in this house up to the time his death.

He was connected in an executive capacity at various times with the Seattle Mattress & Upholstering Company, the Harper Hill Brick Company, and the Pacific Products Company, the Northwest Trust & Saving Bank and the Northern Life Insurance Company. He built the Lippy Block at Third Avenue and Columbia Street, and for years has been president of the Seattle General Hospital.

The only time he sought political preference came in 1917 when his friends prevailed upon him to become a candidate for port commissioner in which capacity he served for several years. Mr. Lippy who was 71 years old is survived by his widow, Salome, two brothers, L. W. Lippy of Seattle, and C. H. Lippy of Snohomish, and two sisters, Mrs. L.

E. Ross and Mrs. M. A. Gordon.

ALASKA WEEKLY, Sept. 18, 1931

WILLIAM LOERPABEL

William Loerpabel was born on a farm in Wisconsin of German and Irish parentage, March 14, 1855. At the age of 18 he left home to begin rafting on the Wisconsin River. As a boy of 20 he joined the gold stampede to the Black Hills of South Dakota, while the Indians were still hostile there. Going overland by ox train he arrived in Deadwood in the spring of 1876 when the town consisted only of a few tents and log cabins and before any law was established there. He was a member of the Society of Black Hills Pioneers.

Joining the gold rush to the Klondike he and his party packed their outfit over the White Pass at Skagway, constructed boats at lake Bennet and, continuing on down the Yukon, reached Dawson just after the spring breakup in 1897.

He arrived in Nome in 1899 and in 1900 took his family there. For many years he operated a claim on Iron Creek, about 50 miles from Nome. He was a member of the Pioneers of Alaska.

In 1918 he came to the Outside and since 1921, with his wife, has lived near Edmonds, Wash.

Loerpabel died on August 9, 1938 near Edmonds, Wash. At the age of 83. He is survived by his widow, Sarah, and by his son, William Harrison, a mining engineer, for many years employed by the American Smelting and Refining Co. in Mexico.

ALASKA WEEKLY, Aug. 12, 1938

JOHN LOT (MRS.)

Mrs. John Lot, 94-year-old Peterburg native, was drowned recently when she fell from a float in the northern city, according to word received here yesterday. In spite of the fact that she was removed from the water almost immediately, attempts to restore her life by means of artificial respiration failed.

Both she and her husband, married for the past 51 years, were residents of the Peterburg district before the advent of white men and before the Territory became a possession of the United States.

KETCHIKAN ALASKA CHRONICLE, May 16, 1934

GEORGE J. LOVE

George J. Love was born in Keokuk, Iowa in 1858, and is a son of Judge Love of the Supreme Bench of that state.

He is a graduate of the University of Iowa Law School and is a member of the bar in Alaska. He arrived in Nome in 1900, but moved to Valdez in 1901 where he has since resided. From 1913 to 1922 he held the position of U.S. Commissioner at Valdez.

Mr. Love is the business manager of the Pathfinder of Alaska.

PATHFINDER OF ALASKA, July 23, 1915

MABEL EMILY LOWE   (See Vol. 1)

Mabel Emily, beloved wife of Albert J. Lowe, died in this city on Sunday morning, January 29, from a severe attack of pneumonia. The deceased was born in Chelsea, Mass., in September, 1867. She comes from an old Puritan family on her father's side, her mother's parents being resident of New Foundland.

She was wedded to Mr. Lowe in November, 1886 in Boston, Mass., and three children, Frederick, Marion, and Herbert, are the fruits of their marriage. Previous to coming to Nome to join her husband, Mrs. Lowe and the children resided in New Highlands, Mass. She arrived here in July 1902

NOME SEMI WEEKLY, Feb. 1, 1905

SAMUEL G. LUCAS

Died, at Juneau, Alaska Friday, September 18, 1908, Samuel Lucas, aged 46 years.

Samuel G. Lucas was born in the state of Kansas, and came to Alaska about 12 years ago, locating at Haines where he made his home until the time of his death. For the past ten years he has been associated with Mr. Henry Brie, of this city, in business enterprises at Porcupine, Haines and Douglas. He was a member of the Arctic Brotherhood at Haines, and was well known throughout Southeastern Alaska as one of the foremost business men of the district.

He leaves a wife, to whom he was united about four years ago and who was with him at the time of his death, and three children by a former marriage to mourn his loss. His father and mother, Mrs. and Mrs. David Lucas, are living at Pasadena, California.

THE DOUGLAS ISLAND NEWS, Sept. 23, 1908

IVAN SIMENSON LUKEEN

Gold was first discovered in Alaska on the Anauk river, a tributary of the Kuskokwim river, which joins the latter stream about twenty-five miles below the trading post of Kalamakofisky. The Anauk river was discovered by Ivan Simenson Lukeen in 1832, at which time he built a fort, called Lukeen's fort, on the Kuskokwim river, twenty-five miles above the mouth of the Anauk.

In 1832 the headquarters of the Russian American Trading Company were at Sitka, and supplies were transported from thence to Lukeen's fort by way of Nashagak river, Tic-chic river and lake, and down the Anauk river to the Kuskokwim river and thence upstream twenty-five miles at the fort. In 1837 the yearly supplies were sent in by way of the mouth of the Kuskokwim river, and the old way abandoned now as a summer route and used only the purpose of sending out the mail during the winter by dog teams. It was the only winter route the Russians ever used from any point on the Yukon to the outside (Sitka), and was only abandoned for the purpose after they left the country. It was while on one of these trips in 1832 [?] that the Russians discovered gold on the Anauk, and it is known today as the Yellow river of the Russian. It is not known whether they ever attempted mining on any large scale, or whether they found gold in paying quantities, but it is thought to be the first time or record of gold being found in this country.

Lukeen was born of Russian and Spanish-American Creole parents in the Ross colony in California. He was well educated at the Sitka school, and proved to be an active, energetic and intelligent officer. In 1863 Lukeen ascended the Yukon river from St. Michael to Fort Gibbon, then at Hudson's Bay company trading post, which was built by McMurry, who descended the Porcupine river in 1847. Lukeen was the first man who connected the Pelly river of Campbell and the sea. He returned to St. Michael that fall. In 1866 the Russian garrison at Klamakoff redoubt, in charge of Dementoff, was withdrawn, the United States having purchased Alaska from the Russian. (Ketchikan Mining Journal, & Seward Gateway, Jan 27, 1906)

VALDEZ NEWS, Feb. 3, 1906

SAMUEL S. LYNCH

Samuel S. Lynch, 69 years old, Indian and World War veteran and Seattle resident since 1890, died Monday at his home, 1902 19th Avenue, after a long illness.

Mr. Lynch was a native of Elizabeth, Pa. He served with the First U.S. Cavalry during the Indian uprisings in Montana and Wyoming as a private, corporal and later as a sergeant, and for a number of years on the police force at Helena, Mont. He came to Seattle in 1890 and made his home here until 1897 when he went to Valdez, Alaska. He returned in 1898 to enlist in the Spanish-American War, but arrived a day late. During the World War he served as sergeant in the 87th Repair Squadron of the Aviation Section.

Mr. Lynch was employed in the utility department at Fort Lewis in 1919. From there he was transferred to the post office here where he was watchman until his retirement more than a year ago. He was a member of the University Post No. 11, American Legion.

Mr. Lynch is survived by his widow Mrs. Mary Lynch; two daughters, Mrs. Edith DeWolfe of Seattle and Rolland Guernsey of Stanwood; and a son, Samuel S. Lynch, Jr. of San Francisco.

ALASKA WEEKLY, Mar. 23, 1934

THOMAS R. LYONS

Judge Thomas R. Lyons, 74, widely known in Pacific northwest and Alaskan legal circles died here last Saturday after a lingering illness

Lyons was Assistant United States District Attorney in Juneau from 1900 to 1903 and was Federal Judge there from 1909 to 1913. He was associated for many years with L. P. Shackleford, Juneau attorney of that time, in the practice of law.

WRANGELL SENTINEL, Jan. 10, 1941

DONALD MACGREGOR

The following article, from the Ottawa Journal, is bound to have an appeal for all Yukoners, particularly those of the early days who will read with regret of the passing of Colonel Donald MacGregor, "Father of the Yukon."

Colonel MacGregor is dead, His passing may mean little in the present generation of Canadians, yet Donald MacGregor in every cubit of his six feet and two inches of stature was a great son of Canada, one of the most gallant and picturesque of all the brave and colorful figures that Glengarry has given to our history. Born 88 years ago, Donald MacGregor had in him the best blood of those Scotsman whose intrepid hearts have carried them to the far ends of the earth, and in 1864, three years before Confederation, and long before Donald Smith and Mount Stephen dreamed of conquering the Rockies, he was on the Pacific coast. He was among the dauntless few that went through the Caribou gold rush; 40 years later–when more than 60 years old–he went to the Klondike in 1899 via St. Michael. He became known as the "Father of the Yukon." He edited a newspaper in Dawson city; he sat in the parliamentary press gallery in the spacious days when Blake and Macdonald crossed swords; and he heard Sir John deliver his unforgettable "A British subject I will die." oration.

In the Yukon, Donald MacGregor became almost a legendary figure. He was famous as the unrelenting foe of graft; he fought transgressors in high places and in low; and on more than one occasion his tact and his courage put down open rebellion. When he left the Yukon the Yukon Morning World paid him this moving tribute:

"'Among the outgoing passengers tomorrow will be the redoubtable and always-to-be-remembered Colonel Donald MacGregor, hero of a hundred battles, friend of all mankind, and fairy godfather to every child in the territory; and with his going Dawson will lose a character unique and greatly beloved.'"

STROLLER'S, June 18, 1927

HANS MADSEN

Stampeding from San Francisco to the Cassiar diggings, on the Canadian territory, after the discovery of gold there had been sent out by McCullough and Tibbitts in 1873-74, Hans Madsen was numbered among those who took passage on sailing craft for Fort Wrangell, near the mouth of the Stikine river, the following summer. Madsen had followed the mining game in Colorado and Montana and was ready for anything when the news of the discovery came to his ears.

When he reached Fort Wrangell, then one of the two places in Alaska where white men were located, the territory was under the control of the military forces entirely. From Wrangell he went up the Stikine river to the Cassiar diggings, where he prospected. The Cassiar strike was not the first to be made in the Stikine district, for placer mining had been going on for ten years or so on the Stikine proper.

Atlin was visited by Madsen, and when the Klondike was

discovered he was among those who joined in the rush over Chilcoot to seek a fortune in that district. In Dawson he mined until the news of the Fairbanks discoveries came, and he stampeded again. In Fairbanks he now is, and in Fairbanks he intends to stay. His extensive placer holding are being looked after with a vigor that is remarkable for a pioneer 71 years of age.

ALASKA HISTORICAL LIBRARY, Biographical File
(Undated)

JOSEPH ANDREW MAGILL

Joseph Andrew Magill, well-known canneryman of Anchorage, Alaska, passed away Tuesday evening [Sept. 10, 1929] in the Cobb Building surgery from a gunshot wound inflicted by himself.

Mrs. Magill, widow of the departed, had gone into the kitchen for a moment. She had scarcely turned her back when a short rang out behind her, and she turned to see her husband stagger and fall to the floor, a bullet wound in his head.

Magill had arrived from Anchorage a short time ago, and was on the verge of a serious nervous breakdown, incident to the strenuous work of the season and a very successful salmon pack, the biggest he had ever had. Ever since he came South he had been under the watchful care of Mrs. Magill, as he had threatened to end it all. Mr. Magill's attorney, Mr. Brackett, says Magill's finances were in excellent condition.

Mr. Magill was the president, general manager and controlling owner of the Alaska General Fisheries, with a cannery at Anchorage and office in Seattle.

As a youth 18 years of age, he ran away from his Tacoma home and joined the stampede to the Klondike. That was in 1898. He made some money on this venture. He was in the thick of the Tonopah boom, and then returned to Alaska, making Cordova his headquarters for some years while the Copper River and Northwestern Railroad was under construction. He had been a resident of the Cook Inlet country for a number of years.

Joseph A. Magill was 52 years of age. Besides his widow, he is survived by two sisters, Mrs. Mary C. Robinson and Mrs. Anna Fisher, and two brother, Johnson and William A. Magill, all of Tacoma.

THE ALASKA WEEKLY, Sept. 13, 1929

JULES A. MARION

Mr. Jules A. Marion, well known old Yukoner, died last Sunday morning at his home in Sedro-Wooley. Mr. Norman Marion of Seattle, a cousin, was practically the only Northerner present. Mr. Marion leaves a wife and one daughter, Nora, who is a student at the Holy Names Academy in Seattle.

Mr. Marion went north before the days of the Klondike rush. He went into the Cassiar country and Dease Lake for the Hudson Bay Company early in the nineties. In 1897 he went to Dawson and in 1899 worked for the A.C. Company as superintendent for the mail service from Eagle in Tanana. He later lived in Fairbanks and had headquarters for some time at Tanana where he was in the employ of the N.C. Company.

After leaving Alaska, he bought a farm in Alberta where he lived for four years and then moved to Sedro-Wooley where he has lived since. He was in the employ of the Northern Hospital there until his illness.

At one time before going North he went with Buffalo Bill to France, Italy, Germany, England, and other European countries with a group of Sioux Indians from North Dakota.

STROLLER'S WEEKLY, Feb. 16, 1929

V. L. MARION

V. L. Marion went to the Northland in 1898, joining in the gold stampede to the Klondike. From Dawson, he went to Nome, arriving there with the rush of 1900. Here he engaged in mining for a time, and then set out on a prospecting trip which took him to the Kobuk country. While on this trip he visited the Siberian coast to take a look at the mineral possibilities of that remote land.

During the years 1903 and 1904 Marion mined in the Nizina country, Copper river valley. Then he passed a few years in prospecting at the head of the Tanana river and in the White river country. Marion had the first contract for transportation on the Alaska Railroad, then operated by the Alaskan Engineering Commission. During his years of mining, prospecting and fur trading in the Northland, Marion has been all along the coast from Seattle to the Kobuk. He is the president of the Copper River Fur Trading Company and the owner of the Silver Fox Ranching Company.
ALASKA WEEKLY, Aug. 16, 1929

KNUTE THEODORE MARKSTROM
Knute Theodore Markstrom, well known resident of Juneau, died at the Home May 16th. He was born in Sweden Feb. 2, 1852, and came to the United States in 1868, arriving in Alaska the same year. From 1891 to 1896 Markstrom spent in South Africa, returning to Alaska to mine and prospect.
ARROWHEAD, May 25, 1935

DAVID MARTIN
David Martin was born in England 63 years ago and moved to San Francisco with his parents when a small child. He first came to Alaska in 1869, landing at Wrangell and going to the Cassair country, from there by way of the Stickine river in 1871. He returned to Alaska, and lived subsequently at Wrangell, Haines and Sitka, at which place he was interested in business with his father.
In 1881 he came to Juneau and established a general merchandise store where Winter & Pond are now located. He did a big business for a number of years, but later gave it up. Since that time he has been engaged in the fur business in Juneau. He had lived here continuously since 1881, with the exception of one trip made to Nome where he spent about a year.
Before coming to Alaska he and a brother were engaged

in the theatrical business in San Francisco.

Martin died April 3, 1916 at St. Ann hospital from a complication of organic troubles. (Daily Empire, April 3)

THE DOUGLAS ISLAND NEWS, April 5, 1916

JESSE C. MARTIN

Jesse C. Martin died at his home in San Diego, California December 22, 1928 with the flu. He was 57 years eight months old, and was born in Illinois. He is survived by his wife, Ada Martin; his daughter, Bernice, both of San Diego; a brother, Walter Martin who lives in Chico, California; and a sister, Mrs. John W. Carter of Lambert, Miss. He was a member of South Dakota Elks.

Jesse Martin joined the stampede to the Klondike in 1897 and in 1900 or thereabouts, went to Valdez, Alaska, where he made his home continuously until he came south some ten years ago, and located in San Diego. Most of the time during his long residence in Valdez, he was the agent of steamship companies. For a few years before he came south to live, he was engaged in the salt salmon industry in Prince William Sound.

ALASKA WEEKLY, Dec. 28, 1928

J. T. MARTIN

News of the death of Capt. J. T. Martin, Alaskan pioneer and police chief of Juneau in 1914, reached Charles E. Naghel here through a letter from E. R. Jaeger of Pasadena, California, in which city the former Juneauite was residing.

According to the letter written by Mr. Jaeger, the aged man had shown signs of failing on New Year's Day, at which time Mr. Jaeger had visited him.

The funeral which was attended by Mr. and Mrs. Jaeger, John Scott, also a former resident at Juneau, and about a dozen G. A. R. members and their families was held in Pasadena on January 3.

ALASKA PRESS, Jan. 25, 1935

M. E. MARTIN

M. E. Martin may justly be styled the father of the city of Ketchikan, being the first white man to locate here. Around his home has grown what is now known as the "First City in Alaska." It was August 15, 1885 that this hardy pioneer landed here from the steamer Ancon, commanded at that time by Captain James Carrol. This was more than twenty-one years ago and great changes have come to pass since that early day. Three years after landing here Mr. Martin located a saltery at this point. Out of this start finally grew a store where furs were bought from Indians and for a long time Ketchikan was one of the best trading points in Alaska. Circumstances contributed to make Ketchikan a place of importance. The growth of the town made the founder well to do in worldly goods–a fate which does not always follow the pioneer.

Mr. and Mrs. Martin left here in October to spend the winter in Portland and the family residence is now occupied by Fremont King and family.

ALASKA MINING JOURNAL, Jan. 1907

JAMES MASON, (SKOOKUM JIM, See Vol 1)

Skookum Jim, more exactly speaking James Mason, one of the discoverers of gold on Bonanza creek, in the Dawson camp, died several days ago at Carcross, according to the Dawson News of recent date.

Skookum Jim passed away at about the age of 62 years. His only child, Miss Daisy Mason of Seattle, came North several weeks ago on hearing of her father's illness, and remained with him until the end. He was buried, as he long had desired, beside the grave of his long-time friend, the famous Yukon pioneer missionary the Right Rev. Bishop William Carpenter Bompas.

Skookum Jim, George Carmack, and Tagish Charley made the discovery on Bonanza August 17, 1896. Skookum Jim was on the creek two or three years after which he returned to his old home district in the Tagish lake country and made his home at

Carcross. He spent much time prospecting in that country and last winter was on a stampede to the headwaters of the Liard. He was taken ill this spring on his return, and was in the Whitehorse hospital for some time.

IDITAROD PIONEER, August 19, 1916

JOSEPHINE MASON

Josephine Mason was born in Towanda, Pennsylvania, January 4, 1865, and came to Wrangell with her husband, the late Julius A. Mason in 1904.

She was a charter member of the Eastern Star and American Legion Auxiliary here and was one of the founders of the Wrangell Women's Civic Club. She was an active member of the Presbyterian church and through the years had taken active interest in civic and social affairs of Wrangell.

Josephine Mason, Wrangell pioneer woman and well known in all southeast Alaska, died Monday, June 11 in Seattle. Surviving are two sons, Julius W. Mason of Wrangell and Eugene H. Mason of Seattle and three grandchildren, Gordon and Kenneth Mason, sons of Mr. and Mrs. Julius Mason, and Carolyn, daughter of Mr. and Mrs. Eugene Mason.

THE WRANGELL SENTINEL, June 15, 1915

BERT MAYCOCK

Captain Bert Maycock is dead. Word of Maycock's death was brought to Juneau today with additional information that death occurred apparently Wednesday morning.

Captain Maycock was aboard his motorboat Pheasant, which was anchored at Windfall Bay on Seymour Canal when he died. Cause of death as yet, is not known. Captain Tom Smith, a long time friend of the deceased's left today for Windfall Bay to return with the Pheasant and her captain's body.

Friends here report that Maycock was approximately 55 years old, and had not been feeling any too well for several months past. His last visit to Juneau was during the middle of

January this year when he was here to load supplies.

Maycock was born in Pennsylvania, and came to Washington in the late 1890's. He engaged in logging there for a couple of years before coming north.

When Maycock first came to Alaska he settled on Nevada Creek where he was employed in mining operations. When the company he worked for finally moved out, he stayed on with a couple of friends and worked properties in his own interest.

In 1913 he bought Windfall Island and started fur farming. Several years later he developed logging interests on Seymour Canal which he followed until he was burned out. Following the fire he came to Juneau and went to work on the gasboat Pheasant, which at that time operated under the mail contract between Juneau and Petersburg. Later he became part owner of the Pheasant and finally owner. In recent years he had been chartering his boat out to hunting parties and prospectors.

Last fall he left with two prospectors and two trappers aboard. It is believed that one of the prospectors was with him shortly before he died, that probably they had gone to Windfall Bay to pick up the trappers and bring them back to Juneau.

Juneau friends of the dead man believe that he is survived by at least one brother and two sisters, all living in Pennsylvania, probably in the vicinity of Erie.

THE ALASKA PRESS (Juneau), April 12, 1935

WILLIAM JENNINGS BRYAN McAULIFFE

Dr. William Jennings Bryan McAuliffe, M.D. died suddenly yesterday morning of a heart ailment. Dr. McAuliffe was born 38 years ago in Louisville, Kentucky to a prominent bluegrass family. He attended public schools in his native city, and later graduated from the University of Louisville Medical School. After a short while in private practice, he moved to San Francisco and became surgeon there for the United States Public Health Service. Six years ago he was appointed surgeon aboard the Coast Guard cutter Northland, stationed in Alaska waters.

After a year aboard the vessel he assumed charge of the federal hospital in Juneau, and held that post for five years. Early this year he returned to private practice in the capital city.

Surviving the doctor in Juneau are his wife, Mrs. Hazel McAuliffe, and small daughter, Joan.

THE ALASKA PRESS, July 5, 1935

ANGUS G. MCBRIDE

Angus C. McBride, aged about 84 years, died in Seattle last Tuesday. Mr. McBride, in company with Fred Henshaw, started the Fort Wrangell News, the first edition being published on the 8th day of June 1898. Mr. McBride also practiced law at Fort Wrangell for the duration of the time he was there.

Making a trip to Douglas in early October, Mr. McBride returned to Fort Wrangell and moved the printing plant to Douglas, where with Charles Hopp he started the Douglas Island News. The first issue came out on November 23, 1898, the day before Thanksgiving. Mr. McBride remained in Douglas until about 1903, when he sold his interest in the Douglas Island News to Charlie Hopp, going to Nome, where he acted as United States Commissioner until he removed to Seattle, where he remained until his death.

After going to Seattle he was named assistant prosecutor for King county, and was universally admired by all who was acquainted with him. A man of deep convictions he took an enthusiastic stand on local questions, often to the detriment of the paper.

On our shelves today are files of the Fort Wrangell News, probably the only ones in existence. They carry the name of McBride & Henshaw at the masthead and are devoted to an enthusiastic description of the town and surrounding district. We also have several case racks with the name "McBride & Henshaw, Fort Wrangell" on them.

Mr. McBride left a widow to survive him.

THE STROLLER'S WEEKLY, April 15, 1932

JAMES McCLOSKY

James McClosky, 69-year-old resident of Juneau and chief jailer in the capital city, died in a Portland, Oregon clinic.

Well-known throughout the Territory, McClosky was very active in civic life in Juneau, having served a term as chief of police in 1925-26 and also having been many times a member of the city council. Born in Madison, Wisconsin, he came north from his former home in Montana in 1896 and remained there since with exception of two years spent in the Atlin country as a miner.

He was active in the Pioneer lodge having served as a trusty to the Pioneer home and was a member of the Elks and Knights of Columbus orders.

Five immediate relatives survive him: his widow and a son, John of Juneau; a son, Gene of Albuquerque, New Mexico; a brother, John of Juneau; two sisters, Mrs. M. J. Tory of Milwaukee, Wisconsin, and Mrs. Catherine Lynch of Sioux city, Iowa.

KETCHIKAN ALASKA CHRONICLE, Sept. 20, 1934

M. F. McCONKEY

M. F. McConkey, a prospector and miner known throughout the west, died of Pneumonia, April 2nd, at Loomis, Washington. The deceased crossed the summit in 1883, and the following season was one of the party which first discovered gold on Forty Mile creek. He did not however remain long in the interior but returned to California and in 1890 went to Okanogan and located and developed several quartz claims in Horse Spring coulee, and he was in a fair way to secure a fortune.

He was born in Ohio in 1850 and in 1876 moved to New Mexico, where he was the pioneer of the Black range, and sold his milling property to a syndicate including Colonel Robert Ingersoll, Senator Plummer of Kansas and others, for $80,000. He was proprietor of the stage line between San Marcial and Chloride, and on one of his trips killed two masked highwaymen who attempted to hold up his stage. He leaves a married sister in Seattle.

THE ALASKA MINING RECORD, April 21, 1897

DUNCAN MCCORMICK

Duncan was born in Port Huron, Michigan on the 10th day of March, 1862. He first came to Alaska in the year 1900, landing in Juneau in April. Mr. McCormick came to Anchorage October 15, 1915, and has lived here ever since. He is a carpenter by trade and a miner and prospector by occupation at the present time. He has friends and relatives at Cass City, Michigan.

ANCHORAGE WEEKLY TIMES, Nov 22, 1917

ANDREW MCCRACKEN

Andrew McCracken, a real, sourdough, who was among those who attended the picnic, on the Umpqua River near Roseburg, Ore., demonstrated to the crowd's satisfaction that he could still pan pay gravel in record time. Mr. McCracken went to the Klondike in 1897 and remained in Klondike and Alaska twenty-seven years. He mined and prospected in the Tanana country twelve years. He resides on his poultry ranch four miles south of Roseburg, on the Pacific Highway, and specializes in fancy egg production. "I have explored the idea that a man can't quit mining after having followed that line all his life until past sixty-five years of age and then embark in another line of business and make a success of it," said Mr. McCracken. He is making good in the poultry business.

ALASKA WEEKLY, Sept. 13, 1929

JAMES McDONALD   (Charles Grant)

One of the most violent deaths that a person could meet was that which overtook James McDonald, a pioneer of Juneau, on Saturday morning last. Mr. McDonald in company with William Prior and two natives, was out on a prospecting trip in the vicinity of Seward city. After having been out for some time

the men became separated, but not so far but that each could hear the other. All at once an outcry from McDonald fell upon the ears of his companions and they ran to learn the cause of alarm, when they were horror-stricken to see McDonald in a hand-to-hand conflict with a huge bear, and before anything could be done or assistance rendered in any way poor McDonald had received a death blow from the paw of the powerful animal. The brain was penetrated by the claws of the brute and several other bruises were found upon the body. It is supposed that he came upon the bear and her two cubs before he was aware of it, and not being armed he was unable to defend himself in any way. Mr. McDonald was fifty-one years of age last winter and had lived in Juneau for several years, having come here from Leadville, Col. His real name was Charles Grant and he was a distant relative of Gen. Grant. His boyhood's home was in Pennsylvania. His remains were brought to Juneau on Tuesday afternoon last, and the funeral occurred on Wednesday under the auspices of Seward post No. 36 G. A.R.
ALASKA SEARCHLIGHT, July 20, 1895

R. D. MCDONALD

R.D. McDonald was born in Nova Scotia on the 15th day of September, 1862. He came to Alaska in the year 1898, arriving in Skagway in the spring. After visiting many of the camps in the territory he finally settled in Anchorage in 1914. Mr. McDonald is a bridge carpenter by occupation but has spent much of his time in Alaska in the hills looking for the glittering sands. His relatives reside at Smithers, B.C.
ANCHORAGE WEEKLY TIMES, Feb. 14, 1918

P. W. MCDONNELL ("PATTY")

P. W. McDonnell owner of the McDonnell Rooms and one of the camps most familiar figures, passed away in Stewart General Hospital Wednesday.

"Patty" McDonnell, as he was familiarly known

throughout the length and breath of the North, also, possessing the distinction of being one of the early day pioneers of Alaska and the Yukon and a member of the valiant band of trailblazers who braved the stormy Chilkoot en route to Dawson in 1896.

After several years in the famous Yukon camp, he joined the gold rush to Nome, arriving there in the spring of 1900. During the intervening years, he resided at various periods in Fairbanks, Ruby, Long City, Valdez, and other points. Coming to the Portland Canal District about the year 1919, he became for a time a resident of Stewart and operated a roadhouse on American Creek for a while before taking up residence in Hyder and engaging in the hotel business, in which he continued up to the time of his death.

Patty McDonnell was a native of Ireland but came to the United States at the age of six. He was a man of quiet habits and unostentatious ways. He is survived by one son, W. R. McDonnell.

HYDER WEEKLY HERALD, Nov. 26, 1927

CHARLES M. MCGRATH (MRS.)

Mrs. McGrath died in Portland, Oregon on March 4th after a long illness. She is survived by her daughter Mrs. Jack Conway, Sitka, Miss Agnes Manning, a sister, and a brother James Manning, both of Juneau.

Mrs. McGrath had lived in Alaska for ten years before coming to Sitka, where her husband founded the present Conway Ganty store & dock, and became a prominent property owner. Both were well known throughout Southeastern Alaska. Mr. McGrath passed away several years ago.

Mrs. McGrath continued the business in Sitka for some time until it was taken over by Jack Conway and Pros Ganty somewhat over a year ago. Mrs. McGrath then spent much of her time in the south because of her health.

THE ARROWHEAD (Sitka), March 16, 1935

CHARLES M. McGRATH

The sudden death of Charles M. McGrath at Sitka Saturday deprived Alaska of the service of one of her best and squarest citizens. He was an Alaskan in all that the term implies. He was a young man in his twenties when news of the Klondike strike swept over the country and like thousands of other young men, he was caught in the resulting stampede and never quit until he reached Dawson. It did not take him long to decide that his future home would be in the North, but he quickly decided that he would follow the pursuit that he knew best and he became the Alaskan representative of one of the strongest wholesale grocery houses of the North Pacific, locating in Juneau. Here he brought his bride and here his daughter was born. About fifteen years ago Mr. McGrath went to Sitka and entered in business for himself. He was a success as the representative of a wholesale house in Alaska and he succeeded as a merchant at Sitka.

WRANGELL SENTINEL, March 11, 1926

MAY MCINTOSH

On Tuesday afternoon last at the Columbus hospital in Seattle death released the soul of Mrs. Archibald McIntosh from its pain racked body. May McIntosh four years ago was honored by her Pioneer sister to preside at their meetings as "Lady of the Golden North."

Archibald McIntosh, husband of the deceased, is well known to early day Yukon Pioneers. He too was honored four years ago when elected Chief of the Alaska-Yukon Pioneers of Seattle. A Pioneer of 1898, he went North in charge of the Government hospitals of the Yukon Field Force, and later was connected with the White Pass & Yukon Railway in an executive capacity.

Mrs. May McIntosh was born in Biglow, Kansas, almost fifty-nine years ago; during her life she was prominent in social, church and charitable affairs.

Mrs. McIntosh was a member of the Queen City Chapter No. 148 Eastern Star, also a Past Lady of the Golden North, and, Past

Master, United Artisans Seattle Assembly.
ALASKA WEEKLY, May 20, 1932

BRUCE MCKAY

On April 28th, one of the best known of the Alaskan navigators in the early days, Bruce McKay, died at the Sailors Snug Harbor in New York City.

Captain Bruce McKay commanded many vessels known to the old-timers, and had the good fortune to be listed with those skippers who never lost a ship. At various times he commanded the old Dora on the westward run, where he was assigned for many years, the Excelsior, the Seward, and the Bertha. He had served also as pilot for a long period of time on other vessels plying in southeastern and southwestern Alaska. He was one of the most capable and best navigators that ever sailed in the north.

He leaves one brother, Captain Archie W. McKay of this city, employed by the U.S. Shipping Board.
CORDOVA DAILY TIMES, May 4, 1922

DUNCAN MCKINNON

Duncan McKinnon, the leading merchant and property owner at Wrangel, died at that place last Saturday of apoplexy, aged 52 years. Mr. McKinnon was a Scotchman by birth, but lived most of his life in Alaska. He was a sergeant in the United States army when this country took formal possession of Alaska. When his term of enlistment expired he engaged in the Indian trade with headquarters at Wrangel, where he has been for twenty-three years. Duncan McKinnon was well known in the Stikine river country.
DAILY ALASKAN, Jan. 18, 1900

JOHN MCKINNON

During the civil war in the sixties, being then a California pioneer and miner, he joined the First Regiment of California Volunteers, and served three years and was honorably mustered

out at Fort Humboldt, California, after which he enlisted in the Ninth U. S. Infantry, stationed at the Presidio, and on the transfer of Alaska to the United States in 1867, was present with his company at Sitka, and hoisted the stars and stripes for the first time, as the indicator of future possession of the Territory of Alaska by the Republic of the United States.
ALASKA NEWS, Feb. 7, 1895

P. C. McMULLEN

P.C. McMullen, former Mayor, councilman and one of the leaders of the Democratic Party in the Third Division, merchant, died in his sleep last night as a result apparently of heart trouble.

McMullen was born in Texas and lived in Nome in the early days. He came to Seward over 20 years ago and was employed by Brown and Hawkins for a number of years and then established his own grocery store. He was to have left tomorrow for Fairbanks to attend the meeting of the Territorial Board of Education of which he was a member.

Survivors are his wife, young daughter, and son.
THE DAILY ALASKAN EMPIRE, May 13, 1938

SADIE MAY McMULLEN

Sadie May McMullen died in Fairbanks [?] Alaska in September 1914. She was born October 11, 1874 in Manitoba, Canada. The earlier years of her life were spent on a farm but at the age of 15 she moved with her parents to Seattle, Washington. In the year of 1896 she came North to Juneau and the following year she went to Dawson, mushing over the Chilkoot pass in the early days of the Klondike strike. After spending the winter in Dawson she went Outside to see her parents again, but soon returned to Dawson. Two years later she took the steamer down river to Nome, and the next year went on to Seattle. Being unable to resist the call of the North she again departed for Dawson in 1902 and that winter mushed across country to Fairbanks. This was a hard trip as the weather was cold and the trail unbroken most of the way.

After several years in Fairbanks she went to Iditarod, where on September 20th, 1910, she was married to Peter McMullen. Today is the fourth anniversary of what she has often repeated to her friends as the happiest four years of her life, most of which has been spent in this place.

FAIRBANKS DAILY TIMES, Sept. 22, 1914

SAMUEL McNEICE

Samuel McNeice was born in Heriday, Scotland, June 14, 1867. He came to Canada in 1883 where he worked on the Canadian Pacific railway in construction work three years. He went to Duluth, Minn., in 1885, where he was engaged with the Duluth Iron Range railway in the construction period. He then went to Dawson in the Klondike rush in 1898, He was in Fairbanks for years; later went to Valdez in 1909. He pioneered with others as a settler at Anchorage in 1916, and has made his home in this section ever since.

For the last two years, he was foreman in charge of a section of the Alaska Railroad in Wasilla.

McNeice died May 24, 1933 in Anchorage, Alaska. He is survived by his widow Mrs. McNeice, and their daughter May.

ANCHORAGE WEEKLY TIMES, May 25, 1933

DAN MCNEIL

A host of friends today mourned the death of Capt. Dan McNeil, 52 years old, veteran skipper of Alaskan vessels and for many years in the service of the Bureau of Fisheries. He died at Port Townsend, Washington.

Captain McNeil was stricken with a heart attack last week and died at the United States Marine Hospital at Port Townsend. He is survived by his parents in Portland, where it is expected his body will be sent for burial.

For a quarter of a century Captain McNeil had piloted ships from Seattle and Puget Sound ports to the Far North, having been much in demand in recent years as pilot for the yachts of wealthy, big game hunters to Kodiak Island. He formerly was master of floating canneries and cannery tenders in Alaskan waters.

Born in Western Washington, Captain McNeil once worked as reporter for a Seattle newspaper and retained his many friends of the craft and his membership in the Press Club. In his youth he studied medicine as the old College of Physicians and Surgeons in San Francisco. He frequently brought his medical knowledge into play in emergency aboard ship or in remote Alaskan camps.

The mariner was a contributor on occasion to Pacific Motorboat and his verses-"My Herring Choker", "Take Me Back to the Ugashik." "The Doreymen," and others-had a wide popularity among Northlanders.

THE WRANGELL SENTINEL, Jan. 23, 1930

FRED MEEKER

The Yukon Sun of February 2 confirms the telegram published in these columns as to the death of the son of Ezra Meeker, which took place at the Good Samaritan Hospital in Dawson on the evening of the 1st instant. Fred S. Meeker was only in the hospital five days, and died from a severe attack of pneumonia.

The deceased was born in Steilacoom, the oldest town in the state of Washington, 38 years ago. He married Miss Clara Messmore of Portland, Or., who is now in Dawson, and was with him til the last. He leaves no children. The father and Mrs. Roderick McDonald, wife of the Dawson wharf manager of the N. A. T. who is his sister, are also in the city. Other members of the family are in Puyallup, Wash., the former home of the deceased. For the greater part of his life Fred Meeker lived in Puyallup, near Tacoma, and was there associated as junior member with his father in the hop business. They were the most extensive growers and shippers of hops in the world and supplied the London market to a large extent. They sent hops across the continent by trainloads. Fred became one of the foremost hop experts on the Pacific coast, and for two years was in London watching the market and studying hops. He also toured Europe.

Fred Meeker was a skilled chemist and made a specialty of chemistry as applied to the manufacture of beet sugar and took a year's course in that line in California. In the summer of 1898 Mr. Meeker went to Dawson and has since been engaged chiefly in mining. Of late he assisted his father in his Dawson store. The father is one of the pioneers of Puget sound.

DAILY ALASKAN (Skagway), Feb. 19, 1901

MARY HILL MEIER

Mary M. Meier came here from Finland in 1892. In 1894 she was married to John Meier veteran of the civil war. For several years she followed her husband into various camps bearing two children along the way. About 12 years ago she returned to Juneau that her children might have a proper education. She died in Juneau on October 6, 1921.

Her husband, John Meier, and two children, John A. Meier Jr., and Mrs. Clarence Smith of San Pedro survive her. She has a brother, Oscar Hill, in Oregon, and sister, Mrs. John Peterson, in Sitka. Her niece Miss Lillian Peterson is living at the Meir home and attends the Juneau High School.

John Meier is now at the St. Ann Hospital, where he will live in the future under the care of the sisters in that institution. He is very feeble in health and it is thought best that he live at the hospital where he will receive constant medical attention.

THE STROLLER WEEKLY, Oct. 8, &15 1921

HENRY W. MELLEN

Henry W. Mellen came to Juneau and vicinity in 1893, and has reside continuously in Alaska ever since. He was for three years United States commissioner at Juneau under a democratic administration and before that expiration of his term accepted a position with the Juslin mine which was operated up under his supervision. For the last six years Judge Mellen has been devoting his time entirely to the mining industry. He built a large smelter at Coppermount for the treatment of ores taken from the mines of the Alaska Copper Company of which he is president.

Judge Mellen was born in Warwick county, Indiana in 1864. He was raised on a farm, and on attaining young manhood attended De Pauw University. He later took up the study of law, was admitted to the bar, and for six years practicing his profession at Boonville, Ind. During his practice he became interested in civil engineering, gradually progressing along this line until he was induced to accept a position with the Monon railroad where he worked for several years. –(Record Miner).

THE VALDEZ NEWS, Aug. 11, 1906

L. H. METZGAR

L. H. Metzgar, General Superintendent of the Alaska Juneau Gold Mining, died in San Francisco Sunday morning, [July 2, 1940].

The Daily Alaska Empire states that Mr. Metzgar and his wife had been on a six weeks' trip to the East Coast and arrived in San Francisco Friday morning.

Mr. Metzgar was born in Clay Center, Kansas, February 29, 1876. He is survived by his widow, their son, Frank, who has just completed his fourth year at Notre Dame University; two daughters, Mrs. John Gordon of Seattle and Virginia Metzgar of Bellingham; his mother, Mrs. L. H. Metzgar of Fayette, Iowa; Mrs. Margaret Jackson as sister who lives in Kirkland, Wn.; and his brother, John Metzgar of Seattle.

PETERSBURG PRESS, June 7, 1940

A. A. MEYER

A. A. Meyer died at his residence in Sitka yesterday (Friday) at 3:10am, and was buried today at 2:30pm.

He was about 51 years of age and was born in Baden, Germany. He enlisted in the 6th U.S. cavalry 9th August 1872 for 5 years, honorably discharged as sergeant, enlisted in the U.S. M.

Corps Jan. 1882, promoted to corporal June 1882, and to sergeant, Sept. 1882, finally honorably discharged as first sergeant 3rd Jan. 1887.

ALASKAN, July 1, 1905

GEORGE F. MILLER

George F. Miller died yesterday at the Providence hospital, Seattle, according to a wire received last night.

George Miller was in the early days of the camp a cook. His first business venture was the operation of the Circle City hotel in partnership with Lockie McKinnon. This partnership continued until Lockie chased the paystreak to the interior. By cautious as well as sound investments, Mr. Miller secured considerable improved realty in Juneau. He was also a director in the First National Bank of Juneau.

George F. Miller always showed an interest in city affairs. He was city councilman for many terms on different occasions. A year ago he resigned before his term was up on account of ill health.

George Miller is survived by a widow who will bring the remains to Juneau for internment.

DAILY ALASKAN (Sitka), June 21, 1918

JAMES MILLER

James Miller died in Seattle on February 26, 1920. He was 84 years old, a native of Scotland, but has lived in America for a number of years. He was one of the first men to operate a fish saltery in Alaska., and was on of the first white settlers on the west coast of the Prince of Wells Island 40 years ago.

Mr. Miller is survived by four sons and two daughters. They are Alex, Andrew, Bert and Craig Miller; Mrs. R.B. Bell, Seattle, and Mrs. W.A. Bryant of Ketchikan. A nephew, Donald Sinclair, lives in Wrangell.

WRANGELL SENTINEL, Mar. 11, 1920.

O. B. MILLET

O. B. Millet, pioneer miner and prospector of the Northland, and who for the past twenty years has been located in the Iliamna district, Western Alaska, has concluded his first trip outside in a score of years and took passage on Saturday's northbound boat, en route home. He is concerned in both placer and copper property in the Iliamna district and says it is only a question of time when that mineral field will interest capital, as the mineral wealth is there.

When Mr. Millet travels, he travels in style. He had an entire stateroom on his trip south on the steamer Yukon, and thus became something of a marked man. The fact that he was making his first trip outside in twenty years was noised about the ship, and a lady tourist from New York City expressed a wish to meet him. That was easily arranged, and after the customary greetings Mr. Millet asked why the lady wished to meet him particularly. "Well, I just wanted to meet and talk with a real 'he-man'; they are scarce in the big centers of population," she said.

Mr. Millet went to the Klondike in the stampede days of 1898 was the original discoverer of gold on Chechako Hill, from which he mined out a very substantial sum. From Dawson, he went to Nome, remaining in that camp for several years. He then went down to the Kenai peninsula; remained in Seward for a year or more, and then went into the Iliamna country, where he has remained.

Mr. Millet's trip south was to visit his daughter, who is married to a Seattle banker, and to have some dental work done.
ALASKA WEEKLY, Oct. 1, 1926

J.E. MILLIGAN

During the period that Morrison was establishing a strain of Alaskan silver black foxes, he partner-to-be traveled another trail. J. E. Milligan, a native of Prince Edward Island who for many years had traded on the Yukon, was visiting his home and learned of the big money to be made in the sale of black foxes for breeding. Thousands of dollars were paid for a pair of this stock. So, with a new thought Milligan returned to the Yukon where finer fur was to be obtained. Two years later he returned to Prince Edward Island and had realized $64,000 from his two years catch in the Yukon.

With the money realized from the sale of these foxes, Milligan started for the trading post opened by George Morrison and mushing seven hundred miles over winter trails arrived at the Morrison stronghold where a partnership deal was consummated with fifteen pairs of choice silver black fox from the Morrison ranch a farm was started on Prince Edward Island. It is interesting to know from this stock six years later, these partner found themselves with 100 pair of the finest breeding stock in the world.

On their farms at Northam Prince Edward Island, Canada, there are 235 pens devoted to the breeding of fox. Incidentally Milligan and Morrison own a herd of blooded Holstein cattle. A young bull, the son of a world's champion cow, Dam Countess Abbekerk Heimke, was recently sold for $3,000.

ALASKA WEEKLY, July 3, 1931

WILLIAM MILMORE (MRS)

The citizens of Sitka were shocked to learn of the tragic death of Mrs. William Milmore who was drowned at the mouth of the Sinrock river June 26th. Mrs. Milmore and her husband had been wintering in Kotzebue Sound; they both had rheumatism so badly that they decided to go to Nome and started in an open boat. They encountered the severe storm of June 26th and 27th and in trying to make a landing the boat was overturned. Mrs. Milmore sank and never rose again. Capt. Milmore managed to get ashore and after many hardships, reached Nome.

Mrs. Milmore was a very bright woman and contributed many articles to the leading magazines. In 1896 she went to Circle City as a government teacher, it was there she met Capt. Milmore who was then Collector of Customs at Fort Yukon. In 1899 they

were married. She lived in Sitka for about a year.
THE ALASKAN, August 3, 1901

ELMA M'NAUGHT

The selection of Mrs. M'Naught as a delegate to the Alaska convention is recognition of a women who owns mining property, and a just tribute to an intelligent and honorable woman who has been identified with the Northland since 1898.

Mrs. M'Naught's interests on the Seward Peninsula comprise near 2000 acres of mineral ground. She is the wife of John M'Naught, managing editor of the San Francisco Call, and one of the oldest journalists in the west.

NOME SEMI-WEEKLY NEWS MINING EDITION, Oct.13, 1905

WARREN E. MOODY

Warren E. Moody died at the Pioneer's Home on January 16th. He was born in South Handly, Mass., in 1847, making him over 82 years of age. He came to Valdez, Alaska in 1902 and prospected in the copper river country until the Tanana gold excitement attracted his attention to the Interior country and has reside there mining, prospecting, and trapping ever since. He had many friends in the northland.

He had a son and daughters but their whereabouts are unknown, as he has not heard from them for many years.
SITKA WEEKLY, Jan 26, 1929

EPHIM MOONIN

The death of Chief Ephim Moonin at his home on English bay, Monday, May 18, marks the passing of tribe leadership to his section. The late chief was born on Spruce Island, Kodiak, 76 years ago, the son of a prominent Russian missionary of those early days. The Russian church, with headquarters in Sitka, appointed the father of Ephim as missionary, counselor, guide to the native tribes living along Cook Inlet.

In his youth Ephim was a noted sea otter hunter, and many years ago was selected as chief of the English bay tribe, in which community he passed the last 45 years of his life. He was twice married and is survived by a son, Peter Moonin.

THE SELDOVIA HERALD, June 6, 1931

I. H. MOORE

Landing in Skagway on the old S. S. "Topeka" in December 1897 Dr. I. H. Moore enthusiastically cast his lot with Alaska. He was a brilliant surgeon who graduated with honors from the University of Pennsylvania medical school, Dr. Moore had been surgeon for the Union Pacific railroad in Pocatello, Idaho, and for a few years superintendent of the Idaho State Hospital for the Insane. He did the first abdominal operation ever done in Alaska–on a major of the Northwest Mounted Police. Soapy Smith breathed his last in Dr. Moore's arms after the famous duel between Frank Reed and Smith, in which both were killed.

Dr. Moore followed Dr. F. B. Whiting as surgeon for the White Pass railroad. From 1901 to 1906 he was surgeon for the Treadwell Gold Mines on Douglas Island. "Lucky Ike," as he was affectionately known, was an Atlin stampeder who left his luck at home.

He also operated a claim (or at least paid for it) on Porcupine Creek back of Haines Mission for two years with indifferent success. In 1911 he developed the Buckeye claim on Long Creek back of Ruby without much "golden reward" as he expresses it, except the reward of a host of rich new friendships in the interior.

His brother, Judge Alfred S. Moore, served eight years as a Roosevelt appointee as federal judge of the Nome district. This doctor's family, his wife and daughter Helene, went to Alaska in 1898 and are local sourdoughs.

ALASKA WEEKLY, July 12, 1929

WILLIAM MOORE

Having to his credit what is perhaps the longest continuous residence in Alaska of any pioneer living in the Territory today, Capt. William Moore has cast his anchor among other sourdough friends at the Pioneers' Home at Sitka. He came from Anchorage on the steamer Alaska yesterday. Capt. Moore who has spent over 60 years of his life in Alaska, is noted as one of the discoverers of Deese Creek gold placers in the Cassiar in the Stikine country.He is as a veteran Yukon River steamboat pilot, and the only surviving son of the founder of Skagway, Capt. William Moore, Sr., noteworthy as the man who brought the first steamboat to Alaska.

Last April the famous pioneer celebrated the sixtieth anniversary of his arrival in Alaska by taking his first airplane trip in a spin over Anchorage and Cook Inlet.

Before his departure from the westward, Capt. Moore was guest of honor at a luncheon given jointly by the Pioneer Igloo and Pioneer Auxiliary. He set sail for Sitka with the well wishes of countless old friends.

THE ALASKA PRESS, Feb. 9, 1934

CASEY MORAN

A born wanderer is Casey Moran, well known impresario and journalist of early Yukon days, who is now directing the editorial destiny of "The Tropical Sun" at Maracaibo, Venezuela, South America. He became associated with that publication on January lst of this year and avers it is his twenty third venture in the journalistic field.

He was a lad in his teens, decided to try his luck in the fastness of the Northland before gold was discovered in the Klondike.

He first set foot in Alaska in the winter of 1895 when he stepped ashore at Juneau. The following spring we find him on the Dyea trail packing his outfit in company with Oscar Ashby, Harry Ashe [?], and others better known when news of the

Klondike strike leaked out at Circle City where Casey made his debut as a maestro of the opera.

Apparently he did not care to try his luck with a "muckstick" He did not aspire to be a gambler or a bartender so entered the theatrical game. It was rather a hard matter for him to secure the talent necessary to stage the first comic opera he wrote. However, He was persistent in his efforts, and one day with his pot of lampblack, placarded the saloons of Circle City with announcements of his first operatic venture. It was a success financially and enthused Casey Moran to further fights of fancy as a playwright.

During the late fall of 1896, news of the strike on Bonanza and other creeks reached Circle City and when Casey Moran decided to abandon the stage for the creeks the theatrical world lost a great impresario. Casey Moran bade good-bye to the creeks of the Klondike and wandered into Dawson where he stepped across the threshold of a newspaper office and became inoculated with the virus of the "Fourth Estate." His remarkable imagination became evident in print as he perpetrated more than one delightful hoax on his readers and on the press agencies throughout the country. His ability was recognized and for a time after leaving the Northland, he was on the staff of one of the New York dailies where again he made a name for himself.

Casting aside the spell of the "Great White Way," Casey Moran stampeded into the Porcupine country where a rich strike had been made and entered the newspaper game there. With the wane of the boom in that section of Canada, Casey decided to seek pastures new and for a time his whereabouts were known but to himself. Some years later he appeared on the surface away down in one of the Latin-American Republics.

Early-day Dawsonites and Fairbanksans will be pleased to hear that the Hon. Casey Moran is still in the land of the living. With a smile they will recall his story of the recovery of the remains of Noah's Ark which the outside newspapers swallowed hook, and line and sinker. Many of us hope that Casey will make

the pilgrimage to Los Angeles this fall and renew the friendships so firmly established in the Land of the Midnight Sun.
ALASKA WEEKLY, Feb. 3, 1933

ALBERT P. MORDAUNT

Capt. Albert P. Mordaunt, one of the founders of Council City, and one of the discoverers of Ophir creek, died Nov. 25 in San Francisco, death being due to a "complication of diseases brought about by hardships experiences in Alaskan wilds." Capt. Mordaunt went to the outside last fall. He founded the Pioneer Commercial co. which owned valuable claims on Ophir creek to which place he headed an expedition in 1897. Capt. Mordaunt was a native of Norfolk, England, and he leaves a widow in San Francisco. He was a Mason and the funeral was under the auspices of that body.
THE NOME NUGGET, Feb. 18, 1903

ELIZABETH URBAN MORIARTY

A feeling of sadness was occasional by the death of Mrs. Elizabeth Moriarty, wife of Mr. Charles Moriarty, superintendent of the Tanana Valley railway. The deceased, after a few days illness at her Chena home was removed on Friday, January 31 by special train to St. Joseph's hospital at Fairbanks where she died on February 4, 1908. Mrs. Moriarty came to the Tanana last summer from Roseburg and has resided here since that time.

Mrs. Moriarty was a native of Niblock, Mo., eight miles from St. Louis. Her maiden name was Elizabeth Urban, and she was married when 15 year old to Mr. Moriarty at Minot, North Dakota. She was of German descent on her father's side and of Yankee on her mother's.

In 1902 they moved to Butte, Mont., where Mr. Moriarty became general roadmaster of the Montana Central. After that the family lived at Kalispel, where John Moriarty, the first child was born, when the father was roadmaster for the Great Northern. In 1894, Tim Moriarty was born in Spokane and Maureen Moriarty

was born at Leavenworth, Wash. and seven years ago Eileen, the baby was born in Roseburg, Ore., where the mother's parents now reside.
TANANA MINER, Feb. 9, 1908

CLYDE L. MORRIS   (See Vol.1)
Clyde L. Morris, pioneer Alaskan transportation and mining man died Wednesday night at the Seattle General Hospital.
Mr. Morris, whose wife died in 1932, is survived by two daughters, Clydene Morris, executive secretary of the Washington State Bar Association, and Allice May Morris, and a son, Robert, A sister, Mrs. W. J. Mahan of Port Townsend, and a brother, Clarence Morris of Amity, Ore., also survive.
Morris was born in Pomeroy, Garfield County, on September 2, 1876. Mr. Morris went with his parents to San Francisco and later to Seattle. He was in the mining business in British Columbia in the last century, and in 1900 went to Nome, where he entered the contracting business. He moved to Seattle in 1904, but retained his Alaskan interests for many years.
ALASKA WEEKLY, May 13, 1938

EDWARD C. MORRISEY
Edward Morrisey came to Alaska with the United States Signal Corps, and was engaged in the military telegraph office in Fairbanks. Previously he had been an associated press telegraph operator and newspaper reporter. When his term of enlistment was up several years ago, he accepted a position with the Fairbanks News Miner and has been engaged there since that time until Delegate Charles E. Sulzer appointed him as his personal secretary.
THE DAILY ALASKA EMPIRE, April 8, 1918

GEORGE L. MORRISON
George Morrison was born in the lumber woods of Pennsylvania where with his brothers he learned to hunt and to

trap. At the age of 13, young George read the history of the Hudson Bay Fur company. The experiences of those early traders inspired him and in March 1896 he left home determined to become a fur trader. So he worked his way to Seattle where he saw boatload after boatload of prospectors and adventurers sail for the north country in quest of fortune, and following his bent he joined the stampede.

He worked his way north under the Arctic Circle and with but little capital established a trading post. Shortly after a gold discovery was made and prospectors came in from all points. In consequence George enjoyed an excellent business, from the Indian and white trappers and from the miners.

It was Morrison's idea that if he could raise silver black foxes in pens he would have a constant source of supply. That he could kill when the pelts were prime and that he would have skins unmarred by the ravages of wild forest life. He considered that by scientific breeding and feeding he could produce a pelt of infinitely finer quality.

Knowing that the silver black fox was a freak of nature, Morrison began to conduct accurate and scientific breeding experiments with his stock, to establish a strain of foxes which would produce silver black pelts. After five years of careful experimentation, in which time he handled four or five hundred foxes, he possessed but fifteen pair of satisfactory breeding stock from which he could, without variation, obtain silver fox pelts of perfect texture and coloring. During the period that Morrison was establishing a strain of Alaskan silver black foxes, J. E. Milligan, a native of Prince Edward Island, made $64,000 trapping on the Yukon, contacted him and a partnership was formed. [See J.E. Milligan biography]

ALASKA WEEKLY, July 3, 1931

WILLIAM S. MUNZ

Senator Munz, a comparative newcomer to Alaska, arrived in the Territory in 1934 to engage in mining but a few years later turned to an earlier interest, aviation, and now operates the Munz Air Service out of Nome. He combines sport with business when conditions are favorable by pursuing wolves over the frozen tundra with a plane and has bagged as many as seven of the predators in a single day.

ALASKA LIFE, June 1947

WILLIAM R. MURDOCK

William R. Murdock, husband of Barbara E. Murdock, died at Douglas City, Alaska, on Saturday, May 9" 1903, of heart failure, aged 59 years.

The deceased was born at Picto, Nova Scotia. He came west to California in the early seventies, and when the first stamp mill was built on Douglas Island he came here and was employed in its construction as a carpenter and millwright. Most of the time since he has lived at Treadwell and worked for the company. He has seen the growth of the mining industry on Douglas Island from its beginning until nearly a thousand stamps were pounding away on the quartz.

DOUGLAS ISLAND NEWS, May 13, 1903

ABNER MURRAY

Abner Murray was a native of Nova Scotia and came to the states in young manhood, coming to Alaska in 1887. For many years he was a millwright in the employ of the Treadwell company. He acquired much property in Douglas in the early days of that town, constructed and operated a sawmill, gave the town a water system, constructed and owned numerous businesses and dwelling houses.

After the Treadwell cave-in he razed many of his building in Douglas and scowed the lumber to Sitka and built a number of houses there including the Bayview, the most pretentious hotel in town.

His brother, John, who joined him in Alaska nearly 40 [?] years ago, died about 10 [?] years ago. The latter also acquired considerable property during his life time. Neither Abner or John ever married and their only known relative H.F. Murray who formerly was in Douglas in now in real estate in Los Angeles where he resides with his wife and son. .

Abner Murray was between 83 and 85 years of age. He died in Sitka on September 13. 1928.

THE ALASKA WEEKLY, Sept. 28, 1928

JOHN D. MURRAY

Capt. John D. Murray, whom Alaskan pioneers knew as the "kid captain" during the days of the Klondike gold rush of 1898, died suddenly Sunday of acute indigestion on the Stewart River boat Keno, operated by the White Pass & Yukon Railroad. The body will be brought to Seattle for burial.

Starting in his teens, Capt. Murray had been piloting steamers on the territorial rivers for more than thirty-five years. With his brother Frank, he had been a pilot on the Stikine River during the gold rush. The brother, with whom he had gone north, is now captain of the Tana on the Kuskokwim.

He is survived by his widow, Mrs. Emily L. Murray, two daughters, Mabel and Marjorie, living at the family residence, 555 N. 84th street [Seattle]; his brother Frank and a niece, Mrs. Frank Durgan.

ALASKA WEEKLY, June 30, 1933

MARTIN MURRAY

Murray was born in England, May 19, 1867. He came to Alaska in the year 1898, along the great Klondike rush. He has been in many of the Alaskan camps and has made mining and prospecting his business in the north. His relatives reside in Seattle.

ANCHORAGE WEEKLY TIMES, Feb. 14, 1918

FRANK F. MYERS

Frank F. Myers, aged 77 years, veteran journalist of the

Northwest, died last Sunday [Dec.10] in Port Townsend, his passing recalling the fact that in his adventurous newspaper career he was one of the early publishers in Alaska and battled with his pen against bureaucratic government as against the welfare of the Territory. He started the Juneau City Mining Record in 1888 and through it assailed politicians then controlling the Territory as corrupt and inefficient, despite libel suits and bitter trials.

After returning to the States from Alaska, he resided at Port Townsend for 40 years and was correspondent for Seattle and Portland papers in the days following the panic of the 1890s, and during the gold rush in the Klondike. His newspaper experience included work on the old Seattle Gazette, forerunner of the Post-Intelligencer.
ALASKA WEEKLY, Dec. 16, 1932

HARRY NAKAMOTO
Harry Nakamoto, proprietor of the Wrangell Bakery, died at 10:20 Sunday evening. Nakamoto was a Japanese and 49 years of age. Early in life he was married in Japan. Later, he and his wife separated and she now resides in Korea. He has a son who this year graduated from the University of Tokyo

Nakamoto owned the building on Front Street in which the Wrangell Bakery is located. He left only a small amount of money and the total value of the estate will probably not exceed $3000. Owning to there being some question as to the cause of Nakamoto's death an inquest was held. The principal witnesses at the inquest were Louis Wigg, Maggie Gunyah, Sarah Lott. The substance of their testimony was that on September 29, 1921, they saw Charlie Lynch beating up Nakamoto at the rear of the building occupied by John Fanning as a fur store.

After viewing the remains and hearing the testimony of witnesses the Coroner's jury made a request for an autopsy. U.S. Commissioner Wm. G. Thomas granted the request and appointed Dr. A. B. Jones of the Wrangell General Hospital to perform the autopsy.

Dr. Jones performed the autopsy at 10:30 Tuesday morning and in the afternoon he delivered to the jury a summary of his findings. Dr. Jones reported that Nakamoto's death was the result of blows traumatism or injuries inflicted upon his body by some external force to him unknown, and that he did not die from natural causes. On Tuesday afternoon the coroner's jury reported that after viewing the remains, hearing the testimony of witnesses, and reading Dr. Jones' sworn report of the autopsy they were of the opinion that Harry Nakamoto's death was the result of injuries inflicted at the hands of Charlie Lynch. A warrant was issued at once and Charlie Lynch was arrested by U. S. Deputy Marshal, H. D. Campbell.

THE WRANGELL SENTINEL, Oct. 20, 1921

J. B. M. NELSON

Another of Alaska's rapidly diminishing pioneers made the final trek last week. He was J. B. M. Nelson, merchant of Chitina, prospector and mine owner of the interior.

J. B. M. Nelson was 57 years old and his birthplace was Nova, Scotia. He came to Alaska in 1896 and from that day until his death, he had never set foot outside of the country. He was attracted to the gold rush that started from Valdez in 1898. He made the long journey over the Valdez Glacier and was one of the earliest prospectors in the State Creek district. This was about 1901. Later he worked for a Valdez merchant, A. L. Levy, and then when copper sent a road of steel to Kennecott, he was sent to take charge of the S. Blum and Company store at Chitina. He later became its owner, and since that time has enjoyed a lucrative business in the interior town.

His survivors so far as can be learned, are two sisters in Everett, Massachusetts, and a brother, Avery, in the same city, according to the Cordova Daily Times.

ALASKA PRESS, Sept. 7, 1934

MARGURETE KELLOGG NETTLES

Margurete Nettles died February 1, 1903 in Skagway, Alaska. She was 44 years old and left a husband and two sons. She was married to Mr. Nettles, July 16, 1885 and joined her husband in Skagway in 1900. She was a native of Boston and her maiden name was Kellogg. She was buried in the family plot in Mt. Hope cemetery, Roxbury[?]

J.A. Nettles was formerly in the foundry business in this city [Boston], but later established that of a plumber and tinner, when he went to Alaska in 1898. There he has become prosperous and prominent in city and is now serving on the city council. (Boston Globe)

ALASKA DAILY GUIDE, Mar. 9, 1903,

JOHN G. "GUS" NORD

Alaskans were grieved to hear last month of the tragic death of Captain John G. Nord. Captain Nord, who was pilot of the S.S. Alaska, together with Captain O. C. Anderson, master of the Alaska; Capt. Roy Wheeler, master of a government vessel, were riding in a car near Haines, Alaska, when the car skidded on loose gravel, overturned, and submerged in a river. The other officers were able to extricate themselves and were saved. Captain Nord drowned before help could reach him.

Capt. John G. Nord was born in Oland, Sweden, February 20, 1868. He arrived at Port Townsend after a trip around the Horn at the age of 14, and spent the remainder of his life at sea. Since about 1898 he had been continuously on the Alaska run. Among the vessels commanded by Captain Nord were the Northwestern, Victoria, Jefferson, Alaska, and Aleutian.

He is survived by two daughters, Mrs. Frances Nordine, Seattle, and Mrs. Ann Gustafson, Los Angeles.

ALASKA LIFE, August 1939

JOHN NOVAK

John Novak, well known old-timer of Alaska, and who for

the past two or three years made his home at McGrath, passed away at the latter place last Wednesday afternoon.

John Novak, about 50, was born in Southern Austria quite close to the Italian boundary line, came to America as a young man, and for many years has been a resident of the Northland. He leaves a sister, Marie Novak, and a couple of nieces at Los Angeles to mourn his loss. He was a member of Flat Igloo of Pioneers.

THE KUSKO TIMES, May 23, 1931

BRIDGET CREGAN O'CONNOR

The passing of Mrs. John P. O'Connor takes away another notable pioneer of the Northland and mother of one of the best known families of the Yukon Territory and Alaska. Bridget Cregan O'Connor died in Fairbanks April 29, 1933.

Mrs. O'Connor (Bridget Cregan) was born at Barry-Gone, Limerick County, Ireland, February 2, 1850, emigrated to New York City in 1870, married John P. O'Connor in New York in 1876 and bore him eight children, four boys and four girls.

John P O'Connor died in April 1928. He came North in 1900 and located at Dawson. The family moved to Fairbanks in 1904 and the parents and two sons had lived there continuously since. A daughter, Mrs. Mary Beraud died in August of 1928 in Chula, California. Son William died in 1892 in Tacoma, Washington.

Surviving children are Pat O'Connor, deputy U.S. marshal at Fairbanks; Jack O'Connor, Alaska game warden, Anchorage; Mrs. James Cody, Dawson, YT, wife of the manager of the Northern Commercial Company store; Jos. O'Connor, merchant at Catania; Mrs. Margaret Abercrombie, Anchorage; Miss Kate O'Connor, Fairbanks.

SEWARD DAILY GATEWAY, May 2, 1933

ASA OFFICER

Asa Officer died as a result of a mining accident 70 miles

from Whitehorse when he was injured in an explosion. He was carried by sled to Skagway where he succumbed in the hospital from his injuries.

He was born in eastern Oregon where his parents were pioneers. He joined the gold rush 1898 and spent the rest of his life in the North.

When the United Stated entered the war, he tried to enlist and when he failed, he went to Canada and joined the Canadian Engineers and served in France, where he was badly gassed and injured. After the war he returned to the North. He was 66 years old. He is survived one known sister, Mrs. L.D. Luce of Tacoma.

THE ALASKA WEEKLY, Mar. 29, 1929.

HARRY I. O'NEILL

A man who came here 19 years ago and who has worked toward one goal ever since–that in brief is the story of Harry I. O'Neill.

Harry's family were of the pioneer stock from the start, and they pioneered with the cheerful aggression that only sons of Erin were capable of. His father and mother were both Irish, though his mother was born in America and his father in England.

Harry was born in Fargo, ND in 1885, one of the frontiers of America. The O'Neill's stayed there for five years after Harry's advent into the world, but soon it became too populated for them and they pushed farther west in 1900, coming to Seattle. In the Queen City, Harry went through the grade schools and later attended the first night school in that city. While attending school he helped pay his way by working as a clerk in a dry goods store and it was with this job that he started on the career which was to be his life work.

Soon, however, Seattle lost its charge to the pioneering O'Neill family and Harry's father joined a party of Dakotans and Minnesotians and left for the Klondike rush.

In 1904 while working in the dry goods store, romance entered Harry's life and he married a Seattle girl, Miss Florence

Leahy, a lass from old Erin parentage. But soon the call to pioneer entered Harry's veins and in 1908 he boarded the old "Portland" and struck out for Cordova. Cordova was a boom town then, the railroad was under construction, the saloons were running full away.

Harry's career since he landed in Cordova in the fall of 1908 is probably pretty well known to most Cordovans. He began by working as a carpenter on the present Times building. In the spring he flunkied for M. J. Heeney. He then worked for Joe Diggs. Next he worked for S. Blum & Company in 1910.

Then in 1912 he started out for himself along with Henry A. slater under the firm name of "O'Neill-Slater Company." In 1915 he consolidated with S. Blum & Company under the name of the "Blum-O'Neill Company." And in 1925 he bought out the Blum interests and has since been operating as "O'Neill Company."

These facts don't tell about how Harry raised 12 children and raised them well.

It was Mrs. O'Neill who accomplished at least a mighty share of this tremendous task. Here again Harry showed his sagacity for only a wise man could possibly have married so good a woman. The O'Neill family was like a regular little army, they say. Each child with his or her specific duties to do and a specified time in which to do them, and army discipline when they disobeyed. They are grown up now, some of them, and some of them are still growing up, but all of them show the wise and careful training of their childhood. Harry and his wife made a business of raising their children and that is perhaps why they were as successful in that as Harry has been in building his present business.

CORDOVA DAILY TIMES, Sept. 17, 1927; PATHFINDER, Nov., 1911

STEPHEN O'NEILL

Stephen O'Neill hailed originally from Wisconsin, having

been born in Stevens Point in 1853. He made his first trip to Alaska during 1885 on the old S. S. Ancon. Steve returned to the States at that time, however, and did not locate permanently in the Territory until 1899, when he came on the Atlin stampede. From Atlin Mr. O'Neill went to Valdez in 1901, and from that day to this he has never left the Territory, not even on a trip to the Outside. He makes Nenana his winter headquarters. He has taken part in almost every stampede during Alaska's mining history, and owns some promising looking quartz ground on Valdez Creek.

PATHFINDER, August 1923

MARY AGNES ORENSHAW

Mrs. Mary Agnes Orenshaw, 64 years of age, died at her home in Juneau one day last week.

Mrs. Orenshaw came to Juneau with her husband and their three children: Ida, Quinton, and Margaret, over 25 years ago and had lived here most of the time since. She was born in England, coming to the United States when a young lady.

Her son Quinton was drowned near Haines a number of years ago and her husband died shortly afterwards in that district. Her daughter, Ida., who is Mrs. Archie McKay, wife of the port captain for the Pacific Steamship Company at Seattle, and Margaret, who is Mrs. Robert A. Columbia, wife of a fruit merchant of Seattle, and Mrs. Columbia's little daughter, Peggy, survive her.

ALASKA WEEKLY, Nov. 13, 1925

VIOLA CODDING ORTON (Mrs. Ira)

Mrs. Viola Codding Orton, Alaska Pioneer and Seattle resident for four decades, died Friday after a short illness.

Born in Michigan, she went to Nome, Alaska in 1900 and married Ira D. Orton, an attorney there in 1902. They came to Seattle in 1908.

Besides her husband, she is survived by a son, Allen

Orton, at Nome, Alaska, and two daughters, Mrs. Leslie J. Brown and Mrs. C. F. Schlosstein, both of Seattle.

Ira Orton has maintained his law practice in Nome since the early days, going to Nome each summer. This is the first year he has remained in the States, as he wished to be near his wife in her illness.

All three of Viola Coddington Orton's children were born in Nome..

THE NOME NUGGETT, June 28, 1948

LARS OSTNES

Lars Oatnes of Marshall and Fortuna Ledge has decided to sell his mining equipment, but makes it clear to his friends that he does not intend to retire.

When Lars disposes of his mining equipment he is going prospecting again–and for gold, too, because that is the one mineral he knows a lot about. He will be off on a new creek.

The lure of gold took Lars Oatnes to Dawson in 1902 and later to Fairbanks. After four years there he joined the Iditarod stampede in 1909 and mined in that vicinity for many years. The Texas oil fever then got him but the Lone Star State has a climate "too severe" for the old-timer and after four and a half years he went back North. He did a little 'wild-catting' in Washington State and established a home in Seattle, but it wasn't too long before he headed for the lower Yukon country.

Lars and Elise have three children born in Texas, Alaska and Washington. His son, Leif Ostnes lives in Fairbanks and for many past summers has been mining with his father at Marshall.

ALASKA WEEKLY, Jan. 7, 1955

LEE PAGE

Lee Page, well known oldtimer of this section, who for many years has made his headquarters up on the West Fork of the Nixon came to the end of life's trail some weeks ago, according to word recently brought here by Alex Mengel

The end of the trail for the oldtimer came at a point about five miles from his headquarters up the West Fork on a sandbar, on reaching which after a hard day of poling up the stream, he apparently had set up his mosquito tent and laid down for a night of rest, according to Mr. Mengel, who only a few days ago left here on a trip to the same location.

Mr. Mengel, on reaching the spot noted, went ashore. No one there to greet him. Looking around, it was a gruesome sight that came within his view. The tent, part of it still standing, was badly shredded, no one within it. Continuing his search, not many feet distant, he came across a human skull, while a little farther away was found a human breastbone. An inspection of the poling boat revealed much disorder–clawed and torn open, a general overturning of the craft, much of it spoiled–apparently the work of bears. The exact date of Mr. Page's passing and how the end came will, of course, never be known. Did the end, after the hard day's work, come from a natural cause, such as heart failure, or was he attacked in the tent by either wolves or bears and killed at disadvantage? These, of course are matters of conjecture.

Lee Page, at the time of his death about 68 years of age, was of French Canadian extraction. He was in Dawson in the early day of the camp. He came to Ophir at a very early date, spending a couple of years there, following which he came to McGrath, spending a year or so here, and then leaving for the headwaters of the Nixon. His headquarters up on the west fork of the Nixon had been his home for the past 23 or 24 years, where he followed the occupation of prospector, and trapper. He visited McGrath early each year of the open season, purchased his supplies and again departed for his isolated home. He again purchased his usual supplied at McGrath and left here in the later part of June to return to his camp.

THE KUSKO TIMES, August 12, 1933

JOHN P. PALMER

John Palmer made the voyage on the schooner *Leslie D.*

which was wrecked when they arrived off Nunivak Island, forcing the passengers to take the steam scow off the schooner and go on to Nome on that. He arrived in Nome in 1900, having come from Seattle. He has also resided at St. Michael and Ketchikan and now at the Pioneers' Home at Sitka.

ALASKA DISPATCH, May 5, 1922

LILA PRIOR PALMER (See John Olds Vol. II)

 Mrs. Palmer, well known Juneau pioneer woman and owner of the Occidental Hotel on Front Street passed away at the home of her daughter, Mrs. D. J. Sinclair this afternoon. Lila Prior was the daughter of John Prior and Eliza Sellar of Sitka.

 She is survived by her husband, by the three daughters, Mrs. C. E. Carpenter of Seattle; Mrs. A. L. Mathews of Grand Junction, Ohio; and Mrs. D. J. Sinclair of Juneau; and a son Harry Olds of this city. She is also survived by seven grandchildren: Lila Sinclair, Shirley and Donna Olds, all living in Juneau; and Dolly and Claris Carpenter of Seattle; and Myra Ann and John Lester Mathews of Grand Junction, Colo.

DAILY ALASKA EMPIRE, March 28, 1939

WILLIS H. PALMER

 Word of the death of Willis H. Palmer, 98, was received by friends here this month from Los Angeles where the Civil War veteran lived for the past two years.

 The distinguished looking, white bearded former miner and later truck gardener of Valdez was said to have been the oldest living Alaska resident up to the time of his departure for California in 1937. Palmer told acquaintances here his original visit to Alaska in the vicinity of Wrangell was made before the Civil War. He went back to fight for the Yankees, served for a while as an Indian Scout under General Custer and then came back to Alaska prior to the gold rush. He came to Valdez when it was a tent camp, shared in its heyday and decline, and lived to see it thrive again as a transportation center. His later years were spent raising garden stuff for sale, his chief products being large red strawberries. His greatest desire was to live to be 100.

Mr. Palmer made frequent trips to the States and each time became good "copy" for metropolitan newspapers with his tales of Alaska. He left several survivors in California.

WRANGELL SENTINEL, July 28, 1939

GEORGE ALEXANDER PARKS

George A. parks of Alaska (Republican), Eleventh Governor of Alaska. Born Denver, Colorado, May 29 1883, unmarried. Elementary and high school work in Denver public schools. Graduated from North Denver high school. Enrolled in Colorado School of Mines, Golden, and was graduated in 1906 with the degree of E. M. (Mining Engineer). Followed the profession of mining engineer in Western United States, Mexico, and Alaska during the year 1906 and 1907. Entered government service as mineral examiner for the U.S. General Land Office in Alaska in 1908 to 1917. During the years 1918 and 1919 served as first lieutenant and then as captain of engineers in the United States Army. At the conclusion of the World War was division gas officer of the Ninth Division, U.S. Army. Now holds the rating of captain, Officers Reserve Corps. Returned to Alaska in 1919 and for four years was chief of the field division of the U.S. General Land Office in Alaska. In 1924 held the office of assistant supervisor of surveys and public lands in Alaska.

Mr. Parks was appointed governor of Alaska by President Coolidge and assumed the duties of the office on June 15, 1925. His general knowledge of Alaska and its problems, gained from years of travel and personal contact with resident of all sections has fitted him to an unusual degree for the position. His present address is Juneau, the capital.

ALASKA SCHOOL BULLETIN, Jan. 1929 (Vol. XI)

LLOYD C. PARSONS

Lloyd C. Parsons was born in Menominee, Michigan,

September 18, 1892. He spent most of his childhood in Fayetteville, Arkansas, and was educated in the schools of that state. He graduated from the University of Arkansas in 1916, receiving the degree of Bachelor of Electrical Engineering.

After graduation, he entered in the U.S. Army and served on the Mexican border from August 1916 to May 1917 as Captain of Company "B" Second Arkansas Infantry. He served throughout the World War and was overseas with the 54th Infantry, 6th Division.

In 1920 he was transferred from the Infantry to the Signal Corps and in May 1921 arrived at Valdez on detail as officer in charge of the 2nd Section of the Washington Alaska Military Cable and Telegraph System.

Captain Parsons is married. His wife was formerly Miss Blanche Bridger of Parsons, Kansas. They were married at Chattanooga, Tenn., on December 22, 1917.

THE PATHFINDER, March 1925

JOSEPH C. PATTERSON

Joseph C. Paterson was born in England, Jan. 19, 1866. He came to America at the age of 17 years and spent several years in the States, principally in the state of Washington, coming to Alaska Treadwell in 1897. In 1901 he and Margaret Hudson were married at Douglas where they made their home continuously until six years ago, when they moved to Juneau.

Joseph C. Patterson died at his home in Juneau Nov. 19, 1928. Surviving are the widow, one daughter, Mrs. Margaret Agnes Grigg, and one son, Charles Patterson.

STROLLER'S WEEKLY, Nov. 24, 1928

JAMES PAULSON

James Paulson, aged 60 years, passed away at the Columbus sanitarium, Seattle, Sunday evening, February 19, 1928.

James Paulson went to the Klondike in 1897 and had lived

in the Northland ever since those early days. For the past ten years he, and his wife had resided in Seward, where they operated an apartment house. At one time, Paulson served as chief of police of the town.

ALASKA WEEKLY, Feb. 24, 1928

FRANK PERATROVICH

Another Alaska-born Senator, Frank Peratrovich of Klawock, started his first term in the Senate this year after having sat in the House in 1945 and 1946.

Graduating from the Indian Industrial School at Chemawa, Oregon, Senator Peratrovich served two years with the Navy during World War I, then joined the famous Haskell Indian Football Team for a triumphant tour of the country during which it won games from coast to coast.

He returned to Alaska, engaged in fishing for a number of years, and now operates a general merchandise establishment at Klawock, on Prince of Wales Island.

ALASKA LIFE, June 1947

KATHERINE L. PERKINS

At the age of 92, Katherine L. Perkins, widow of the late Col. W. T. Perkins, died in a Rest Home near Seattle last Sunday morning [March 19]. Born in Dennison, Iowa, she attended the University of Michigan, and was one of the first women graduates in medicine. Here she met her future husband, who graduated the same year in law.

The couple were married in 1884 at the time of their graduation, and spent 63 years together as constant companions. Col. Perkins died on Dec. 21, 1947, a few days after their wedding anniversary.

After practicing their respective professions in Bismarck, N. D., for several years, they went to Nome where Dr. Perkins delivered the first white child born there. The Colonel was interested in properties in Siberia and the North, and later was instrumental in plans of the Seattle Chamber of Commerce which resulted in the building of the Alaska Railroad. He was also interested in the Portland Canal district.

Mrs. Perkins was one of the early members of Chapter A. P. E. O. and of the Woman's Century Club. Surviving relatives are a nephew, Carl Frederick Kuehnle, and a niece, Mrs. E. A. Howard, both of Winnetka, Ill., and six other nieces and nephews in Conn., Iowa, and California.

ALASKA WEEKLY, March 24, 1950

W. T. PERKINS

Col. Perkins is known from Skagway to Nome, and from the Kobuk to Valdez. Born in Buffalo, New York in 1858, he comes of a family, the male members of which have made their marks in many enterprises. Graduating from the New Hampton Institute in 1877 he pursued a course of study at Bates' College, Maine, graduating from there in 1881 with a degree of Bachelor of Arts.

Col Perkins then took up the study of law at the University of Michigan and attained his degree as a Doctor of Law in 1884. He then took up his residence in Dakota practicing law and engaging in the banking business, for four years occupying the position of vice-president of the First National Bank of Bismark.

He then entered mining at Cripple creek, and in 1898 joined the rush to Alaska, landing at Skagway and engaging in mining at various points along the Yukon, coming to Nome in the fall of 1898. The present Northwestern Commercial Company was formed soon afterward and Mr. Perkins was made a auditor of the company which position he occupies today.

NOME SEMI-WEEKLY NEWS, June 26, 1904

MARY BERNEDT PHILBIN

Funeral services for Mary Bernedt Philbin, wife of Peter J. Philbin, fox rancher at Midway Island, Pybus Bay were held yesterday.

Mrs. Philbin was born in January 12, 1884 in Dakota before there was a North or South Dakota. She left there at the age of three, coming west with her parents to settle in Seattle before the fire which destroyed so much property at that time. During her childhood days she spent a summer with her father, Anton Osten, near Nome on a gold mining claim. Her father went over the Chilkoot Trail during the gold rush days into the Klondike.

She was married in Seattle and her four children, Eunice, now Mrs. Frank Wooton, Donald, Marnee and Peter, Jr. were born there. They as well as her husband survive her.

In May of 1934 the family came to Alaska, joining Donald who was staying with his aunt and uncle, Mr. and Mrs. Wm. Abbess, who with her husband now lives in Seattle, is one surviving sister and Mrs. Florence Hegland is the other.

PETERSBURG PRESS, April 18, 1941

JOSEPH L. PIDGEON

Capt. Jos. L. Pidgeon, who is the father-in-law of Capt. E. W. Johnston, is the discoverer of gold on the famous No. 8 Cooper Gulch claim. The discovery was of great importance to the Nome mining district, as it indicated the possibility of the extent of the beach line eastward. After the discoveries on Little Creek and Portland Bench a great many shafts had been sunk to bedrock to locate the eastward extension of this beach line, but no pay was found in any of them. Apparently a sort of promontory extended into the ocean at the time Bering Sea laid down this beach deposit, covering the ground where fruitless prospecting had been done. When Capt. Pidgeon found the paystreak on No. 8 Cooper Gulch, work started which resulted in the discovery of pay along several miles of the tundra in mines which have produced millions.

Capt. Pidgeon is a native of Prince Edward Island. He spent his boyhood days in Boston. He was in the service of the

United States Navy during the war, being wardroom steward on the Albatross from 1864 to 1865. He went to Nome with Capt. Johnson in 1909 and spent several years in fruitless prospecting and unrewarded endeavor. When he began work on No. 8 Cooper Gulch, in the fall of 1905, he was ridiculed and laughed at by his friends. The first shaft reached bedrock at a depth of sixty-five feet. He put in two thaws and drifted a distance of twelve feet, when he struck a concentrated deposit of beach sand which would average about twenty-five dollars to the pan. In all probability this gold mine contained the richest spot ever found in a placer gold mine. When he located the paystreak Capt. Pidgeon was working the property under lease. Before the expiration of the lease he had extracted enough of the precious metal to take care of him for the remainder of his life.

ALASKA-YUKON MAGAZINE, March 1909

GEORGE E. PILZ (See Vol. 2)

George E. Pilz was the first mining engineer to work in Alaska after the transfer of the Territory to the United States. He was born in Warochnitz, in Saxony, which is in a mining and smelting region. He worked his way through a college or polytechical course of three years. After his graduation he studied Geology under Bernhard von Cotta, and in 1863 he was sent to the Berlin University to hear a series of lectures of Alexander von Humboldt on American Continent geology and mineral resources. He became strongly impressed about the course of the mineral belt running through the whole continent from the Andes through Central America, Mexico, California, British Columbia and to the northwest through Alaska. He also forecast that it would continue across into Siberia.

He then was sent by the Saxony government to bore for coal in a district near Lienzic. In 1866 he was called into the war service, when Prussia took Saxony. After hard trials he secured a furlough to come over to America in 1867, worked in Pennsylvania, in Vermont and New Hampshire, and later at the famous Calumet and Hecla Mine in Michigan. He then went to California in 1869, in 1870 to Nevada, installing furnaces, afterward returning to San Francisco, where he was an engineer on the blowing out of the "Blossom Rock" in the harbor.

In San Francisco he met Nicholas Haley, who had worked under him as an ore sorter in a mine in Placer County, California. Haley had been to Alaska as a soldier at Fort Sitka, and had ore from prospects he had found there.

Pilz was satisfied that there were grounds for profitable gold mining near Sitka. He bought Haley's claims, the Stewart and the Haley, then with a complete outfit of provisions, tools and power, took some hard rock miners from California, and sailed on the April steamer.

Arriving in Sitka, Pilz got his equipment to work at the Stewart mine, and put men to blasting out the ore, while the Indians worked on putting up the mill. By the fall of 1879 Pilz had a ten-stamp mill installed at the Stewart mine. He bought the old sawmill of the Russian American Company from the Alaska Commercial Company that had lain unused for a decade, repaired it, put in flues and steam power, and put the old steamer Rose in repair to tow logs. He sent a schooner load of Alaska cedar to San Francisco, where the government seized it under the lack of law to export lumber from Alaska.

On Christmas Day 1879, a three days' run had been made on the ore of the Stewart Mine, and a cleanup was made of $1200. This was the beginning of lode mining in Alaska. The returns did not pay sufficiently to justify working the ore. Pilz began to look for better prospects. He sent out men throughout Southeast Alaska prospecting for gold. To those Pilz paid $4.00 a day and outfitted them and giving them the third claim on each vein, he to have the choice of two out of those filed. To the region about where Juneau now is, he sent Richard T. Harris and Joe Juneau, two Cassiar miners that were at Wrangel.

Chief Kowee, a Tlingit Indian, showed the two prospectors some rich ore. Pilz described it as: "The richest ore we saw in or around the Basin."

Harris and Juneau put in a blast and bull-dozer and carried down to the beach ore sacks of the richest chunks, hiring Kowee's Indians to do the packing. Harris and Juneau staked the claims and planned out a mining district.

Pilz had been on a trip to Nevada, and returned two days after Juneau and Harris came to Sitka with the ore, and Captain Glass of the U. S. S. Jamestown had taken charge of it.

Pilz went to the new camp and staked the Kowee Claim opposite Gold Creek.

"Then I located along the beach with power of attorney of Pierre Erussard (French Pete), and by power of attorney of E. Bean, the Mattison claim. He cleared out the streets and built the first cabin, and another back on Seward Street. This is from the story of how the gold was found at Juneau, and the claims were first located on the ground of the Treadwell Gold Mining Company.

For years Pilz tried to get capital interested. He went to San Francisco to secure it, but no one would take an interest. In 1882 he met Treadwell in San Francisco. Treadwell was broke and wanted to come to Juneau and try out there. Pilz took him over the ground. He tried 18 months at different places on the divide between gold Creek and Sheep Creek, then gave it up and went to San Francisco, later to return. Pilz allowed Treadwell to sack ten tons of ore and take it to San Francisco. Treadwell returned by the next steamer and gave him an option on the Paris Claim. Pilz went on working while Treadwell went to San Francisco, organized a company, and assessed a $2.50 assessment per share, and squeezed Pilz out, for he had used all his money trying to get the mill working.

Pilz went to law over it, but as he said, "It left me plumb on the turf. Capital kept me down and out." In 1889 he sold the Kowee Claim and he put the money into a Huntington mill and a Pelton waterwheel. He placed this in the Basin but "scarcity of labor and high wages took all I had," and "That winter a snow slide came down the gulch and carried all buildings, mill and everything, even the watchman, out into the center of the basin, ground up to a total wreck under 100 [?] feet of snow.

He says he was broke and had to hunt employment to support his family. He went to Honduras to set up a stamp mill for a Philadelphia company. He worked for the Pacific Iron Works, traveled over Honduras, Nicaragua, San Salvador and Costa Rica, then down to Venezuela and Columbia. He came up into Mexico, put in furnace plants and other works for the Guggenheims. From there he returned to California, and finally came back to the North. He wound up in the Forty Mile. He spent his last years there, trying to strike pay in the next gulch.

In the autumn of 1926, Pilz, 82 years of age, decrepit and ill, was put on a horse, taken to Eagle on the Yukon, and in September 12th of that year he died. He was buried in that village in the cemetery by the Order of Red Men.

ALASKA LIFE, Feb. 1944
ALASKA MINING RECORD, April 8, 1896
ALASKA WEEKLY, March 21, 1924

A. W. PIPER

A. W. Piper, who has been a resident of Seattle since 1873, and who was one of the best know pioneer business men of that city, died in the morning of November 11th at his residence, 1523 Boren Ave., at the age of 76 years.

Mr. Piper was born near Kissingen, Bavaria in 1828, and came to America when 19 years of age. Mr. Piper had been educated as an artist, and he was attracted to the uninhabited parts of the country. He came to California by way of the Isthmus of Panama in 1853, settling in San Francisco, where he was married the following year. He lived in San Francisco about twenty years, and then came to Seattle, where he went into the bakery business, remaining in that business until a few years ago. The rush to Alaska attracted him, and he spent two years in Nome, 1900 and 1901.

Mr. Piper took an active interest in politics, and on one occasion ran for mayor of Seattle on the Populist ticket. He was one of the earliest cartoonists in the City of Seattle, and for that matter, in the State of Washington. Mr. Piper also had considerable ability as a sculptor.

THE NOME SEMI-WEEKLY NEWS, Jan. 27, 1905

MARY C. PLEIN

Mrs. J. F. Plein passed away at Fortuna Ledge on Saturday in the presence of her devoted husband with whom she pioneered Alaska for the past thirty-two years. She died in Fortuna Ledge, Alaska on December 31 [?] 1932.

Mrs. Mary C. Plein was born in New Orleans 71 years ago. She was educated in Louisiana and several years later was married to Joe F. Plein. When Nome was struck he departed for Nome and was shortly after followed by Mrs. Plein. During her stay in Nome, Mrs. Plein was active in all charitable and Masonic affairs and for a time was Worthy Matron in the Eastern Star, Anvil Lodge.

In 1916 Mr. and Mrs. Plein left Nome for Marshall where they have resided ever since. The Plein residence which stands on the bank of the Yukon River, was the community center for Fortuna Ledge. There Mrs. Plein planned many pleasant surprises for the miners and prospectors. Mrs. Plein cared for the native women and children, when in sickness or distress. She will long be remembered in that little Lower Yukon mining camp as well as in Nome.

THE KUSKO TIMES, Nov. 15, 1932

S. A. PLUMLEY

S. A. Plumley, a well known pioneer resident of Ketchikan, passed away Saturday, January 9, 1926, a victim of a paralytic stroke. He was 75 years of age. He is survived by three married daughters and a son, all of whom reside on the outside. He was buried under the auspices of the Pioneers of Alaska, of which order he had long been an active member.

Judge Plumley, who was an attorney by profession, went to Ketchikan from Fort Townsend, Washington, in the early days, soon after the town was established, and that place had been his home until two or three years ago when he was named U. S. commissioner for the Craig recording district. He resigned this position due to failing health and came outside over a year ago. The change seemed to do him good and he felt able to return to the Northland. He left Seattle for Ketchikan about a month ago.

ALASKA WEEKLY,   Jan. 15, 1926

ERNEST PODBOY

Ernest Podboy was born the at Seisenberg, Austria. The date of his birth is January 5, 1882. He came to Alaska in the year 1900, landing at Valdez. He came to Anchorage in 1915, and at the present time is engaged in the mercantile business, dealing in auto supplies. He has been to Dawson, Fairbanks, Iditarod, and the Kuskokwim. His place of business is on Fourth Avenue near E street.

ANCHORAGE WEEKLY TIMES, Jan. 31, 1918

BERT PORTER

Bert Porter, an old time prospector and miner of the camp, died at 6:00 yesterday morning at the Good Samaritan hospital. He had been there since the day after Christmas. He was in a general state of debility, and gradually wasted away. Mr. Porter lived for years on Little Blanche creek, a tributary of Quartz, where he owned a number of claims. At one time he held most of the claims on that creek. He was 56 years of age, a native of Ontario, and was raised in Minnesota. He told friends not long ago that he had not heard from any of his relatives in twenty years. He never was married. Before coming North he was a lumberman in Minnesota.

DAWSON DAILY NEWS, Oct. 2, 1916

JACK PRATT

Thirty-Thirty Jack (his mail comes that way), left his home in Alabama as a kid. He ran away to sea on a windjammer, drifted for a while, lived briefly in Chicago about forty years ago, and then went to Alaska.

When "30-30 Jack" came up to Columbia University Engineering School from Auburn College in his home State of Alabama, he could have gone on to become an engineer just like every other engineer.

But Klondike gold called and he left before completing the course. He hasn't been back since.

It was in the Klondike he got his nickname because he carried a 30-30 carbine when all the others were toting six-shooters.

From there on his life led him all over Uncle Sam's largest Territory and he became by turns nearly everything there was to become. He operated one of the first halibut fleets in Alaskan waters, shot bear for the shakos and coats of the imperial Russian Army (bear skins brought a good price then); operated a jack-hammer under water, arrested murders, made and lost small fortunes in gold and finally wound up living in a little cabin on Anan Creek.

There he traps mink, otter, fox and ermine, protects the great runs of Humpback and Coho salmon that crowd the waters of the creek in spring and acts as warden for the Anan Creek recreational area and bear sanctuary, recently created by the United States Forest Service and located practically at his front door step.

He also guides sportsmen in his spare time and it is by this means that he maintained contact with the outside world. For the Hollywood celebrities and millionaires of the Pacific Coast came to know of the veritable fishing and hunting paradise which lay at his front door and it is not uncommon to see glistening yachts lying at anchor in the deep fjord into which the creek flows.

Thirty-Thirty now lives in a cabin on Anan creek, near

Wrangell. His expenses are about $20.00 a month, and his only steady companion is Bosco, his cat. (Bosco is now staying at the best hotel in Wrangell at a cost to Jack of $5 a month).

Anan creek is in the best hunting and fishing country in the North and Jack often plays host to yacht owners from the United States, Jack Barrymore, Lewis Stone and other movie stars are good friends of his. His favorite stars are Loretta Young and Dolores Costello. Loretta, however, "gets the darndest yen" to clean up Jack's cabin and once she threw away some of his best winter clothes, claimed they were worn out, he said.

Jack has never married, although he admits that once in a while, during the three months' nights, he gets a little lonely. He says the prettiest girls he ever saw, bar none, are the half breed women of Siberia. Twenty five years ago the prettiest girl in the north was the dance hall proprietor now known as "Dirty Maude." Maude, Jack says, is still a fine looking women. She gets her name from her habit of chewing fine cut tobacco and spitting over her shoulder as she dances.

Thirty-Thirty Jack is one of the sourdoughs who swarmed into Alaska in 1898. This is his first trip to "civilization" (and you can have it, he says) in thirty eight years. He's one of the real pioneers, still sturdy and young despite his 66 years, and he intends to stay that way..

He's been a deep sea diver, prospector, game hunter, "Mountie," fisherman, trapper, saloon keeper, and government agent. He and "Tex" Richard were partners in a saloon in Nome, and he knew Rex Beach, Robert W. Service, Jack London, and "Tex" Guinan. "The last time I saw Jack London," says Thirty-Thirty, "he was sittin' on a beer keg in front of a saloon in Nome. And the keg was just as empty as Jack was full. He was a typical hobo. Said he had his name in every jail from coast to coast."

WRANGELL SENTINEL, Feb. 24, 1939
CHICAGO TRIBUNE, Feb. 20, 1939
THE EVENING STAR (Wash. D.C.), Oct. 13, 1938
WRANGELL SENTINEL, Nov. 11, 1938

CHARLES D. PRICE

Charles D. Price, (64), son of John W. Price and Orlena McDanields, was born in Butte, June 14, 1877. In 1893 he moved to Douglas, Alaska, where he was engaged in mining work for 28 years.

He came to Portland 23 years ago and operated several garages in this city.

Charles Price died in Portland, Oregon on Saturday March 15, 1941. He is survived by a daughter, Mrs. Charlotte Mahaffy of Marshfield; two sons, Willis J. of Astoria, and Douglas C. Price of Portland; two brothers, Thomas C. and Martin Price, both of Anchorage, Alaska; and a sister, Mrs. Charles Cragg of Portland.

PORTLAND OREGONIAN, March 17, 1941; State of Oregon Death Certificate # 884

THOMAS C. PRICE (See Vol. 2)

Mr. Price was born in 1874 in Grizzly Gulch, near Helena, Montana, and attended school in Butte. His parents moved to the Pacific Coast in 1899 and settled in Portland, Ore., where Mr. Price learned the plumbers' and sheet metal trade and worked at his trade in Portland and towns in Washington. He joined the stampede in Unick river, Southeastern Alaska in 1893, and during that fall located in Juneau with his parents. He has four brothers and one sister, and the Price Homestead, near Juneau, is a well known landmark to all old timers. He and his brothers for years were the owners of the Salmon creek power rights, which finally lapsed and were taken over by the Alaska-Gastineau company. Mr. Price was in business in Juneau from 1895 until 1904 under the firm name of Price Bros., and during that period made a trip to Dawson during the Klondike stampede. He was in business in Ketchikan and Douglas and went to Cordova in 1909 and was in business there during the construction days of the Copper River & Northwestern railway. He left there in 1915 and located the firm of Price & Bennett in Anchorage. Mr. Price was married in July 1899, to Miss Lois Evans in Juneau. Lois Ethel Evans-Price, the one daughter, was born in Arlington, Wash., May 1900. Mr. Price was admitted to the bar to practice law in the Third Division in June 1915. He was a member of the council and fire chief of both Juneau and Cordova, and organized the first fire fighting force in Anchorage and was the first chief.

ALASKA MAGAZINE, May 1917

SARAH E. PRITCHETT   (See Vol.3)

Mrs. Sarah E. Pritchett, former owner and publisher of the Wrangell Sentinel and for 22 years prominent in the community, was in Wrangell this week, arriving on the Princess Norah and returning to her home in Seattle on the return trip of the same boat.

Though here only a short time, Mrs. Pritchett was entertained by many old time friends. She is making her home with her son in Seattle. Mrs. Pritchett came up to wind up business affairs and dispose of property. She sold her Front Street home to Mrs. And Mrs. William E. Byrd. Following the death of her husband, James Pritchett, ten years ago, Mrs. Pritchett, for eight years ably occupied the editor's chair of the paper

WRANGELL SENTINEL Feb. 13, 1942

LYDIA PRYOR

The funeral of Mrs. John Pryor who died Monday night, was held Thursday afternoon from the Methodist church.

Pryor was born in England and was 77 years of age on May 14, 1921. When she was four years of age she came to Michigan with her parents and was married to John Pryor in May 21 1861.[?] They came West shortly afterwards and settled at Grass Valley, Cal. In 1879 the came to Sitka.

Mrs. Pryor was the first white woman to arrive in Juneau, coming here from Sitka in 1881, following the discovery of gold in Silver Bow Basin. Her husband, John Pryor, had come to Juneau the previous year and was engaged in mining in the basin.

They built a cabin on the corner of what is now fourth and Main streets and here Mrs. Pryor has lived since that time.

Mr. Pryor died in 1908, and the year of the death was the golden wedding anniversary of the couple.

Mrs. Pryor had three children born to her, two sons and a daughter. The sons are dead and she is survived by her daughter, Mrs. A. J. Palmer, and four grandchildren: Mrs. C. E. Carpenter; Miss Klondyke Olds; Miss Lydia Olds; and Harry Olds; children of Mrs. Palmer. And a great grandchild, Corville, daughter of Mrs. C. E. Carpenter.

STROLLER WEEKLY, Sept. 3, 1921
ALASKA MONTHLY MAGAZINE., October 1907

DANIEL D. PULLEN

Extraordinary heroism in action in the Bois de Cuisey, France, has won for Colonel Daniel D. Pullen, former University of Washington student and first cadet from Alaska to enter West Point military academy, the distinguished service cross, according to official announcement made in Seattle. The award was made by General Pershing for the distinguished gallantry and leadership of an officer in directing a tank attack on the Bois de Cuisey and for rallying a disorganized force of infantry, after which he led it in the face of violent machine gun fire and successfully occupied the ground taken by the tanks.

Colonel Pullen is the son of Mrs. H. S. Pullen of Skagway, Alaska, one of the most widely-known women in the Northland, and a brother of Capt. Royal Pullen, who last summer married Miss Eloise K. Newlands, daughter of Mr. and Mrs. George Newlands of Medina, Wash.

In 1905 he entered the university of Washington, and was in his third year when given an appointment to West Point by President Roosevelt.

At the University of Washington Pullen–and he is known only as "Dan" to all Alaskans and friends in Seattle–first won fame as one of the best tackles that ever played on the football team, and later at West Point he gained more laurels as right tackle. As a student Colonel Pullen also stood high at West Point, and was one of the honor graduates. He was graduated in the class of 1912, and immediately afterward was commissioned as second lieutenant of infantry. His promotions have been rapid. Shortly after the outbreak of the war he was sent to Europe as a lieutenant colonel of a tank corps regiment. After a brief service in France he was promoted to colonel.

Colonel Pullen was born in Clallam county Washington April 25, 1885. In 1897 he went to Skagway, Alaska with his parents and has claimed the territory as his home since that time.

THE SEWARD GATEWAY, Feb. 13, 1919

JAMES PULLEN

James Pullen, on Monday, March 28th, died by drowning. The deceased came from Maine to California in 1858, going from there to the Carriboo district in British Columbia. After a few years spent in the Cariboo, he went to Amineca, and from there to Cassiar in 1874. He came to Juneau, in which place he resided until the time of his death. He has two sisters in Maine, and also a family, but it is not know where they reside.

JUNEAU ALASKA FREE PRESS, April 2, 1887

LOUIS PAUL PYREAN

Louis Paul was born at Nanaimo, British Columbia. His father was a Frenchman and his mother a Tongass native. He took the name of Paul as the last name of his father was too hard to pronounce by his people. His father was a trader and was murdered somewhere about Victoria when Paul was a little boy. His mother returned with him to his place, where she died. Louis was raised by Yaah-noosh, his grandfather. After working in the mines in Alaska, Louis went to school in Wrangell where he married Tillie Kehrian on January 8, 1882. On the 10th of January, 1877, she gave birth to a little boy.

On December 13, 1876, Louis left with S. A. Saxman, a

missionary for the Presbyterian church, set out by canoe for Old Tongass, an Indian village to determine the feasibility of establishing a mission there. They were never seen again. The canoe was found smashed and driven under a rock by a winter storm.

THE ALASKAN (Sitka), January 29, 1877

GEORGE RAABE

Captain George Raabe, 77, for 30 years connected with boats on the Yukon River between Whitehorse and Dawson, died at his home in Portland, Oregon, on December 1 [1929].

In 1898 Captain Raabe came north and spent the first year on the Stikine River. Then for 30 years he was pilot on the Yukon River, traveling between Whitehorse and Dawson. For several years prior to his retirement in 1928, he was pilot on the Whitehorse flagship of the White Pass and Yukon Route. Although he had his master's papers in the United States, he could not be a captain in Canada without becoming a citizen of the country, and he preferred to remain a pilot. Captain and Mrs. Raabe had celebrated the 53rd anniversary of their wedding about a week before his death. Besides his widow, Mrs. Nannie Raabe, he is survived by a daughter, Mrs. Nellie F. Johnson of Beaverton, and a son, Captain Clyde Raabe, of the Columbia Pilots' Association.

THE VALDEZ MINER, Feb. 1, 1930

EDNA HAZEL RAY

Edna Hazel Ray is the wife of Attorney L. V. Ray of Seward. She was born in the State of Washington in the year 1889. She came to Alaska in 1901, her people going to Iliamna. Later she came to Valdez, where she resided for several years. It was here that she met Lee Vincent Ray, then a young lawyer, serving as Assistant District Attorney, and married him. They have two children, Hazel Patricia born in 1909 and Lee Vincent born in 1918. Mrs. Ray has also resided in Juneau where she is well know in social circles, her husband having been the presiding officer of the First Territorial Senate. Mr. and Mrs. Ray have a home in Seward overlooking Resurrection Bay.

THE PATHFINDER, May 1920

LEE VINCENT RAY

Lee Vincent Ray was born in Hyde Park, Massachusetts and came to the Territory in 1903 first stopping at Ketchikan. For several years he served as Assistant United States Attorney, residing at Valdez.

He was a member of the first Territorial Senate and was elected President of that body. Since residing in Seward, his present home, he has served the municipality in different capacities, chiefly as attorney. Senator Ray is a married man and has two children, one born in Valdez, and the other in Seward. As an attorney he has a wide and extensive practice throughout the Territory.

THE PATHFINDER, May 1920

JOHN T. REED

John T. Reed, Hyder's first U. S. Commissioner, who served from April 1 1920 until he was succeeded to John W. Frame Dec. 1, 1921, died in Seattle Feb. 24 [1923] and was buried in that city the following day.

John T. Reed was born in St. John, New Brunswick, October 29, 1855. He joined the big rush to Dawson in 1898, and in 1900 went to Nome, where he resided until 1910. Three years later he returned to Alaska, settling in Juneau where he was connected with the district court until his appointment as commissioner for Hyder. On leaving here it was his intention to first take a vacation in the south and then return to Ketchikan and open a law office.

He is survived by a wife and two sons who live in Boston.

HYDER ALASKA MINER, March 8, 1923

JOSEPH L. REED

Judge Joseph L. Reed, an attorney of the Third division, was found dead in his office Wednesday afternoon.

Joseph Reed was well known in Alaska, having lived in Seward several years before coming to Valdez, in the early part of 1915, where he has resided since engaged in the practice of law.

Judge Reed was the descendant of a very noted line of barristers. Born in Louisville, Kentucky in 1875, he spent the years of schooling there, graduating from the Louisville law School. After his graduation he attended the University of Virginia, the Michigan Law School and Center College of Virginia, graduating from all of them with honors.

While yet a young man he came west, finally to Alaska, where he settled in Seward in her boom days. Later he made a visit to Washington, where he met and married Mae G. Ryan, who survives him. They were married in Bellingham, Washington, October 10, 1914, coming to Valdez the following year. Two children blessed the union, Alice and Richard, both of whom are now students at the University of Washington.

Judge Reed's family included four U.S. senators, five congressmen, a number of judges, many prominent lawyers and doctors. Four were presidents of colleges. There were a score of generals, colonels, and captains. Two feminine relatives were the wives of President Rutherford B. Hayes and Benjamin Harrison. A cousin Letitia Green married Vice President Adlai Stevenson. His great-grandfather Joseph Reed was secretary to General George Washington and later became first governor of Pennsylvania. Judge Reed was a member of the Sons of the Revolution and a Son of the Confederacy.

Judge Reed has long been active in political and local circles, occupying a number of positions during the past twenty years. The past year he has acted as city attorney and as treasurer. He has been an active member of the Masonic order and was also past grand master of the Valdez organization.

Judge J. L. Reed passed away at the age of 61. His widow, Mae Ryan Reed, a daughter Alice, and a son, Richard; two sisters, Mrs. Hobson, wife of Judge Hobson of the Supreme Bench, Louisville, Kentucky, and another, the wife of a prominent physician in Bakersfield, California, survive him. His father and mother died years ago.

THE VALDEZ MINER, March 6, 1936

RALPH REED (MRS.)

Mrs. Ralph Reed, long time resident of Seward left Tuesday to live "Outside." She will be greatly missed by her many friends both old and young.

Mrs. Reed and husband, the late Ralph Reed, came to Hope, Alaska, in 1915. That same fall they went to Anchorage where they lived until 1919. They came to Seward on the first train out of Anchorage over the new line, October 5, 1919. They left Anchorage at 7 a.m. and arrived here the next day at 2 a.m., taking 19 hours to cover the 114 miles trip, being delayed by rock slides.

They first lived in the Harriman Building (now the Ray Building). Mr. Reed was in the Department of Justice for 20 years. They resided in Moose Pass from 1937 to 1947, where Mr. Reed passed away.

Mrs. Reed became well known to the younger generation as librarian of the Community Library from September 1948 until September 1951.

SEWARD SEAPORT RECORD, July 4, 1952

PATRICK RENWICK

Patrick Renwick, one of the earliest residents of Skagway and well known to everybody in Skagway, died at 2:30 o'clock this morning at the White Pass hospital from heart failure and other contributory causes.

Mr. Renwick came to Skagway in the fall of 1897 from Nevada and Idaho. He has lived in Skagway ever since and has many friends in town for he was open hearted and generous. At one time he was very wealthy but of late years he has owned little beside some local property.

Mr. Renwick is survived by a wife who lives in Seattle.

He was a member of the Elks and the local lodge will take charge of his funeral.

THE DAILY ALASKAN, June 1, 1909

H. E. REVELL

H. E. "Colonel" Revell, a pioneer of Alaska for the past 47 years, died here today of heart failure.

Revell came to the North from Port Townsend, Washington, where he was born in the old sealing days. For a time he served as a boat puller, and afterward as a seal hunter. At the time of the placer strike at Sunrise on Turnagain Arm, he owned and operated a pack train running from Hope and Sunrise to the Moose Pass district.

For many years he was a licensed big game guide and during his career piloted many hunting parties throughout the North. He was the first contractor to handle the Seward-Iditarod mail, furnishing a weekly mail service from Seward to the Interior placer camp with the dog teams.

In recent years he and his wife have been operating the Rapids Roadhouse near the famous Rambling Glacier, as well as operating freight trucks on the Richardson Highway.

H. E. Revell is survived by his widow, two sons, and one daughter.

ALASKA WEEKLY, Sept. 1, 1939

RALPH M. RHOADES

Ralph M. Rhoades was born near St. Joseph, Missouri where he spent most of his youth. He acquired the Alaska fever and came north to Nome where he remained until 1912. He left Alaska to homestead in Montana. Remaining there scarcely two years, he returned to the Seward Peninsula and thereafter spent most of his time in Alaska.

He finally went to the Cordova section and located there in 1924 and engaged in the selling and buying of furniture. He was a member of the city council and chamber of commerce.

He died in Seattle in May 1933. He was 62 years of age. He is survived by a brother, J.A, Rhoades and a nephew, J.W. Rhoades.

THE ALASKA PRESS, May 5, 1933

CLARENCE RHODE

When Clarence Rhode, Alaska Game Commission wildlife agent for the Cordova District, modestly remarks that he's been brought up in game management work, you'd be surprised to know how literal that statement really is.

Clarence's dad, C. J. Rhode, was the first Fish Commissioner for Wyoming away back in about 1905. Later he went into game and fish propagation work in Washington where Clarence was born in the living quarters attached to a fish hatchery, brought up on a game farm, steeped in game management and wildlife work. Adventure from the North called when he saw Alaska-bound boats leaving Washington harbors for the land of gold and abundant wildlife.

He hit Skagway, went down the Yukon to Eagle, where he worked, boomed into Fairbanks, got a job–eventually ended up in the Forest Service at Seward where Jack O'Connor, Anchorage AGC officer, saw a good game warden going to waste. July 1, 1935, the Alaska Game Commission won another good officer when Clarence Rhode joined its force.

He made a successful Westward and Bristol Bay patrol in 1937 and that same year became acting assistant executive officer to Frank Dufresne, chief of the AGC. Again Rhode returned to field work in January, 1938, with station at Cordova, where he has been doing a first class job and has perfect cooperation in his district.

ALASKA LIFE, March 1940

BESSIE MORTON ROBERTS

Mrs. A. R. Roberts, who with her husband Dr. Roberts, was resident of Seward for 16 years, passed away in Portland, Oregon, Saturday evening, September 14.

Mrs. Roberts was Bessie Morton, and it was in her home town of Ontario, Oregon, that she met and was married to Dr. Roberts. They were married following the World War in which Dr. Roberts served as an entry from Seward, where he lived prior to the outbreak of hostilities. Dr. and Mrs. Roberts have lived in Seward continuously since their marriage.

Mrs. Roberts is survived by her husband and 14-year-old son Gerald: her mother, who lives in Ontario; and by two sisters and two brothers. One sister Ollie lives with her mother. The other is Mrs. Mae Beatty, a resident of Oakland, California. The two brothers are Estes of Heppner, Ore, and Murray also of Ontario.

Miss Eva Roberts, Dr. Roberts sister, received the sad message Sunday morning. She immediately dispatched a similar message to her brother at Kodiak, who is expected to return to Seward on the first available ship.

SEWARD GATEWAY, Sept. 17, 1935

PETER ROBERTS

On January 1, 1863, at Stafford Springs, Connecticut, Peter Roberts was born. He came to Alaska in 1884, landing first at Juneau. He came to Anchorage in 1915 and has been engaged here ever since. His vocation is that of a "lumberjack," but here in Alaska he has done considerable prospecting and he has been in all the towns on the Yukon from Forty Mile to Nome. At the present time he is engaged with the Alaskan Engineering commission on Turnagain Arm. His home address is Anchorage.

ANCHORAGE WEEKLY TIMES, Nov. 22, 1917

ENOS ROBINSON

Enos Robinson had been in the territory since 1904, and

at the Pioneer's Home for two years. He came from Fairbanks, where he had been mining and prospecting. Robinson was born in 1852, Washington County, Ark.

ARROWHEAD (Sitka), May 25, 1935

JOHN HENRY ROBINSON

John Robinson, Pioneer Alaskan, for years located at Anchorage where he was special investigator for the Alaska Railroad, died in Pasadena, Calif. last month.

John Henry Robinson, 66, for 23 years a United States marshal in Alaska, assigned to Valdez, Eagle, and Fairbanks districts, and also part time with the Alaska Railroad as special investigator at Anchorage, was born in Everton England, and came to the United States when a young man. While at Valdez, Alaska, he served as deputy United Sates marshal under Frank Brennerman, now a resident of Long Beach.

Surviving are his widow, Mrs. Jessie L. Robinson; a brother, Henry Robinson of Everton England, and a nephew, John W. Robinson of Seattle.

ALASKA PRESS, Dec. 7, 1934

LEO W. ROGGE

Fourth member of the Fourth Division delegation to the Senate is Leo W. Rogge who has spent at least a part of every winter in the Fourth Division for the past forty-seven years. Born in Davenport, Iowa, Senator Rogge came north in Gold Rush days and mined at Dawson and in the Forty mile country before moving on to Fairbanks. He began his legislative career in the House ten years ago and this is his second session in the Senate.

ALASKA LIFE, June 1947

LOUISE D. BULLOCK ROMIG   (See Vol. 3)

Mrs. Louise D. Romig, 66, died yesterday afternoon at Providence Hospital four days after her husband, Robert died from a heart attack.

She came to Anchorage in 1922 and she and Romig were married here in 1924. She was born July 31, 1895 in Minnesota.

Surviving are two sisters, Mrs. George Capstick of Anchorage and Mrs. Pearl Rouleau of Yakima, Wash.; and two brothers, Grant Bullock of Walla Walla, Wash., and Harry Bullock of Yakima, Wash.

During her 38 years residency in Anchorage, Mrs. Romig was well known. During the twenties and early thirties she successfully managed Gordon's Department Store, a ladies clothing business.

Her husband, Robert Romig, was born in Bethel in 1897, the son of the famous "Dog Team Doctor," J. H. Romig, and Ella Mae Romig, missionaries on the lower Kuskokwim River at the turn of the century. The father died in 1951, the mother in 1937.

Robert Romig started one of the first insurance agencies in Anchorage in 1922 and still operated it at the time of his death. In addition he was part owner of Alaska Fuel and Transfer Co.

AK. STATE LIBRARY BIO FILE (Undated, 1-19-1962?)

ERNEST W. ROSE

Resident of Western Canada for 52 years, 11 of which he lived in the Yukon, Ernest W. Rose, aged 62, died in Lethbridge hospital on April 30.

When only 18 years of age he mushed with his father overland from Edmonton to the Yukon in 1897 taking 18 months for the arduous trip. For several years he and his father worked claims on the Sulphur and Hunker Creeks, and later he was a special constable with the R.N.W.M.P.[Royal Northwest Mounted Police] at the Dawson town station.

Coming out in 1918 he settled in Lethbridge and married Miss Hettle Collings. About seven years ago he went into the bee business with considerable success, and it was while carrying on the work of getting his apiaries prepared for the summer that he suffered the stroke which proved fatal.

Besides his widow, Mr. Rose leaves a sister, Mrs.

Malcolm Young; and three brothers, James, Harry, and Fred. The Lethbridge Old-timers Association attended the funeral.

ALASKA WEEKLY, May 10, 1935

MARTIN W. ROSLUND

Martin W. Roslund died from heart trouble the night of the 18th of August. He was born April 20, 1876 in Malmo, Sweden. After finishing his apprenticeship as blacksmith he worked in some large shops as machinist, then went to sea. After a few voyages in British ships he came to New York and worked in manufacturing shops. In 1906 his brother came back to Seattle from the Klondike and Martin came to Seattle and went with Carl to Dawson. They were mining on Hunker Creek until 1916 when they went down to Iditarod. Martin was mining on Otter until 1936 when he sold out and went to Goodnews Bay and staked some claims. He was working for the Goodnews Bay Mining Company when he died the 18th of August.

He is survived by his brother and family in Seattle, one sister in Malmo, Sweden, and another sister who is a major in the Salvation Army stationed in Java, East Indies. He was buried at Platinum by the Goodnews Bay Mining Company August 20.

ALASKA WEEKLY, August 25, 1930

MARY F. NESLER ROUSE

Mary F. Rouse died suddenly Wednesday afternoon from heart failure. She was preparing to return to her old home in Indiana expecting to start for there about the first of May. She came to Sitka four years ago with her sister Mrs. Judge Tuttle and her daughter Mrs. Heimlinger. For nearly fifty years she was a consistent member of the Baptist church. While in Sitka she always attended church when her health permitted.

Mary Nesler was born in Posey County Indiana, May 5, 1839, but moved to Henderson, Kentucky with her parents when an infant. There she was married in Dec. 1858 to Jacob S. Rouse. To them three children were born, two of whom are living–Mrs.

Heimlinger of Sitka and Dr. H. R. Rouse of Nashville, Tenn.

Her husband died Dec. 1879 [?]. Most of her life was spent in Columbia City Indiana. She was one of eleven children only two of whom now remain–Mrs. Judge Tuttle and Mrs. Johnson of New York.

SITKA ALASKAN, April 13, 1901

JULIUS MARINE RUFFNER

Julius Marine Ruffner, a pioneer resident of Seattle and for the past thirty years concerned in mining operation in the Atlin, British Columbia, district, passed away Monday morning, April 29, 1929, in Monmouth, Ill., at the home of Mrs. Ruffner's parents, where he was recuperating from an illness that started in the Atlin country many months ago. He was 60 years of age and is survived by his wife.

Mr. Ruffner went into the Atlin, B.C. mining camp in 1898, the year following the original discovery by Fritz Miller, Lockie MacKinnon and others. Here he engaged in placer mining and for many years was in active charge of a great hydraulic mining company which had acquired the discovery claims on Pine creek and other claims on the same stream. When this big operation was worked out, Mr. Ruffner became concerned in silver-lead properties in the Atlin district, later forming the Atlin Silver-Lead Mines, organized under the unit system. He carried on extensive development work on these properties for a number of years.

Mr. Ruffner had carried on negotiations for the sale of control of the mines to a syndicate organized in Buffalo, New York, for the past two years, and was in the East to close the deal when stricken. The syndicate had sent an engineer to the Properties and his report was favorable. Ruffner had just completed the organization of a mining corporation, instead of the unit system, which was preliminary to the closing of negotiations, when illness came on which confined him to his bed until the summer came.

Mr. Ruffner's associates in Seattle inform the Alaska Weekly that the deal will be carried through and that the engineer who examined the properties on behalf of the Buffalo syndicate, will be placed in charge of the operations.

The Atlin Silver-Lead enjoys the reputation of being a very large mining property, ready for the production stage. It was the departed's dream to develop a great mine in the camp which had so long been his field of operations.

ALASKA WEEKLY, May 3, 1929

JAMES B. RUSSELL

Many oldtimers are acquainted with James. B Russell, known as the "gun store man" of Juneau who died suddenly at Chichagof on Oct. 31, 1931. The Empire, speaking of his death says:

"James B. Russell came to Juneau about 30 years ago and for a time operated luncheon counters. For many recent years he was proprietor of Russell's Gun store on Lower Front street. Last summer he was engaged in house painting residing on Eleventh street where he owns property.

"Mr. Russell came from a prominent family in the middle-west. His father, known as Major Russell, was one of the three men who established the first pony express from West Point landing, now Kansas. The Juneau pioneer is believed to have been born in Montana. As far as known, there are no surviving relatives,"

KETCHIKAN ALASKA CHRONICLE, Nov. 10, 1931

R.S. RYAN   (See Vol. I)

R.S. Ryan was born in the city of Waterford Ireland and was educated at the famous Clongowes Wood college. He early adopted the engineering profession and entered the office of his father who was the head of the contracting firm of John Ryan and Sons. Mr. Ryan came to the United States in 1891. Then in 1899 he came to Nome and has since been prominently identified with

the life of the camp.
THE NOME SEMI-WEEKLY NEWS MINING EDITION, Oct. 13, 1905.

INJVALD RYSTAD

Rystad is a native of Norway. He was born April 3, 1868. After traveling over a large portion of the United States he finally came to Alaska in February 1898 with the Klondike rush. For many years he followed mining and prospecting, but by trade he is a carpenter. He came to Anchorage in 1915 and has been doing carpenter work since coming here. His relatives live at Great Falls, Montana.
ANCHORAGE WEEKLY TIMES, Feb. 14, 1918

CHARLES SANFORD (See Vol. 4)

Charles F. Sanford, U.S., Commissioner at Hyder since 1913 has resigned that office due to ill health, and with his younger daughter, Frances, left Hyder this week for Seattle to make his home with another daughter, Mrs. Charles E. Smith, formerly of Wrangell. After many years spent in newspaper work in Southern California, Mr. Sanford went to Nome in 1900 where he was associated with the Gold Digger Daily and later with the Nome Nugget. He went to Hyder in 1922 and established the Hyder Herald until 1934.
THE WRANGELL SENTINEL, Oct., 13, 1936

FREDERICK SARGENT

Frederick Sargent, one of the oldest pioneers in Alaska, died at Kodiak in his 94th year. To him belonged the honor of having raised the Stars and Stripes in Sitka when Alaska was transferred to America by Russia in 1867. Mr. Sargent was a member of a party which crossed the great Canadian wilderness between Winnipeg, then a Hudson Bay trading post known as Red River, and the Rockies in the early fifties. When the party left St. Paul they were equipped to protect themselves from the

Indians, but they were aided by the Red man, when accident happened to the Red River carts, huge wooden affairs constructed with out as much as a nail, the natives were always ready to assist them. Many members left the party an returned to their homes in the Eastern states. Sargent and others kept pressing on and wintered at Edmonton. The following spring they crossed the mountains and landed on the headwaters of the Frazier river. He drifted to the North and took up residence at Sitka despite the efforts of the Russians who resented the American encroachment.

In telling of the ceremony when the transfer was accomplished, Mr. Sargent said the Russians and Americans were lined up in state array when the order was given by the Russian officer to lower the flag of the Czar. The cord caught when the flag was about half mast, and it required an effort to shake it loose so the flag could be taken off.

When the Stars and Stripes began the journey up the pole, the cord again halted and an incipient cheer broke out among the Russian soldiers. The cheer was checked by one of their officers. The cord was relieved of the obstruction and the flag ran to the top. When the ceremony began there was not a breeze and the Russian flag hung limp at the pole. When the American flag was raised to the top of the pole, it was caught and waved by a breeze.

Mr. Sargent came to Kodiak with the first party of Americans in the employ of the Alaska Commercial company when the concern took over the holdings from the Russian Fur Trading company. He has remained in the North ever since, never returning to his old home.

FAIRBANKS WEEKLY TIMES,. May 10, 1911

MARGARET A. SAXMAN

Funeral Services for Mrs. Margaret A. Saxman, who died on April 3 were recently conducted in Pasadena, where she had made her home for the past fifteen years.

Mrs. Saxman went to Alaska in 1886 as a missionary under the Presbyterian Church. She taught in the native schools of Juneau and at the Sheldon Jackson Institution at Sitka. Her husband, together with Louie Paul, a native were lost at sea while on an expedition to locate a mission at Metlakatla.

For a number of years since her retirement Mrs. Saxman had made her home at the Monte Vista Grove Home for retired ministers and missionaries. Services were conducted by Rev. Wm. H. Manshardt, her former pastor.

ALASKA WEEKLY, April 15, 1938

S. A. SAXMAN

S. A. Saxman was born in Armstrong county Pennsylvania in 1854. In the 1880s he and his wife came to Alaska as missionaries for the Presbyterian church. They taught the Indian children at Loring, later moving to Tongass to take charge of education in that area.

On December 13, 1876 Saxman, along with Louis Paul, and an Indian, Wah-koo-so-at set out in a canoe to visit Old Tongass village to determine the feasibility of starting a mission there. They were to return in 5 or 6 days. The day they left the seas were rough and winter storms developed. When the men failed to return on time, the people feared that they may have been drowned, but the weather precluded any search efforts. On December the 31st, the winds and seas abated and Capt. C. F. took his boat and began the search for the men. He took with him George Paul, Louis's brother and Harry, a young Indian. On January 6, the party returned, reporting they had found the canoe driven under a rock by the storm. The bodies of the men were never recovered.

THE ALASKAN (Sitka), Jan. 29, 1877

JAMES SCHMIEG

We are sorry to have to chronicle the death of our fellow townsman, James Schmieg, who departed this life January 22nd, from a sudden attack of pneumonia. Mr. Schmieg was one of our earliest pioneers as he came to Alaska when the country was first turned over to the U.S. government in 1867. He has resided at Cook Inlet, Kodiak, and Fort Wrangel. For many years he has been engaged in the drug business at Sitka and Juneau.

He leaves a widow and six children to mourn his sad loss.
JUNEAU CITY MINING RECORD, Jan. 28, 1892

TOLBERT P. SCOTT

Another old-timer both in Alaska and in the Legislature is Senator Tolbert P. Scott, a native of North Carolina and a resident of the Second Division for more than 40 years. Senator Scott, whose home is at Nome, is one of the most experienced gold dredge operators in the north, having started his career along those lines in 1907. He was first elected to the Legislature in 1933 and is now completing his first term in the Senate.
ALASKA LIFE, June 1947

JAMES SHEAKLEY

James Sheakley, Alaska's fourth governor, was born in Mercer country, Pennsylvania, April 26, 1829. His father was one of the early pioneers in the state of Pennsylvania, having located in Adams county where his ancestors had settled before the revolution. James' early ambition was to be a lawyer but he was dissuaded in this by his mother, his father having died when he was only ten years old. At the age of 16 he went to Meadville where he learned the furniture business while attending the Meadville academy. He returned home in 1839 and lived with his mother until 1851, when he got the gold fever and went to California by the way of Nicaragua. He remained in California until 1854. He returned to his old home in the east and in the year 1855 was married to Miss Lydia Long. Sheakley followed the old business until 1874 when he was elected in the 44th congress on the democratic ticket.

In 1884 when congress passed the act giving the then district of Alaska a civil form of government, to consist of a United States district court and four lower courts, the judges to be known as United States commissioners, Mr. Sheakley was one of the commissioners appointed, and placed at Fort Wrangell. He was also appointed superintendent of the Alaska government schools.

He was a warm friend of Rev. Sheldon Jackson and was the co-worker with him in the establishment of Alaska schools, and the natives who loved him to this day refer to him as "Little Father."

At the Democratic national convention in Chicago in 1892, Mr. Sheakley and judge A. K. Delaney were the delegates representing Alaska. President Cleveland in 1893 appointed Mr. Sheakley governor of Alaska.

He took office in Sitka on August 28 of that year. His record was such that President Harrison reappointed him, notwithstanding his opposite political affiliation. After serving a total of nine years as an officer in the territory and being in his 58th year, he resigned and returned to his home at Greenville, Pa., where he lived up to the time of his death. James Sheakley died December 10, 1917 at the advanced age of 89 years.

ANCHORAGE WEEKLY TIMES, Feb. 14, 1918

ROBERT E. SHELDON

Fourteen years old, Bobby landed in Skagway with his father, headed for the Klondike during the rush of '98. His father died, leaving young Bobby to carry on. He sold newspapers to Soapy Smith and did odd jobs. At sixteen he was rated a "natural" pile driver operator. He steamboated in Southeastern Alaska and was engineer at the Light and Power Company in Skagway. Quietly he took correspondence courses and avidly read everything.

In 1905 Sheldon built the first car in Alaska. It is now displayed in the University of Alaska Museum. He drove the first automobile over the Valdez Trail (and it was just a trail!). Later Sheldon pioneered auto transportation in Mt. McKinley Park.

In 1908, he moved into Interior Alaska where he

In 1908, he moved into Interior Alaska where he immediately became active in public affairs, business, politics, a member of the Territorial Legislature, active in the Chamber of Commerce, Ice Carnival and other public service work. For the past seven years Bobby Sheldon has been popularly rated as the only "First Class Postmaster in a Second Class Post Office" in the Department.

ALASKA LIFE (By Kay J. Kennedy), July 1940

LYNN SHORT

Though Lynn Short is not the oldest in point of residence he has spent more time in the north than any other living Fort Yukonner. He is 87 years of dignified age.

The first of August, 1883, Lynn Short shook the dust of Montana from off his feet and struck out for the north. As one might not expect he has never seen salt water, having traveled to the territory by the back door route. He took a considerable number of years getting into Alaska and these were spent in the Yukon Territory. He was associated with the Hudson's Bay Company at such posts as Chipewyan on the west end of Athabasca Lake and Hay River. During the navigation seasons of 1887 and 1888 he cooked on the old Steamer Grahm which plied between Fort Smith and McMurray, the latter now known as Waterways.

Fort Yukon first saw him the spring of 1899 and has been his stamping ground ever since. He operated a roadhouse in the town for many years but has now retired from active business life, enjoys the company his neighbors furnish him and looks forward each year with pleasure in the hunting season when he can pull the starting cord on his outboard motor and head out for some shooting.

JESSEN'S WEEKLY, July 18, 1947

JAMES M. SHOUP   (See Vol. 2)

The marshal is always one of the best known men in

Alaska. His business takes him to all parts of the district. He has ten deputies scattered over the territory within his jurisdiction, but ought to have at least twenty-five. The present incumbent of that office is Hon. James M. Shoup, who is a brother of Senator Shoup of Idaho. He was appointed marshal of this district on 26th day of June, 1897, and thoroughly understands the duties of the office. He is fifty years old and resides in Salmon City, Idaho, before he came to the district. He also resided in Boise. Marshal Shoup was in the navy during the war and was on the Mound city. He escaped injury during that contest but while fighting Indians since then suffered some injuries that have caused him considerable pain and suffering. He was in the hospital for a short time at Tacoma since his appointment, owing to that wounds he received while fighting bad Indians.

Marshal Shoup is about six feet tall and weights about 180 pounds. His hair is prematurely gray and his mustache is of the same color. He is a man of fine appearance, pleasant and agreeable in his intercourse with his fellow men. His deputies all like him, but he holds them to a strict accountability in the discharge of their duties. He keeps a good man as long as he can, but does not hesitate to discharge an unfaithful subordinate.

DOUGLAS ISLAND NEWS, Jan. 18, 1899

JOHN JOSEPH SIMPSON

John Joseph Simpson, old-time Alaskan, died this morning at 10:00 o'clock at St. Ann's Hospital from spinal injuries sustained when he fell from the roof of his home near the Douglas end of the Douglas Bridge two days ago.

Mr. Simpson, who was about 63 years old, was born in England, coming to Alaska in the early days. At one time he owned a grocery store in Juneau near City Dock. Later he moved to Douglas and acquired large property holdings there.

Mr. Simpson's largest purchase of property was the old St. Ann's Hospital site in Douglas. He also acquired the Jensen building property on the Douglas waterfront. The building on this latter property became much traveled after being purchased by the Douglas man. First it was torn down and re-erected on the old hospital site. Then Mr. Simpson removed it to a site just north of the present Douglas bridge. Later hearing that the bridge might be erected near Salmon Creek, Mr. Simpson again wrecked the building and had it reconstructed on Douglas Island directly opposite Salmon Creek.

A homestead was taken up by Mr. Simpson near the bridge and for several years he had been offering free plots of land to anyone who would build upon his acreage.

The Douglas man received a great deal of acclaim for his typical Alaskan sprit when about six month ago while walking in Juneau he found a pocketbook containing $50 and immediately came to the offices of the Empire to insert an "ad" to notify the owner of his finding.

Several years ago, Mr. Simpson became a communicant of the Mormon Church and sold to them property for a church on Douglas Island for a very nominal sum.

Funeral services on Friday afternoon at two o'clock in the C. W. Carter Mortuary Chapel will be under the auspices of William H. Umpley and Wendel B. Fernely, missionaries of the Church of the Latter Day Saints.

The deceased is survived by a daughter, Doris, in Seattle.
DAILY ALASKA EMPIRE, Aug. 18, 1936

WALTER SCOTT SIMPSON

Walter Scott Simpson, Canadian agent for the Cassiar Indians since 1910, died recently at McDames Creek of heart trouble, aged 73 years. For many years before entering the government service he had been prospecting, mining and operating trading posts in the Cassiar district in association with Capt. J. F. Callbreath. He went to McDames Creek more than a third of a century ago as factor for the Hudson Bay company, with which company he had been associated from early manhood. His father, Governor Simpson of the Hudson's Bay company, and his uncle, Sir George Simpson, a high official and explorer for the Hudson Bay company, were prominent for many decades in the Provinces of Ontario and the Dominion.

Walter Scott Simpson for many years has been nicknamed "The Grand Old Man of the Cassiar." He is survived by his widow and three sons and two daughters: Walter Scott Simpson, Jr. of Clearwater, B.C.; John C. Simpson, Telegraph Creek, B. C.; Fred Stanley Simpson, Wrangell, Alaska; Mrs. O. R. Larson, Boise, Idaho; and Miss Florence Simpson, Seattle. He is survived also by one brother, Frank Simpson of Winnipeg, and three sisters: Mrs. Plummer of Winnipeg, Miss Geraldine Simpson of New York, and Miss Algona Simpson of Seattle.

ALASKA WEEKLY, Aug. 19, 1927

ANDREW W. H. SMITH

Word was received here last week end of the passing in Seattle of A. W. H. Smith, for many years General Agent of the Barrington Transportation Company. Mr. Smith died last Friday and word was received here Saturday morning by Capt. Hill Barrington, who had been associated with Mr. Smith through the years. Mr. Smith was born in Montreal, December 19, 1874 and went to Dawson in 1897. He spent several years mining in and around Mayo and then opened a brokerage office in Dawson in 1900 in partnership with Ed Sears. The same year he became associated with the Barrington brothers–S. C. and Hill– in the transportation business, an association which lasted through the years.

Veteran of World War I, Mr. Smith was a Captain of Engineers in the Black Contingent. He won the Military Cross and was wounded just before the close of the war. He was at one time one of Canada's famed hockey players and several times played for the Stanley Cup, coveted prize of hockey.

He is survived by his widow, Mrs. Louise Smith of Seattle and a sister, Mrs. Alma Laurie of Ottawa.

THE WRANGELL SENTINEL, March 24, 1944

BOWEN SMITH

Bowen Smith, pioneer of Stewart City, and the manager of the store of J. E. Lilly & co., on Black Hills, died at the store on Black Hills, Thursday night. Heart disease was the cause of the death. Mr. Smith was between 60 and 70 years of age.

The deceased leaves two sons, a married daughter and a widow. The sons are on Black Hills, where they are engaged in mining. The daughter and the widow are at Stewart City.

Mr. Smith was one of the earliest settlers of Stewart City. He opened a store there, and ran it until two years ago when he sold it to W. B. Smythe. He opened the Lilly store on Black Hills last fall, and has been associated in the enterprise.

The services will be at Stewart City, which is 25 miles over the divide from Black Hills.

THE WEEKLY STAR (Whitehorse), March 13, 1908

FRANK M.. SMITH

Frank M.. Smith, one of the oldest pioneers of Alaska died yesterday in this city at the age of 58 years, says the P.I. of the 9th. Mr. Smith superintended the construction of a Western Union telegraph line in Alaska in 1865. The line started at New Westminster, and was intended to go to Bering straits. A cable was to be laid across the straits to connect with a line being built by the Russian government. The Alaska line was abandoned when this Atlantic cable was laid.

Mr. Smith again went to Alaska in 1869 for a fur company. He was the man who first reported to the United States government that Fort Yukon, then occupied by the British, was on American soil, and his contention was later confirmed.

That same year he made a trip with dog sleds from near the mouth of the Tanana river to Fort Yukon, a distance of 500 [?] miles. From 1878 until 1884 he was United States collector of customs at Unalaska.

ALASKA DAILY GUIDE (Skagway), Feb. 19, 1905

FREDERICK EASTMAN SMITH

Frederick Eastman Smith, son of Frederick M. Smith, was born in Unalaska on September 9, 1882, and believes he was the first white child of American parentage born in Alaska. His mother, Elizabeth Tracy Smith is still living at 82 in Portland, Oregon. Her mother rode horseback from Oklahoma to California in 1850. Smith's father was manager of the old A.C. Co. post in Unalaska and also a member of the group which attempted to put over the Trans-Siberian cable line which was unsuccessful.

PETERSBURG PRESS, Feb. 28, 1941

LYNN C. SMITH

Lynn C. Smith, United States Marshal for the Fourth Judicial division of Alaska, died of a heart attack on Thursday last [March 9, 1933] at Providence Hospital, Seattle. He has brought out prisoners from Alaska, sentenced to serve at McNeill Island.

Mr. Smith was an old-timer of the North, being one of the first on the ground at Rampart, to which place he spent with Volney Richmond, now the well known head of the Northern Commercial Company. He was on the ground at Dawson, at Fairbanks, and later in Ruby, where he was engaged in the jewelry business, and later became manager of the N.C. Co. at that place. He was also in Iditarod, where he served as U.S. Deputy Marshal for some months. He received appointment as U.S. Marshal for the Fourth division during the Harding administration.

THE KUSKO TIMES, March 11, 1933

RICHARD SMITH

Richard Smith was born at Fort Wrangel, May 26, 1874, and died at Douglas, May 15, 1902. He was educated at Chemawa, Oregon, remaining at school for four years. He returned to his childhood home in the summer of 1807, and gave his heart to God some time the following winter, and became an active Christian worker. He accompanied his father to Chilkat and Cluckwan

during the summer of 1899, on a religious visit, and result of which was the conversion of a hundred or more of the native people. May his work tell for eternity.
DOUGLAS ISLAND NEWS, May 21, 1902

WALSTEIN G. SMITH
Returning to the chosen line of endeavor, Walstein G. Smith is busily engaged in official duties at the First National Bank.
Mr. Smith completed twenty-two years of service to the Territory as Treasurer on March 31, when his term expired and he gave way to his successor.
Thirteen years before being elected to his first term as Territorial Treasurer, Smith came to Alaska. He landed at Katalla in 1907, becoming settled in that city Smith was one of those progressive men responsible for the organizing and founding of the first bank at Katalla.
Born in Ohio, Smith became interested in banking when but a lad and started his career as a messenger boy in a bank of his native state. Before coming to Alaska, the ex-treasurer was cashier of the old Northwestern Bank in Bellingham, Washington.
ALASKA PRESS, (Juneau) April 5, 1935

B. F. SMYTHE
B. F. Smythe was born in Franklin, Pa., March 4, 1840, and well known by the printing fraternity throughout the country in his younger days. He was a civil war veteran, serving as a soldier, dispatch bearer, paymaster and in the commissary department of his division. He was Douglas Island representative of the Daily Alaska Dispatch in the years 1903 and 1904. He passed away at the Union Printers' Home at Colorado Springs April 14.
Mr. Smythe is survived by a niece in Washington, D.C., a son who is publisher of the Harrisburg (Va.) Independent, another son in California and a grandnephew who is a member of the Tacoma Typographical Union Many other relatives and friends are located

in different parts of the United States.

DOUGLAS ISLAND NEWS, May 28, 1920

MARY SOKOLOF

Something unusual was noted in the annals of Alaskan history when the golden wedding anniversary of two Alaskan born people was observed here last month. Mr. and Mrs. John Sokolof were married fifty years on November 23, but Mrs. Sokolof did not live long after the event was celebrated. She passed away at the Government Hospital several days later, after being ill for six years.

Mary and John Sokolof were married at Sitka when the bride was just 13 and one-half years old, however, the marriage was not recorded until Mrs. Sokolof was fourteen. Rev. Nicholas G. Mitropolitansky performed the marriage rites, assisted by Rev. A. P. Kashavaroff, who is the present pastor of St. Nicholas Russian Church in Juneau. In 1895 the couple moved to Killisnoo where Mr. Sokolof was lay reader to the late John Soboleff. (Rev. Soboleff was the father of Mrs. Tay Bayers and Mrs. Lloyd Bayers, now living in Juneau.).

Before the turn of the century, the couple moved to Juneau where they lived for thirty-five years. Mrs. Sokolof was known as a kind, patient women and tireless worker, according to Father A. P. Kashavaroff, who was her friend since childhood. Two children were born in the Sokolof union, a daughter Mary, who died at Sitka, and a son, Andrew, who passed away at Killisnoo. A nephew, Alex Sokolof, a radio operator at Chilkoot Barracks, Haines, is the only surviving relative beside the widower.

Mr. Sokolof has made trips with naval boats as interpreter, and has acted as court interpreter on numerous operations. During the past summer, he was a stream warden for the Bureau of Fisheries.

THE ALASKA PRESS, Dec. 21, 1934

ROY SOUTHWORTH

Roy Southworth came north from his native city of Stockton Calif. in the great Klondike rush of 1898, and toiling over the Chilkoot pass, he entered the printing game in Dawson where he was associated the Daily Klondike, the Daily Nugget, and the Daily News for years.

Afterwards he was among the first to stampede to the Fairbanks camp after the big strike there and establish newspapers of his own in that city and later in Nenana. He then came to Anchorage, where for a time he conducted the Daily Alaskan, and finally became associated with The Anchorage Daily News and was editor and manager for years until he moved to Portland, Oregon and bought interest in the Arrow Printing Company.

THE ALASKA WEEKLY, Mar.3, 1933.

ABRAHAM SPRINGS

Abraham Springs, 77, died Friday at his home in Seward . Springs was a leader in Jewish and educational circles. He went to Alaska during the exciting gold rush of 1898 and served as postmaster at Circle Hot Springs. Later he was one of the leaders in the organization of the city government in Fairbanks. He also served as a prosecuting attorney in Fairbanks. He has lived in Seattle for the past 18 years. Two sons survive him.

SEWARD GATEWAY, Sept 26, 1933

MICHAEL STAGNER

Michael Stagner is from the state of Ohio, having been born in Toledo on the 15th day of October 1859. Mr. Stagner is an old timer in the territory, having come to Sunrise in June, 1897. During the most of this time in the north he has been a prospector and miner. He still claims Sunrise as his home and most every spring shoulders his pick and shovel and makes for the hills.

ANCHORAGE WEEKLY TIMES, Feb. 14, 1918

H. STANFIELD

About noon on Wednesday the city was horrified at the news brought from the Island that Mr. H. Stanfield had received his death blow by accident while attending to his duties at Treadwell.

Workman were busy that morning removing the brick lining from a tall chimney, and to inspect the progress of the work Mr. Stanfield stepped into the chimney through a hole cut into it at its base, neglecting to warn the man above him who remained unconscious of his presence. Scarcely had he entered the place when a brick dropped from a point fifty feet above, striking him with terrific force upon the side of the head, fracturing the skull. Mr. Stanfield lingered until 6:00 pm when he died.

The deceased had been in charge of the chlorination works since January. He came to the Treadwell from Nevada City, California, where he had long engaged in a similar calling and where a widow, a son, and stepson are left to mourn his untimely end.

Mr. Stanfield was a native of Bolton, Lancastershire, England, aged about 67 years, and was a pioneer of California.

ALASKA MINING RECORD, Sept. 17, 1894

JOHN STANLEY

John Stanley was the president of the former city council and was elected at the last city election to membership in the new council.

Mr. Stanley was the pioneer blacksmith in Skagway and did business here in the old days when horseshoe nails [?] sold readily for a dollar a piece.

He is a large property owner and one of the most progressive and enterprising citizens of the place.. His popularity was shown by his being elected by the second largest vote cast for any single candidate.

DAILY ALASKAN, Feb. 19, 1899

JENNIE STARISH

Retaining all her natural teeth and her faculties of hearing and seeing and doing household duties almost to the end, Mrs. Jennie Starish died recently at her home in Saxman. She was between 105 and 106 years old. Nearly every native in Saxman was related to her. This remarkable old lady was the oldest living woman of the Thlinget tribe. Several times she refused money from newspaper men to give them a story of her life about the Thlinget tribe.

She is survived by five children, 19 grand children, 15 great grandchildren, and one great great grandchild. The children are: Miss J. E. Olofsen and Miss B. Tolesen of Ketchikan; Mrs. P. Jacobsen, Charles Starish, James Starish of Saxman.

Mrs. Starish was one of the first to move to Saxman with her family and lived there until her death. Almost to the last she packed in wood and did chores and was assisted by her sister's daughter, Mrs. McKay, who is 80 years old. Mike Perez of Ketchikan, whose wife is a grandchild of Mrs. Starish, said she resented any offers for assistance except from immediate members of her own family.

The funeral was held at Saxman in the Salvation Army Hall. All delegates to the Grand Camp of the Alaska Brotherhood and Sisterhood convention being held in Saxman attended. Burial was in the old Indian cemetery on Pennock Island, where one of her children was buried and many of her grandchildren. Her husband died 33 years ago at the age of 78. He was buried at Checate Cove, Behm Canal.

THE ALASKA PRESS, Nov. 23, 1934

HENRY STATES

Henry States died at the Pioneer Hospital on January 15th. He was born in Limico, Ohio in 1849, making him over 80 years of age.

Mr. States was one of the early Pioneers' of Alaska,

having arrived here in 1884, and had become well known to all the early pioneers.

He was the first U. S. Commissioner, appointed by President Arthur, to serve in that capacity at Juneau for a number of years, after expiration of that office he became active in prospecting and had followed that occupation until his health failed and was admitted to the home. He leaves a son, whose headquarters are in Seattle and has been notified through a cablegram to Emery Valentine of Juneau who was a particular friend of his.

SITKA WEEKLY, Jan. 25, 1929

JOHN W. STEDMAN (MRS.)

Mrs. John W. Stedman passed away Friday afternoon, June 5, at Bishop Rowe General Hospital.

Mrs. Stedman is survived by an older sister, Mrs. Frances Sample, who makes her home with the Gurr family in Portland, a brother, Edward Gannon of Holly, Michigan, her niece, A. D. Gurr, whose childhood has been especially dear to her, and by her husband.

The Stedmans were born in Martland, Michigan. They grew up together, were married very young, and on April 17 of this year "celebrated their fifty-seventh marriage anniversary."

They moved from Michigan to Elkhart, Indiana, and in 1891 went to the west coast settling in Fairhaven, later a part of Bellingham, Washington. In 1898 they moved to Wrangell and then to Ketchikan where Mrs. Stedman shared in the pioneer life and development of the town For the past twenty years they have been residents of Wrangell.

WRANGELL SENTINEL, June 12, 1936

WILL A. STEEL

Will A. Steel was a native of Pennsylvania and engaged in newspaper work there before he came to the Coast with his father and brothers nearly forty years ago. He lived for many years in

Alaska, going to Cordova in the early days of Copper City to engage in the newspaper business. Later he was in Juneau for many years and edited the Daily Alaskan owned at the time by Charles E. Herron. He served as private secretary to Judge James Wickersham while the latter was Delegate to Congress from Alaska and later was elected Territorial Senator of the First Division of Alaska servicing for four years.

Will A. Steel died in Juneau, Alaska October 20, 1934. Mr. Steel is survived by his brother Harry G. Steel, owner and editor of the Cordova Daily Times and a resident of Alaska for more than twenty five years, and other relatives residing in Pennsylvania.

ALASKA WEEKLY, August 24, 1934

GEORGE W. STEPHENSON

Died, at his residence on Douglas Island on Monday, March 5th, 1900, George W. Stephenson of pneumonia, aged 47 years and 10 days, after an illness of three weeks.

He was born in St. Louis, Minn. February 23, 1853. When he was four years of age his parents moved to Ohio, where he lived until his 18th year. At that time he came west and located in California, engaging in the business of mining which he has followed ever since. At the age of 36 he went to Venezuela, South America where he lived for about 7 years, at the expiration of which time he returned to California. He came to Douglas Island in 1896 as foreman of the Mexican mine in which capacity he was acting when stricken down by his last illness.

Mr. Stephenson was married in South America and his wife and four children, one boy and three girls, survive him.

DOUGLAS ISLAND NEWS, March 7, 1900

ISAAC NEWTON STEVENSON

Isaac Newton Stevenson died recently in St, Anns hospital in Juneau. He was 68 years old last May. He went to Juneau in 1898 and has lived there since except for a few years

spent at his old home.
VALDEZ MINER, Oct. 15, 1927

B. D. STEWART (MRS.)

Mrs. Stewart, who was born in Fayette, Mo., 55 years ago, is a relative of the famous Byrd family of Virginia of which Admiral Richard E. Byrd is perhaps the most prominent member. Mr. Stewart and she were married in the city of her birth on May 19, 1909, and went together to Alaska in 1911, when Mr. Stewart was an engineer with the Alaska-Gastineau Mining Company. They have made their home in Juneau since that time.

Mrs. B. D. Stewart died Sunday morning, September 17 at St. Ann's Hospital in Juneau, following a brief illness and an emergency operation from which she failed to rally. Mrs. Stewart is survived by her husband, one of the prominent citizens of the territory, five children, all of whom live in Alaska and four sisters, all of whom are married and make their homes in the States.

Four of the children: John Ervin 20; Jeannette 19; Thomas Byrd 14; and Mary Elizabeth 11; make their home with their family in Juneau while the oldest son, B. D. Stewart, Jr. is married and lives in the Interior.
ALASKA WEEKLY, Sept. 29, 1933

DAYTON WILLEY STODDARD

Dayton Wiley Stoddard was born March 16, 1878 in Hutchinson, Minnesota, and afterward lived for years in Portland, Oregon, before coming to Alaska with his family in 1917. At first he was engaged with the Alaska railroad, later was postmaster of Anchorage for a term, afterward was in business here for himself, and later became city clerk and magistrate.

Mr. Stoddard was prominent in the social and public life of the city; was a member of the American Legion; and a member of the local Masonic order.

Dayton Stoddard died in the Anchorage hospital, November 23, 1933. He is survived by Mrs. Stoddard, and their

four daughters: Vivian 19; Fay 16; Dorothy 10; and Beth 9.
ANCHORAGE WEEKLY TIMES, Nov. 23, 1933

THOMAS SUNNY

On Saturday the 21st last, Mr. Thomas Sunny and Miss Marion Murphy were united in the holy bonds of matrimony at the Catholic Church, Juneau, Father Althoff officiating. Miss Murphy is the daughter of D. H. Murphy, attorney at law. Mr. Sunny has been in Juneau for some years past, has large interests in mining property here.
ALASKA FREE PRESS, May 21, 1887

N. J. SVINDSETH

Capt. N. J. Svindseth passed away very suddenly last Wednesday morning [May 19, 1915] at the Swedish Hospital, Seattle, Wash.

Capt. N. J. Svindseth is well-known all over Alaska and has been associated with her growth for many years. He was born in Norway, in 1859, and came to America when but 16 years of age, and for many years made his home in Oregon, and served two terms in the early legislatures of that state.

Since coming to Alaska he has made Wrangell his home the greater part of the time; and was elected and served in the first Alaska Legislature as Representative from this district, at which place he made a wonderful record for himself.

His death was caused by a complication of diseases, principally Brights disease. Mr. Svindseth has a brother, but we are unable to learn his address.
WRANGELL SENTINEL, May 20, 1915

MINNIE. E. SWINEFORD, (See Vol. 3)

Mrs. M.E. Swineford, widow of a former governor of Alaska, died recently in the Ketchikan General hospital, at he age of 70 years. She was born in Marquette, Michigan. Governor Swineford was appointed by President Cleveland to fill the unexpired term of Kincaid, the first governor of the Territory, and later was appointed governor and served a full term. Mrs. Swineford came to Alaska in 1885 and has resided here since that time.

Governor Swineford and his wife went to Ketchikan in 1889 and was the first recorder of the Ketchikan district. He died in Juneau in 1899. Mrs. Swineford continued to reside in Ketchikan, and for the last several years has been librarian at the Ketchikan public Library.

VALDEZ MINER, Oct. 15, 1927

CAROLINE BALLARD TALBOT

Ketchikan this morning lost one of its splendid citizens, telegraphic advices from Seattle telling of the death there of Mrs. J. A. Talbot, Sr., who has been suffering for several months with a cancer.

Mrs. Talbot during her five years in Ketchikan played an important part in its social and civic life, being particularly interested in the American Legion Auxiliary, of which she was national Chaplin at the time of her demise.

Before her marriage, Mrs. Talbot was Miss Caroline Ballard. She was born in Grand Rapids, Mich, in 1870 In 1881 [1891?]she married J. A. Talbot who survives her. Of this union there are three children who also are living: Mrs. H. H. Townsend, daughter, of Seattle; J. A. Talbot, Jr. and Geo. S. Talbot, sons of Ketchikan. Other survivors are Mrs. E. A. Reeves of California, and Mrs. William Lessig of Denver, sisters.

ALASKA CHRONICLE, Aug. 21, 1925

GLADYS TAMAREE

Miss Gladys Tamaree died on August 23, 1924 in Ketchikan at the home of her brother, William L. Paul.

She is survived by her father and mother, Mrs. and Mrs. William Tamaree, a sister, Miss Frances Tamaree, and three older half-brothers; N. Kendall Paul of New York City; Louis F. Paul and William L. Paul all of whom were at her side at the last with the exception of Mr. Kendall Paul.

Gladys Tamaree was born in Wrangell on December 6, 1908. She was always a remarkably sweet girl, beloved by all. Her scholarship was of high merit and in every way she gave promise of an honored and useful life.

WRANGELL SENTINEL, Aug. 28, 1924

NOLLIE MCMURRAY TATE

The sad news of the death of N. M. Tate of Petersburg was received here Tuesday morning.

Nollie McMurray Tate was born in Waco, Texas August 20, 1882. He came to Alaska 14 years ago and was interested in copper holdings near Lake Bay. He was married in St. Philip's Church, Wrangell, June 20, 1912 to Miss Flora Amelia Radloff of Portland. Later, Mr. and Mrs. Tate came to Wrangell to reside and lived here four years previous to going to Union Bay about five years ago. Mr. Tate was interested in the Union Bay Cannery and was superintendent of the plant.

He is survived by his father who resides in Kansas, a sister and a half-brother.

Mrs. Tate is leaving for Scow Bay, where the family has resided the past few months on the Spokane, accompanied by her mother, to pack her household goods and will return here to live. She expects to occupy the apartments in the Lemieux building next to the Starland theater.

WRANGELL SENTINEL, Sept. 15, 1921

EDNA TAVLIN

Dr. Edna Tavlin, dental director of Alaska, Office of Indian Affairs, arrived Sunday on her first visit to Wrangell. She left Thursday morning for Kake.

While in Wrangell she inspected the teeth of all children in the school, both white and Native, and did all the dental work possible in the limited time of her stay here for all children of

Native blood throughout the school.

Dr. Tavlin is a graduate in dentistry from the University of Cincinnati and has had special preparation and experience aside from our five years in dental college to fit her for the position she now holds. For the past three summers she has traveled on the Yukon and Tanana rivers aboard the medical and dental boat of the office of Indian Affairs, doing the dental work of the Indians of that district. Previous to her Alaska work she was in charge of the Missoula County, Montana, Dental Clinic maintained for school children. She was associated in this work with Dr. F. D. Pease and an average of over 2000 children passed under her care each year.

Dr. Tavlin spent the past winter in the Indian villages of southeast Alaska. An accomplished musician and a conservatory graduate, she is enthusiastically received in the villages both for the dental relief she gives, and the beauty of her music of which she gives freely to the Indian citizens.

Little and pretty, charming and accomplished, looking so like a girl despite her white hair, that it is hard to think of her as the mother of a college boy. Dr. Tavlin is filling a big job in a big way.

WRANGELL SENTINEL, April 22, 1932

GEORGE L. TAYLOR

All Whitehorse was shocked yesterday morning when the news was passed around that Judge George L. Taylor had died a few minutes after midnight [Oct.21, 1915].

Taylor retired at about 11 o'clock Wednesday night. Just before 12 Mrs. Taylor entered the room from her own and inquired as to how he was feeling and received the assurance that he was anticipating a good night's rest. Within fifteen minutes his wife heard a gurgling groan and entered the room to find her husband just crossing death's threshold.

The only members of the family here are Mrs. Taylor and their youngest daughter, Evelyn, the latter twelve years of age.

Other members are Mrs. W. R. Hillery of Skagway; Jack, with Borden's Battery now in France; and Wilfrid and Helen, twins and aged 18 years, both attending college in Toronto. Mrs. Hillery, accompanied by her husband, arrived from Skagway on yesterday's train. The body will be taken to Skagway today and embalmed for shipment to deceased's boyhood home, Bothwell, Ontario, next week, accompanied by Mrs. Taylor and Miss Evelyn.

Judge George L. Taylor was born at Bothwell May 14, 1861, and was 54 years of age on his last birthday. While yet a boy he came west to Winnipeg where he studied law in the office of a brother-in-law who was associated with the late Judge Killim. After being admitted to the bar and practicing for a few years in Winnipeg, he returned to Bothwell where he practiced until coming to Whitehorse in 1901 to accept the position of police magistrate, which he held at the time of his death.
WEEKLY STAR (Whitehorse), Oct. 22, 1915

WILLIAM D. TAYLOR

Word was received on the last mail that William D. Taylor died in Seattle on the 13th of December. Taylor will be remembered here as "Fortymile" Taylor

Taylor was injured badly several years ago when he fell from a wagon and never entirely recovered. Burial was held in Seattle on the 15th of December.

Taylor was born in Canada in 1858. In 1897 he stampeded to the Dawson country. From there he went to Circle, and later came to Fairbanks, where he remained until last spring. Mr. Taylor took up a homestead on St. Patrick Creek about six years ago and made his home there, until illness forced him to enter the hospital.
FAIRBANKS DAILY NEWS-MINER, Jan. 2, 1925

E. W. G. "TED" TENNANT

On Saturday's mail W. F. Thompson received the news

of the death of his brother-in-law, E. W. G. "Ted" Tennant in North Yakima, on Christmas eve of diabetes. He leaves a wife and son in good circumstances. Tennant was born in Iowa.

Many old timers here will remember Ted came to Alaska in 1897, and established himself in Skagway. There with Charley Hanson, he ran the Mondamin hotel, next door to Soapy Smith's famous 10x12 hold-in-the-wall. In 1898 Ted traded between Skagway and Dawson, driving a drove of hogs over the White Pass that fall and scowing them to Dawson. With his scows and his "trade" goods he shot the Whitehorse rapids many times and in the last trip was wrecked and lost all he had made in trading on the trail. That was the trip he essayed to take the steamer "Lorelei" through the rapids, as motive power to haul a bunch of scows to Dawson, once through. The Lorelei was never much of a steamboat after that trip, nor were the scows in working order or the goods saleable.

In their dickering Tennant & Hanson staked the "lucky" men of 7 and 11 Jack Wade creek, and made a stake out of that. Ted spent the winter of 1900-1901 in Dawson, and took his wife with a team of bird dogs to Jack Wade creek during the fiercest of the winter. He also mined and milled in the Atlin country and from Alaska went to North Yakima where he ran a hotel. Ted pioneered the real estate boom in the Yakima country and grew rich through that.

ALASKA DAILY CAPITAL, April 20, 1920

DAVID B. TEWKESBURY   (See Vol. 2)

David B. Tewkesbury, one of the best known newspapermen of the Northwest, is a Juneau-bound passenger on the Alaska. He will become a member of the Empire staff.

Mr. Tewkesbury has been connected with the Times and Post-Intelligencer in Seattle at different times, and has served in practically every branch of the editorial work. Until recently for several years he was an editorial writer on the Times. He has done newspaper work in Alaska at Nome, and Anchorage and for sometime he was engaged in the work at Dawson. He acquired a fondness for Alaska through his Northern experience that induced him to accept an offer from The Empire.

THE DAILY ALASKA EMPIRE, July 11, 1930

CECILA MCLAUGHLIN THEILE

Mrs. Karl Theile passed away early this morning at St. Ann's Hospital in Juneau following a brief illness

Mrs. Theile was born Cecila McLaughlin, daughter of a pioneer family, Mr. and Mrs. Dennis McLaughlin. She grew up in Juneau and lived the greater part of her life in Alaska, where she married Karl Theile, former Secretary of the Territory of Alaska.

Mrs. Theile lived in Wrangell for years when her late husband operated the Diamond K. Cannery here.

She is survived by her daughter, Rosemary Theile of Portland, Oregon and son, Karl Theile of Wrangell, two brothers, Joe McLaughlin of Portland and Dennis McLaughlin of San Francisco, her brother John's widow and children of Juneau, and three sisters; Rose McMullen of Juneau; and Anne and Catherine McLaughlin of San Francisco.

At the time of her death, she held the position of administrative supervisor in the office of A. H. Romick, Commissioner of Commerce for the State of Alaska.

ALASKA STATE HISTORICAL LIBRARY, Biography File
Aug. 1, 1961

L. G. THOMAS

L.G.. Thomas, founder and for many years president and manager of the Alaska Furniture and Undertaking Company and the Alaska Casket Company, left today on the steamer Jefferson for Seattle, from which place he will go to Everett, Wash., where he will incorporate and manage the Washington Casket Company.

Mr. Thomas came to Douglas in June of 1903, landing here with but $18 which represented his worldly possessions. But he had his trade, that of a woodworker, and that indomitable energy and "pep" that never fails, and within a short time, seeing the possibilities of this section of Alaska, he was at the work from whence grew the concerns above mentioned, both of which he carried on with satisfaction to his patrons and success in himself until he recently sold out to Sheldon & McKenna of Juneau, who will continue the business here.

Mr. Thomas is owner of the Thomas block, corner of Third and D streets, and one of the most imposing business blocks in Douglas. His son, M. F. Thomas, will remain here to look after his father's interests while the latter is establishing himself and a much larger business on the outside.

DOUGLAS ISLAND NEWS, May 10, 1916

WALTER THOMAS

Walter Thomas was born in Novia Scotia on June 5, 1857, and came to Ketchikan in 1890, and has been here during the past 35 years. During that time he has accumulated property and has all his life taken an active interest in civic and Territorial affairs. From 1922 until 1924 he served as a member of he city council.

Walter Thomas, pioneer of Ketchikan, died yesterday afternoon at the Ketchikan general hospital after a short illness. He had been suffering from heart failure for some months. He was 68 years old.

KETCHIKAN ALASKA CHRONICLE, Aug. 29, 1925

FRED C. THOMPSON

Fred C. Thompson, veteran clerk of the Sonoma County Superior Court, died Sunday night at Sutter hospital in the valley city July 3, 1938.

Thompson, who for 24 years had served as deputy county clerk here, brought to a close a colorful career. In his earlier years he had accompanied Jack London on a trip to Alaska and had participated in the gold rush days to the Klondike.

Thompson was a native of Minnesota and was 73 years of age. He came to California in 1897 and early in 1898 made the trek to Alaska with London, who was an intimate friend until the author's death.

The Santa Rosan spent 17 years in the Klondike, engaging in gold assy work and as representative of large business interests. Only recently Thompson discussed his Alaskan adventures in a radio interview over KSRO.

Surviving relatives include one son, Clarence Thompson of Santa Maria, former operator of a Del Norte county tourist resort; and a sister, Mrs. Ethel Sorensen of Honolulu.

THE ALASKA WEEKLY, July 8, 1938

THOMAS T. THORNBURG

Sitkans will learn with regret that Major Thomas T. Thornburg fell at the head of his command in a desperate encounter with an overpowering force of Utes, at a place near Milk River, Colorado, on the 29th of September.

Old residents of Sitka and Wrangell will readily recall the gallant officer and genial, accomplished gentleman stationed there during the summer and autumn of 1869. A widow and two children survive the deceased soldier.

ALASKA APPEAL (San Francisco), Oct. 15, 1879

C.M. THORNDYKE

C.M. Thorndyke died at the local hospital in Juneau of throat cancer. He was a widely known mining man in the Willow creek gold camp and other districts of Alaska. He was born in San Francisco July 11, 1859. He was a member of an old pioneer family of that western metropolis. During his early life he was engaged in mining in Arizona and Old Mexico and at one time was interested in mining projects in this vicinity. At the time of his death he was interested in mining in the Willow creek section and had just returned from a trip in that country.

The deceased was in charge government transportation during the Spanish American war. He was a charter member of the Manila Lodge of Elks.

He leaves a widow now in Juneau, a sister in the states, and a son who is employed in Goldstein's and another son in Thane.

ANCHORAGE DAILY TIMES & COOK INLET PIONEER, Oct. 6, 1916.

JOHN L. TIMMINS

"Jack" Timmins was born January 28, 1857. He was one the early pioneers of Alaska, reaching Juneau in 1886 and established a mercantile business. He remained there until 1898, when he joined the stampede into the Klondike. He was prominent in the development of Fairbanks and Nome.

In 1912 he came outside and settled in Los Angeles where he organized the Royal Gum Company, of which he was president. He died there July 8, 1924. He is survived by his widow, Margaret Timmins who shared with him the hardships of their early northern days.

ALASKA WEEKLY, July 18, 1924

OLAF TORKELSON

Olaf Torkelson, 46 years of age, passed away at 11 p.m. yesterday in Juneau at his home, 620 West Twelfth Street. Born at Tvedstrand, Norway, Torkelson came to Douglas in 1907. He has been employed by the Treadwell Mining Company, the Perseverance mine where he was carpenter foreman, and the Alaska Juneau mine.

Until August 1935, he was for 12 years city foreman of Juneau. For six months, Torkelson has been in poor health, and last night died from stomach trouble. Torkelson is survived by his wife and three children: Helen, Ruth, and Catherine; a sister in New York; niece in Seattle; and relatives in Norway.

ALASKA DAILY PRESS, March 2, 1936

GEORGE S. TOWNE

George S. Towne, 69, printer resident of Skagway and

well known among old timers of the North, died this week in Columbus Hospital in Seattle following a brief illness.

Mr. Towne went north in the Gold Rush days and was engaged in the printing business in Skagway with his present partner, Mr. Jensen. He was there during the heyday of Soapy Smith and the most colorful days of Skagway. About 1904 he returned to Seattle to engage in the printing business and later he and Mr. Jensen again became associated in the Gateway Printing Company which they have conducted for many years.

He is survived by his wife, a son, George, Jr., and a daughter, Ruth.

ALASKA WEEKLY, August 5, 1938

MINERVA E. LEWIS TROY

Mrs. Minerva E. Troy, 87, former wife of Alaska's governor in 1933-39, died here [Port Angeles, Wash.] yesterday after a long illness.

Her marriage here in 1892 to John W. Troy was the first performed in a church in Clallam County. They went to Skagway, Alaska, in the Klondike gold rush of 1897 and were divorced a number of years later after returning to this state.

Troy purchased the Juneau newspaper Alaska Empire in 1914 and owned and managed it until his death in 1942. He was appointed governor of Alaska in 1933 by President Franklin D. Roosevelt.Mrs. Troy came to Port Angeles in 1890 to join her father, Dr. F. S. Lewis, pioneer physician for the Puget Sound Cooperative Colony which settled in Port Angeles in the 1880s.

She served with the Red Cross in France in World War I and was a prominent artist, musician and vocalist here for two score years. She suffered a crippling stroke six years ago.

Mrs. Troy's two daughters, Mrs. Helen Monsen of Juneau and Mrs. George Lingo of Anchorage, were here when she died.

Funeral services will be held here Saturday in the McDonald funeral home.

ALASKA STATE HISTORICAL LIBRARY Bio. File

TONY A. TUBBS

Tony Tubbs joined the rush to Nome in the spring of 1900, taking with him one of the largest hotel outfits ever brought to Alaska. He immediately engaged in the restaurant and bakery business on River street there, and as an indication of the business he did, he employed at one time thirty-five persons. In the memorable tidal wave in the fall of 1900, which swept River street, Tony's business house went out with the tide. Since that time he has been engaged in paying "dead horses" as a result.

Departing from Nome, he was asked by the Treadwell Company to take charge of its large boarding house on Treadwell island, which position he held for eight consecutive years. When he resigned, the men of Treadwell presented him with a beautiful gold watch and chain as a testimonial of their appreciation of his services.

Before coming to Alaska, Mr. Tubbs was for seven years in charge of the Sullivan-Bunker Hill Mining company's boarding house in Coeur d'Alene, Idaho. Tony's wide acquaintance and personal popularity insure his success in any undertaking he may enter.

DOUGLAS ISLAND NEWS, June 1, 1910

CHARLES B. TURGEON

Eldorado, Bonanza, Dominion, Bear–these are some of the creeks on which Charles B. Burgeon owns claims. From the fact that they are the very best in the Klondike district, it will be no stretch of the imagination for one to surmise that Charlie is "on to his job." Then he has been in the Yukon country for four years, which in these days of tenderfeet is a long time.

Mr. Turgeon has often looked on the seamy side of life. He knows full well that he is in a country of more square miles than meals, and there have been many days in his Yukon experience that brought no beefsteaks. That the future holds but few privations for him–that is if wealth can purchase immunity from them–is a fact generally recognized in Dawson.

Charles B. Turgeon was born in Quebec, Canada, about forty years ago and spent his early life there, coming to the United States in 1880. The year before the discovery of gold near Dawson he spent on Miller creek, where fortune treated him rather more kindly than it did the other pioneers, and when he arrived with the stampeders at the new diggings he was able to buy for cash some splendid claims which cost him—comparatively little money. That his judgment has been more than good is evidenced by the fact that although he bought them while they were yet entirely undeveloped the majority of them are among the choicest in the district.

He first bought No. 8 above Bonanza, but considering Eldorado better and having an opportunity to close on his purchase at a round profit he did so and became interested in 35 Eldorado which he still owns. When it became known that Hunker would turn out well, he purchased No. 15 below on that stream.

Then turning to that wonderfully rich little stream, Bear creek, he secured a half interest in No. 19 above, on French Gulch, where the very latest strikes had been made, both on the hillsides and in the creek he owns No. 14. His attention was then attracted to Dominion creek, which now ranks as third in the district, and on this he secured No. 5 above and Nos. 149, 169, and 174 below discovery. He also owns No. 26 on O. K. gulch, just four miles from Dawson and No. 12 on Dion creek, which is just four miles up the river from Dawson.

Besides these magnificent holdings, he has town property of constantly increasing value, including the celebrated Eldorado saloon. It is hardly necessary to state that No. 35 Eldorado is a rich claim, the mine being just below the mouth of Gay gulch, in which such wonderful pans and buckets of pure gold are being taken, and will alone yield a comfortable fortune.

On Hunker creek the pay is wide and deep at the point where Mr. Turgeon's claim is situated, there being two runs of gold crossing. The outside world will probably be surprised to learn that Bear creek is even richer than Bonanza and this lucky miner's holding–No. 19–will alone produce enough "dust" to make him rich.

While on many of the streams of the Klondike the pay streak is erratic and has the annoying faculty of dodging shafts and drifts, it is generally conceded that it is more uniform on Dominion than on any other creek. Between the two Discoveries values are increasing daily. None of Mr. Turgeons' claims on this latter stream are in the disputed district.

Mr. Turgeon is over six feet tall and is built like a gladiator. He is a noted pedestrian and can climb mountains and scale cliffs that would give a Cheechaka the heart disease. Though a perfect type of the generous, free-hearted miner, "easy come, easy go," will hardly apply to him. He will remain in the Northwest for another year and will then take a trip to Paris to be present at the exposition to be held there in 1900.

THE KLONDIKE NEWS, April 1, 1898

CHRISTIAN TVETEN

Christian Tveten died late Wednesday afternoon, November 13, at his home after an illness of about two weeks.

He was born near Larvik, Norway, December 9, 1872 on a farm. He left Norway as a young boy and spent many years on sailing ships before coming to the United States in 1890.

In 1899, the lure of the North brought him to the Territory. He settled in southeastern Alaska. Beginning in 1903 he and Charles Norberg operated two scows in what is now known as Scow Bay, the place getting its name from that activity. The men bought and shipped halibut, as there was not a cold storage in the vicinity at that time.

In 1911 Mr. Tveten went into the general merchandise business with S. L. Hogue. This was operated successfully for many years. In recent years Mr. Tveten has been wharfinger for the Citizen's Wharf Co., and also has been in the coal business.

He married Mamie Hadland here in 1911 and they have

four children, two sons, Paul and Arthur, and two daughters, Ruth and Margaret, all of whom are living.

Paul is married and works for the Northern Commercial Company in Fairbanks. Arthur, who is also married works for the Peterburg Press. The two daughters are living in Seattle at the present time, Margaret working for an insurance company and Ruth in training as a nurse at the Columbus Hospital.

Besides his widow and four children, other survivors are two sisters and a brother in Norway.

PETERSBURG PRESS, Nov. 15, 1940

JOHN LEWIS VAN LEHN

John Lewis Van Lehn, 62 years old, a resident of Alaska since 1896, died suddenly of heart trouble Saturday night [July 25] in his home on Willoughby Avenue in Juneau.

Mr. Van Lehn was born in Tuacarawas, Ohio. Before coming to Alaska, he lived in Port Angeles, Wash. Nearly all the years that he resided in this Territory were spent in this part of it. He was a carpenter by trade and for a long time maintained a shop in this city. His wife died in 1925. Mr. and Mrs. Van Lehn had no children. His only relatives are believed to live in Ohio. They are not known here.

THE DAILY ALASKA EMPIRE, July 27, 1931

GEORGE R. VANSE

Alaskans have been notified of the death of George R. Vanse who passed away in California last month. He was engaged in mining in Dawson from 1898 to 1902. Then, after a few years in Ketchikan, and Seattle, he joined the Nome stampede in 1904, where he mined the golden sands. In 1909 he came to the Susitna and Cook Inlet country, where he engaged in mining and freighting, making his headquarters at Susitna Station and Knik. When the Alaska Engineering Commission started construction of the Alaska Railroad in 1915, Vanse was placed in charge of unloading freight from steamers at Anchorage. In 1916 and 1917 he was superintendent of the Susitna River Transportation Department, which he organized, transporting supplies and material by sternwheel steamer and tunnel boats from Anchorage, up the Susitna River for the engineering parties, station gangs, and construction forces in the Susitna Valley and Indian River districts.

In 1918 Vanse was appointed assistant superintendent of construction on the line, and at the close of the season's construction work he went for the States where he has since resided on the Pacific coast.

THE ALASKA PRESS, April 5, 1935

MAYBELLE VAN WINKLE

Mrs. Maybelle Van Winkle died in Oakland, March 8, 1955 after a long illness. She was born in Iowa on Feb. 3, 1895, and lived in Seattle until the death of her husband, Jack Hurley, when she went to Ketchikan to help her brother operate Bell Island Hot Spring. It was while there that she married Archie Van Winkle, who survives her.

Other survivors are her brother, Walter C. Blanton, and three sisters; Mrs. Carl (Margaret) Warren, Berkeley; Mrs. John (Myrtle) Erickson, Fairmount, Minn.; and Mrs. Dean Sibley, Oakland, Calif.

ALASKA WEEKLY, March 18, 1955

CORNELIUS L. VAWTER

Cornelius Vawter, after twenty-three years' service as a deputy marshal in Alaska, was in Seattle during the week, seeking a sunny spot in Southern California to rest until he again hears the call of the North.

Prior to 1898 Mr. Vawter was a successful silver mine operator in Montana. Then came the slump in silver and the subsequent closing of many mines throughout the western states. In the year 1898 Mr. Vawter was appointed a deputy United States marshal by U.S. Marshal Shoup and was stationed at St.

Michael. At this time there was but one judicial division in Alaska. The headquarters of the court was at Sitka. In 1898 Vawter took a number of criminals from St. Michael to Sitka, among whom was Homer Bird, who was convicted of murder, after two very sensational trials, and hanged at Sitka. He was the first man legally executed in the Territory.

In 1900, the second judicial division with headquarters at Nome, was established and Mr. Vawter was appointed United States marshal for the new division. Mr. Vawter was marshal all through the stirring days of the regime of the notorious Judge Noyes. He was the officer that took the infamous Alexander McKenzie to San Francisco under arrest upon charges of contempt of court of the circuit court of appeals. Mr. Vawter was an important witness against the Noyes and McKenzie crowd, made famous by Rex Beach's story, "The Spoilers."

Subsequently Mr. Vawter returned as deputy marshal stationed at Unga, and when H. K. Love was made marshal of the Third division Mr. Vawter was placed in charge of the Valdez office.

When the Fourth division was created in 1909, Mr. Vawter accompanied Marshal Love to Fairbanks, and has since served as a deputy of the Fourth division at Iditarod and for the past several years has been stationed at Fort Gibbon.

THE ALASKA DISPATCH (Seattle), Feb. 10, 1923

PAULINE VELTA

Mrs. Velta was born in Prestipieed, Wales in 1872. While still a child of about seven years she was brought to America by her parents who settled in Joliet, Illinois. During the gold rush days she came to the North in 1899. She has been a residence ever since. For the last several years she has been a housekeeper at the Principal Hotel. Mrs. Pauline Velta died at St. Mary's hospital on July 10, 1925.

THE DAWSON NEWS, July 11, 1925.

FERN L. WAGNER

Fern L. Wagner died recently in Lewiston, Idaho, and was a well known mining figure of Alaska, indefatigable in his search for properties.

A native of Louisa County, Iowa, born Jan. 4, 1880, he came west in 1898 and was at Goldfield and Tonopah during the Nevada gold rush. He owned at one time a chain of restaurants in Nevada. Previously he had mined and prospected in California and Colorado.

Mr. Wagner was an officer of the Alaska Exploration Company and the Peters Creek Mining Company with extensive holdings along Valdez Creek in Alaska, in which many Lewiston residents are interested. Until two years ago Mr. Wagner spent his summers in development of the properties.

Survivors include his wife, Mrs. Iva Wagner: three brothers and two sisters; Dr. Charles Wagner and Harvey Wagner, both of Elsinore, California; Frank Wagner, Talkeetna, Alaska; Mrs. Homer Hillenbrand, Corvallis, Ore.; and Mrs. R. W. Slater, Gettysburg, S. D.

THE ALASKA WEEKLY, Aug. 26, 1938

WILLIAM WAGNER

William Wagner was born in Brooklyn, New York in 1878. He resided there until 1898 when, in company with Jos. A. Bourke and Charles Wolf, he came to Alaska, landing on the present site of Valdez in March of that year. For several years he was engaged in prospecting and mining, and later went to Ellmar where he followed his trade of carpenter. He then went into fox raising in partnership with the late Fred Liljigen, and followed this business for several years. He sold his business to his partner and returned to Valdez where for several years he has been engaged in the garage business. William Wagner died at his home on Thursday evening. His only surviving relative, as far as is known, is a niece some where in the east.

THE ALASKA WEEKLY, Sept. 28, 1928

AL WALSH

Al Walsh, one of the best known and most highly esteemed of pioneers of Alaska, passed away yesterday afternoon at the Anchorage hospital.

Several members of his family are outside, while a brother, Barney Walsh, is on Donlin creek, a tributary of Cooked creek, in the Kuskokwim, where the two bothers have been placer mining the last several years.

Mr. Walsh was born in Wisconsin 59 years ago, was in the old Cariboo mines in British Columbia before he came to Alaska in the early gold mining days, and has been a conspicuous figure in many camps of the northland. Besides the brother on Donlin creek, he leaves a number of brothers, sisters, and nephews in Wisconsin and California.

ANCHORAGE WEEKLY TIMES, March 30, 1933

FRANK WARD

A dispatch to the Portland Oregonian, from Astoria, in its issue of April 22nd says: "Frank Ward, a son of Charles Ward of Clatsop, died in this city tonight of consumption. The deceased came down from Alaska several months ago in search of health, but grew steadily weaker from the time of his arrival. He spent several years in Juneau, where he was engaged in mining, and also in publishing The Alaska News. He was about 37 years of age." Frank Ward was well and favorably known in Juneau, having been the predecessor of the present editor of the News..

ALASKA NEWS (Juneau), May 7, 1896

THOMAS MONROE WARD

Thomas Monroe Ward, engineer of bridges and buildings of the U.S. Government railroad of the Seward division to Kern creek and all construction work, docks, warehouses, etc., in Seward the Terminal City.

Capt. Ward was the first engineer of the government railroad established at Seward headquarters and though many have left Captain ward is still with the commission

He is one of the first class engineers having had experience in all branches of railroading, etc. The following list shows some of his achievements:

Preliminary and location surveys and construction building the Atlantic division, sea board air line, Georgia. Preliminary location and construction Ohio So. Railroad. Principal assistant engineer in charge of office Springfield, Ohio, Topographer and draftsman, City of Balti., Md. Later made chief engineer of same. In April, 1898 extended service of U.S. army with the 5th Md. U.S. Volunteers. Infantry, July 15, 1898, Commissioned 1st Lieut. 3rd U.S. Volunteers engineers August 15, 1898. Appointed battalion adjutant. Commissioned captain 3rd regiment U.S. vol engineers. Received surrender of General Molince, Spanish army at Matansas, Cuba, Jan., 1898. Served with the U.S. army of occupation in Cuba. June, July, 1898, asst. engr. In charge of construction of fortifications, Chesapeake bay, Md, corps of engineers., U.S. army.

Elected member of American Society Civil Engineers, N.Y. City, March 1911. Asst. engr. Poland Pack Co. Later associated with the Northwestern Pacific railroad in San Francisco, Calif., and then with the U.S. Government railroad, Seward, Alaska, being appointed by Chairman W. C. Edes of the Alaskan Engineering Commission.

Capt. Ward is a namesake of his uncle, Brigadier General Thomas Ward, U.S. A., retired of Rochester, N.Y.

ALL ALASKA REVIEW, Dec. 1916

FRANK H. WASKEY   (See Vol. 3)

Frank H. Waskey, Alaska's first delegate to Congress, has been a resident of Alaska since 1898, in the spring of which year he came to the Cook inlet country. In 1900 he went to Nome, and has since acquired property in several districts of Alaska. Mr. Waskey is a native of Lake City, Minn., where he was born in 1873. He is an energetic business man and a pioneer and conversant with the needs of Alaska and its miners in the way of helpful legislation. Three years ago he married Miss Edna Blodgett of Ballard, and is the father of a junior Waskey about a year old. Mr. Waskey is a democrat in politics, but he was nominated by the miners and union labor of Nome as well as by the democrats of that place, and all the parties of Fairbanks.

THE DOUGLAS ISLAND NEWS, Sept. 12, 1906

CHARLES ALEXANDER WATSON

Charles Alexander Watson was born at Montross, Scotland on May 10, 1820. At the age of 10 he took a sea voyage to Iceland with his uncle and soon after his return to Scotland began his service for five years as seaman's apprentice. At the expiration of that time he was sent to school by his father who thought him too young to take the examinations and go to sea as mate of a vessel.

After one year of schooling, with the assistance of his uncle's persuasion, he was permitted to stand the test and was awarded papers as first mate. Two years later he passed the examinations and became a full fledged captain.

He was given command of the Thornaby, then in the Baltic Sea trade. His next ship, the Pilot, a fine new vessel, "turned turtle" with him while he was racing with another vessel off the coast of Sweden. Despite the warnings of his first mate, a much older man than he, he carried so much sail that the list of his ship shifted the cargo and the vessel was up-side-down before she had fully lost her headway.

After cooling off for 30 hours in the waters of the Baltic, he and his crew were picked up by a passing vessel. Strange as it may seem, the ship owners thought this lesson fitted him to take command of another new vessel which they were about to launch.

After cruising over the world for nearly 40 years he landed in San Francisco in 1880 and decided to quit the sea, so went to Colfax, Wash. and bought a farm.

Finally tiring of the uneventful life on a farm, he went to

Seattle and built the yacht Hero and began a cruise in Alaskan waters. In 1895 he sold the yacht and Sitka being the nearest place where he could make out the transfer papers he came here and liked the place so well he decided to spend the remainder of his days within sight and sound of the sea.

With this in view he purchased a quit claim deed to a six acre tract on the point at the entrance to Sitka harbor, and named it Watson point. He raised a large family, most of whom are living in New Zealand

THE ALASKAN (Sitka) July 15, 1899, May 12, 1900

CHARLES ALEXANDER WATSON (See Vol.2)

There was something awfully appropriate in the death of good old Captain Watson of Watson's Point whose life was brought to a close last Monday afternoon [Dec. 31, 1900], just on the eve of the new century, when he fell from his boat into the icy waters of Sitka harbor never to rise until the great judgement day when the sea shall give up its dead.

Just how the Captain met his death will probably never be known. He started from home in a small skiff about 11:00 a.m. Monday 31st with a shot gun and fishing tackle. About 12 o'clock the boat was found and brought in by a native. Both barrels of the gun had been discharged, one of them undoubtedly as the gun lay in the bottom of the boat where it was found when the boat was picked up as the charge had blown a hole in the skiff under the after thwart. It is supposed that he had fired at a duck and as he was replacing the gun the second barrel was in some manner discharged causing the old man to lose his balance and fall over board.

Charles Alexander Watson was born at Montross, Scotland May 10, 1820. At the age of 10 years he made his first sea voyage as cabin boy on board an uncle's ship and at the age of 21 he took command of a vessel. After spending over 60 years on the sea he settled on a small piece of property a mile from Sitka where as he expressed it, "He could hear and see the waters of the beloved ocean."

Captain Watson was a devout Christian gentleman, and whenever he was able to be out of his house, he could always be found at a Divine service on Sunday mornings, little matter how rough or stormy the weather.

THE ALASKAN (Sitka), Jan. 5, 1901

RUSSELL G. WAYLAND

Mr. Wayland was born and bred in Seattle. He attended the University of Washington, where his mother had graduated before him, Wayland being the first graduate of the second generation. He took his degree in 1906 in the College of Mines. During his college vacations he gained engineering experience in the Sound region and shortly after graduation obtained a position on the engineering staff of the Alaska Treadwell Gold Mining Co., where he successively held the positions of head surveyor, chief engineer and assistant superintendent. In 1915 he became general superintendent of the Treadwell group.

DOUGLAS ISLAND NEWS, July 28, 1916

A. WEINBERG

Mr. Weinberg was born in Russia, April 14, 1860[?]. He came to Alaska in the time of the great rush to the Klondike and has seen many of the camps of the north. He came to Anchorage in 1916 and engaged in the mercantile business. At the present time he is doing business in Talkeetna. His family resides at Seattle.

ANCHORAGE WEEKLY TIMES, Jan. 31, 1918

WRIGHT WENRICH

Wright Wenrich, formerly of Juneau, died at a hospital in San Diego, California. Wenrich was well know in several places in the North. He spent a period of a few years in the lower Yukon country and later was at Whitehorse several years where he was engaged in fox raising. He came to Treadwell from Yukon and worked something like two years in the Mexican mine. Later he came to Juneau and for a time was a reporter on the Alaska Dispatch. He was deeply interested in the wild life of the country and wrote several articles on that subject which were published in Forest and Stream or similar publications. In the summer of 1921 he was appointed game warden by Governor Bone.

Wenrich was a native of Missouri and about 40 years of age. As he was not inclined to discuss personal matters nothing is known of his family further than that he had relatives somewhere in Missouri.

THE STROLLER'S WEEKLY, Nov. 1, 1924

CHARLES WEPPLER

Charles Weppler died at his home in Chatsworth, Ontario on January 24 of this year. Born in Ontario, Can., Weppler was 62 years of age at the time of his death.

While in Alaska, Weppler worked as a miner, employed by the Ebner Mining Company. While in Juneau he made his home at the Circle City Hotel. About 25 years ago Weppler returned to Ontario, married, and bought a farm near Chatsworth, where he has since resided. For the past two years he has been in ill health, and since last September has suffered from a severe sickness.

Weppler is survived by his wife, living at Chatsworth, Ont., a nephew, Louis Weppler, living at Tara, Ont., near Chatsworth; a sister, Mrs. Robert Clark, living at Whittier, Calif; a sister, Mrs. John Campbell, now living at Kirkland, Wash.; and a brother, Ottomar Weppler, now residing in the state of Washington.

Charles and Ottomar Weppler, Mrs. Clark and Mrs. Campbell are all pioneer presidents of Juneau. Mrs. Clark is better known to the people of Juneau as Mrs. George F. Miller, wife of a partner of Lockie MacKinnon in the Circle City Hotel here for years.

ALASKA DAILY PRESS, March 2, 1936

EMILLE BROSIUS WEYBRECHT

Mrs. Charles Christopher Weybrecht, well known resident of Seward since 1921, died suddenly on the afternoon of June 1st [1934] as the result of a heart attack.

Mrs. Weybrecht was Emille Brosius, daughter of E. H. and Emily Wanser Brosius of Alliance, O. She was the widow of the late Colonel C. C. Weybrecht of the Eighth Regiment, Ohio National Guard, who was in service on the Mexican border during the trouble in 1916. He served in France and died shortly after his return to Ohio in the fall of 1919.

Mrs. Weybrecht is survived by three brothers: William Orlen Brosius of Pittsburgh, Pa.; Edgar E. Brosius of East Pittsburgh; and Cal M. Brosius of Seward.

Mrs. Weybrecht was a member of the Keturah Moss Taylor Chapter, Daughters of the American Revolution of Newport, Kentucky.

THE ALASKA WEEKLY, June 22, 1934

GEORGE WHITE

George White, former Governor of Ohio, died December 15, 1958 in Good Samaritan Hospital. He was 81 years old.

Mr. White came here for the winter with his second wife, Agnes, from Marietta, Ohio. She was with him when he died. His first wife died in 1929.

Mr. White was born in Elmira, N. Y. Graduated from Princeton in 1895. He taught school for a while, worked in the Oklahoma oil fields and prospected for gold during the Klondike gold rush before entering politics in 1905.

From 1911 to 1915 and from 1917 to 1919 he represented the Fifteenth Ohio District in the House of Representatives. In 1920 he was chairman of the Democratic National Committee in Illinois and presided at the convention that nominated James M. Cox for President. He was elected Governor of Ohio in 1931 and served two terms. Mr. White settled in Marietta, Ohio in 1902 and engaged in oil production, to which he returned after his last term

in Congress.
NEW YORK TIMES, Dec. 16, 1953

JOHN I. WHITE

The Skagway Alaskan says that Capt. John I. White is registered at the Occidental. He is an old timer in the north, having made his first visit to this country before many who read this were born. He came to the Stikeen river on the Flying Dutchman when she was brought from the Fraser river in the 50s by Capt. Moore, with whom he is well acquainted. Capt. White was at Bella Bella when William H. Seward came to what is now Alaska in 1862 and from which visit its purchase in 1867 resulted. Capt. White is going into Dawson. This is his fourth trip in there. He has spent ten winters in the interior and two at St. Michaels and traversed the country from one end to the other. He has gone from the head waters of the Yukon to its mouth in a skiff and seen all the hardships which are characteristics of frontier life. Notwithstanding this he is hale and hearty.
DOUGLAS ISLAND NEWS, May 22, 1901

STEPHEN STEUART WHITE

Dr. Stephen White died at St. Francis Hospital, Juneau on May 30, 1899. Dr. White was born near Baltimore, Md., January 30, 1863, having entered the service some twelve years ago, and during his short term of two years at this place, had earned for himself an enviable reputation as a pathologist and practitioner. His death was caused by ptomaine poisoning.

His body was embalmed and shipped to San Gabriel, Cal., where his wife and two children are living.
THE ALASKAN, (Sitka) June 10, 1899

S.W. WIBLE

S.W. Wible was by profession a civil engineer. He surveyed the great irrigation project on the extensive land holdings of Miller and Lax, the California meat barons and for twenty years served as their superintendent.

He came to the Kenai peninsula in 1898 and has yearly passed the summers here, engaged in mining. He became interested with the original Crow creek boys, then acquired extensive holding on Canyon creek.

Mr. Wible had reached the advanced age of 82 years. When he left here last fall his friends feared he would never return, due to his failing health. He was a man of large wealth, possessing oil lands and other properties in California.

S.W. Wible died at his home in Bakersfield, California, September, 1911.

SEWARD GATEWAY, Sept. 30, 1911

HANS C. WICK

Hands C. Wick, long-time Petersburg resident, died Monday morning at 7:30 o'clock at the Petersburg General Hospital.

Mr. Wick was born in Molde, Norway, on March 9, 1882. He came to the United States in 1903, crossing the Atlantic on the same steamer as Erick Ness. Both men went to Bayfield, Wisconsin, and later came to Petersburg. Mr. Ness came to Alaska in 1906, and Mr. Wick in 1908.

After his arrival in Petersburg, Mr. Wick engaged in logging. From 1912 to 1928, with few interruptions, Mr. Wick was City Marshal. During the brief periods when he was not Marshal, he engaged in fishing.

From 1928 to 1934 Mr. Wick was Deputy U. S. Marshal, serving part of this time with Deputy U. S. Marshal C. V. Brown. Since 1934 he served as part-time guard under Deputy U. S. Marshal Chris Christensen and held this position at the time of his death.

Mr. Wick is survived by brothers and sisters in Norway and by a step-daughter, Mrs. Hope Oleson, and a step-son, Bonaparte Cambas, both of Seattle.

PETERSBURG PRESS, Nov. 3, 1939

EDGAR WICKERSHAM

After a lingering illness of two years, Edgar Wickersham died in Pasadena, Calif. On December 16 [1936] at the age of 71. He was born in Patoka, Ill., on November 22, 1865.

Forty years ago he married Elizabeth Chamberlin of Buckley, Wash., and left for the Gold Rush country, going to Skagway in 1898. Here he worked for the White Pass & Yukon Railroad. In 1900 he was appointed U.S. deputy marshal and in 1903 went to Fairbanks in the same capacity.

In 1918 Mr. and Mrs. Wickersham left the northland and made Pasadena their home. Of a cheerful disposition and always ready with a helping hand to assist others, he won a host of friends in his new home as he did in the North.

Besides his devoted wife, Mr. Wickersham leaves three brothers: Judge James Wickersham of Juneau; Harry Wickersham in Buckley, Wash., and Frank Wickersham of Cambric Pines, Calif. who was with him at the time of his death.

THE ALASKA WEEKLY, Dec. 25, 1936

EUGENE S. WILLARD (MRS)

Mrs. Eugene S. Willard, 63 years old, and one of the best known of Alaskan pioneers, died Monday night at her home in Chicago, according to a telegram received yesterday by her son.

Mrs. Willard was born in Newcastle, Pa. in 1832, and with her husband went to Alaska in 1881, where they founded the first mission in the Chilkat country at Haines. In 1886 they founded the first mission at Juneau. They stayed there 13 years and then came to the outside to educate their children.

As the author of "Kinda Shon's Wife," published in 1894, Mrs. Willard attracted considerable attention among ethnological experts and her book received the first prize at the Alaska-Yukon Pacific exposition as an authoritative volume on the habits and characteristics of the Alaskan Indians.

PROGRESSIVE (Ketchikan), Feb. 27, 1915

ROSE SYLVESTER WILLETT

Mrs. Willett, born in interior Canada, came to Wrangell as the young bride of Rufus Sylvester who rose to wide prominence in Alaska and besides being the owner of Wrangell's first mill was a large property owner in the town. In her younger years Mrs. Willett was noted as one of the town's most prominent and most beautiful women.

Mr. Sylvester died many years ago and Mrs. Sylvester later married Oscar Willett, a Wrangell carpenter.

Six children survive. They are Mrs. R. J. Suratt, Mrs. May Gartley, Mrs. James Nolan, George Sylvester, Mrs. Allen Ritchie all of Wrangell and Mrs. Ann Chilberg who lives in California.

Mrs. Rose Sylvester Willett, 75, a resident of Wrangell for almost 60 years died last Saturday evening [July 19, 1941] at the family home at 8 o'clock.

THE WRANGELL SENTINEL, July 25, 1941

ALFRED D. WILLIAMS

Capt. Alfred D. Williams, born in Pennsylvania on November 29, 1864, died in Seattle on June 5 and was buried on the 9th of June 1938.

After spending several years mining in Colorado and Idaho, he had a river boat built and taken from Vancouver, B.C., on the S.S. Tafon to St. Michaels where he launched it and went up the Yukon River in the spring of 1899 to Rampart. He steam boated and mined in the Rampart and Hot Springs district until 1907 when he became foreman for Frank Manley, and later for Tom Aitken. Joining the stampede to Iditarod and Ruby, he mined until 1917 when he bought a reindeer herd at Unalakleet and drove them to the Nelozy Hot Springs near Kokrines. He cared for them so well that they had increased to about 8,000 head in 1928, at which time he sold them to the Dominion Reindeer Co.

On April 4, 1922, he married Mrs. Marie Smitzes in Seattle, who had been one of the popular stewardesses on Alaska boats for many years. She survives him and also a brother C. E.

Williams living in Colorado Springs.
THE ALASKA WEEKLY, June 17, 1938

JAMES A. WILLIAMS

James A. Williams, aged 69 years, passed away on the morning of January 6, 1927 in the government hospital in Anchorage Mr. Williams was one of the old Circle City pioneers, coming down the Yukon river to that point in the spring of 1895, after packing his outfit over the Chilkoot Pass. At one time, he was the owner of No. 13 on Eagle creek, in the Circle district. Hearing of the Carmack gold strike in the Klondike, he went there in the spring of 1897, where he owned and operated a sawmill for three years. Later, he took over the Dawson Light and Power Company, which he operated for seven or eight years, carrying on mining operation at the same time.

From Dawson, Mr. Williams went to Fairbanks, where he was identified with mining on Dome creek for several years. From there he went to the Valdez creek country, in the upper reaches of the Susitna valley region, and finally drifted on down to Gold creek, a tributary of the Susitna river, where he operated a roadhouse and a store for some years. Still later, he came down the river to Talkeetna, where he operated a store and a stopping place, until sickness came on that caused him to go to the government hospital in Anchorage.

Mr. Williams was well known and highly regarded by all the old-timers, who will regret to hear of his passing. He is survived by two sons, James and Henry, who are in Alaska, and five sisters: Mrs. J. R. Howard of Tacoma; Mrs. Margaret Harting of Seattle; Mrs. Mattie Cain of Hayeville, Alabama; Mrs. Anie Gaines of Lapanta, Arkansas; and Mrs. Vina Boreo of Walla Walla, Wash.
ALASKA WEEKLY, Jan. 21, 1927

EDGAR WILSON

Mr. Edgar Wilson aged 50 years died at his home at Dyea

Wednesday morning after a brief illness of about thirty six hours with inflamation of the lungs.

The course of his death was due to over exertion during a long journey through snow the day before. Mr. Wilson with Capt. J. J. Healey established a trading post at Dyea inlet in 1887 from which time he has been in constant attendance. He leaves a wife and one child.

ALASKA MINING RECORD, May 20, 1895

JOSHUA WILSON

Joshua Wilson, who died in Juneau yesterday, was well known in Douglas, residing here at different times, the greater part of the last 25 years. He enlisted with an Ohio militia company during the war and was mustered in later. Owing to the fact that he first joined the Civil war forces as a member of the militia, he could not secure a pension. Some time ago his friends started a movement to place him in a soldiers home somewhere in the states and it was learned today his war credentials and transportation had only lately arrived–too late to do the old man any good. When last in Douglas, he lived in a cabin on the beach but ill health forced him to enter the hospital in Juneau. He was a very quiet man and well liked by whom he came in contact with.

ALASKA DAILY RECORD, April 13, 1911

PERLEY RUPERT WILSON

Perley Wilson, engineer at the Hyder Lumber Company saw mill and one of the camp's best known characters, passed away suddenly in the Ideal Cafe building last Saturday evening as a result of heart disease.

Perley Rupert Wilson was a native of Solon, Maine, and is survived by several brothers and a sister who reside in various parts of the States. He was an old timer in the North, having resided in Alaska and the Yukon for 25 years or more. He was a resident of Dawson in the early days and resided in various Alaska camps between Dawson and Nome at various times. He became a resident of Hyder shortly after the discovery of the Premier mine.

During the course of his residence he became associated in the ownership of the Hyder Lumber Company plant with William Gray, present owner, and Robert Andrews, but later sold his interest to Mr. Gray several years ago and took a position as the company engineer which he still held. During his residence here he became interested in the well-known Ninety-six group of mining claims on Mineral Hill, a short distance north of Hyder, and held a third interest in the property at the time of his death.

HYDER WEEKLY HERALD, March 28, 1931

JOHN WINKIE

In the passing of John Winkie, early this morning at St. Ann's Hospital, Alaska lost another true pioneer. He was a personal friend of many of the pioneers of Juneau, including among other S. Zynda, B.M. Behrends and Charles W. Carter.

John Winkie was born in Scotland. He left there with his parents and settled in Michigan. In 1883 he went to California, where he was employed on a farm. At the age of 20, Alaska lured him, so he came North in 1886. Since that time he has been employed at various mining camps as steward and cook, and for the past fifteen years has been working at his occupation at Chichagof.

Last August he came to Juneau, because he was not in the best of health, and made out his will which he turned over to Howard D. Stabler. About a month later he entered St. Ann's Hospital, where he has been confined.

THE ALASKA PRESS, Dec. 14, 1934

JOHN WINN

John Winn, a resident of Juneau since 1893, passed away at 2:50 pm yesterday at the Laural Beach Sanitarium in Seattle following an illness of several months,. He was the son of Col. William Winn, who died many years ago, and of Mrs. Arina Winn, pioneer Juneau woman.

The deceased was born at Wiota, Wisconsin 62 years ago, and came north in 1893, where he engaged in mining activities. He went South three months ago to enter the sanitarium for treatment.

Survivors include, besides the mother, a brother Burdette Winn, a mining engineer living at Hurley, New Mexico, and a sister-in-law, Mrs. Bess Winn of Juneau. A brother, Grover Winn, well known Juneau attorney died last year.

THE DAILY ALASKA EMPIRE, June 28, 1944

MILTON WINN

The funeral of Milton Winn, 52, formerly of Juneau and a prominent member of the pioneer Winn family, will be held Saturday at Tucson, Ariz. Winn was killed in an auto accident Tuesday night, 65 miles west of Tucson.

Winn served as chief of the Juneau fire department for years. He was one of the city's most popular athletes, taking an active part in baseball, bowling, and other sports.

The funeral will be held under the auspices of the Tucson Elks Lodge, and internment will be in the Elks plot. Winn will be buried beside his wife who passed away 15 years ago. Mr. and Mrs. Burdette Winn of Butter Creek, California, brother and sister-in-law of Winn, will attend the last rites.

ALASKA PRESS, Jan. 16, 1936

LIZZIE J. WOODS

The many acquaintances and friends of Miss Lizzie J. Woods, who for many years was matron at the Cottage Hospital in this city, will be somewhat surprised in learning of her whereabouts and the busy life she leads compared with the average women of today.

Miss Woods has for the past six years been located at Fort Yukon, Alaska, a next door neighbor to the North Pole, where she acts as postmistress, missionary nurse, teacher in the government's

Indian school, head of the Episcopal mission, nurse, physician, infantry captain and has acted as United States marshal. She has also established quarantine and checked the spread of diphtheria and was responsible at one time for closing the river to traffic to stop the plague.

Miss Woods is at present enjoying a brief stay at Santa Monica, Cal., where the Western papers are publishing full accounts of the great deeds of the good woman who did so much for the sick of the city and who will be remembered for many kind acts and management of the first public hospital of this city.

THE PORTSMOUTH HERALD (NH), Dec. 28, 1908

CHARLES WORDEN

Charles Worden, Bonanza King of 26 Eldorado fame, known from one end of Alaska to the other, died suddenly in October on the Kuskokwim river. Mr. Worden took a fortune out of 26 Eldorado, was one of the richest men in Dawson, and became known as one of the original Klondike Kings.

When the Fairbanks strike was made, Worden was one of the first stampeders. He mined in this district for several years. Mr. Worden spent the past five years in the Kuskokwim country, where he was developing a very promising copper property.

He is survived by a wife, who is now living in Seattle, and two sisters-in-law, Mrs. Robert Geis, and Mrs. Louis Golden, of Fairbanks.

FAIRBANKS DAILY NEWS-MINER, Dec. 26, 1924

SIMION IVANOVICH YANOFSKY

One of the first historical events of interest in the records [vital records of Russian Church] is the account of the marriage of Governor Yanofsky to a half breed daughter of Governor Baranoff. Yanofsky was at the time of the marriage a Lieutenant in the Russian fleet stationed at Sitka. The marriage was on Jan. 7, 1818. The record gives the account of the wedding as follows:

"'Jan. 7, 1818, Lieutenant of the Russian fleet, Simion

Ivanovich Yanofsky married the daughter of the Government of the Russian Possessions to America and Governor and Cavalier Alexander Baranov [sic], the girl, Irma, a creole.'"
VALDEZ MINER, Jan. 20, 1917

G. E. "Ed" YOUNG

In an attempted landing on the small Livengood airfield yesterday, Pilot G. E. "Ed" Young, pioneer "ace" of the Pacific Alaska Airways and his two passengers, A. D. "Buck" Roberts and Eric Nelson, were killed instantly. Nelson was a former resident of Seward and interested in the Seward hotel.

In a reconstruction of the tragedy it is said that aviators Young and Robbins left Fairbanks at 12:15 yesterday afternoon for Livengood. Robbins landed first with no difficulty, Young remaining aloft to await clearing of the field.

When Young's turn to come down came he banked his ship and it is presumed slipped into an air-pocket as his crashed to the ground. All three were killed instantly. The plane was NC9765 and the tragedy occurred at about 12:45 pm.

Aviator Young was one of the best known and esteemed flyers of the Northland. He probably had more flying hours to his credit than any other pilot and has been flying in the Territory since the days of the late Lieut. Carl Ben Eielson.

Young was about 40 years of age and is survived by a widow and a son. Mrs. Young is in Seattle at present. It has been the intention of Young to join her next week.

The bodies have been taken to Fairbanks.
GATEWAY TRI-WEEKLY (Seward), Sept. 21, 1933

www.ingramcontent.com/pod-product-compliance
Lightning Source LLC
Chambersburg PA
CBHW060555230426
43670CB00011B/1829

Revolutionary Patriots

of

Calvert and St. Mary's Counties

Maryland

1775-1783

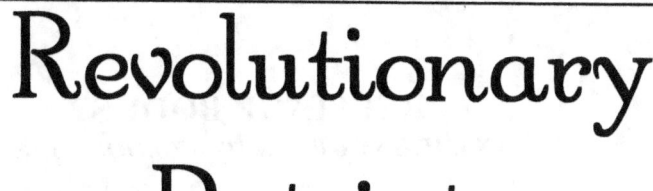

Henry C. Peden, Jr.

HERITAGE BOOKS
2006

HERITAGE BOOKS
AN IMPRINT OF HERITAGE BOOKS, INC.

Books, CDs, and more—Worldwide

For our listing of thousands of titles see our website
at
www.HeritageBooks.com

Published 2006 by
HERITAGE BOOKS, INC.
Publishing Division
65 East Main Street
Westminster, Maryland 21157-5026

Copyright © 1996 Henry C. Peden, Jr.

All rights reserved. No part of this book may be reproduced or transmitted in any form or by any means, electronic or mechanical, including photocopying, recording or by any information storage and retrieval system without written permission from the author, except for the inclusion of brief quotations in a review.

International Standard Book Number: 978-1-58549-402-X